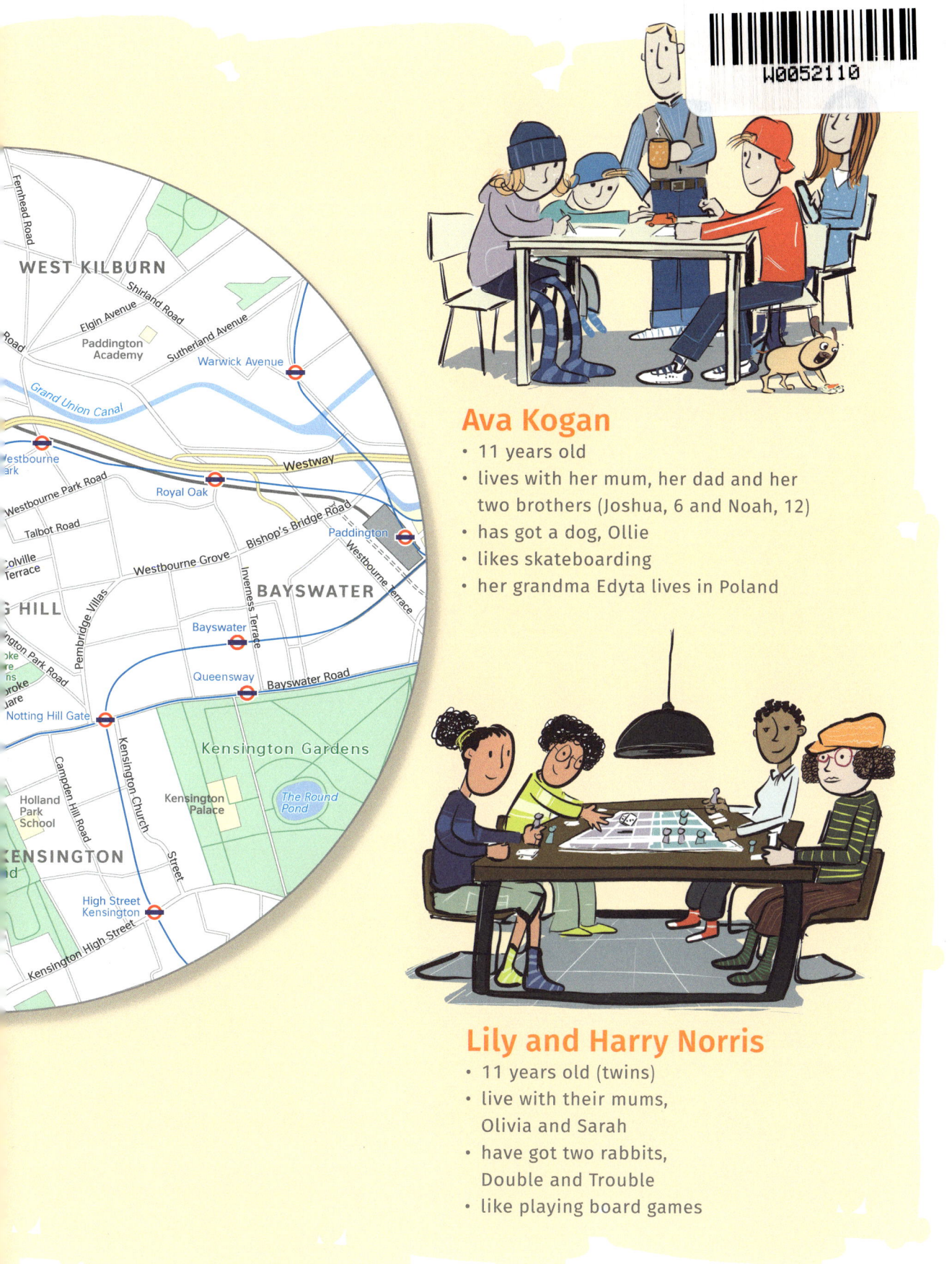

Ava Kogan

- 11 years old
- lives with her mum, her dad and her two brothers (Joshua, 6 and Noah, 12)
- has got a dog, Ollie
- likes skateboarding
- her grandma Edyta lives in Poland

Lily and Harry Norris

- 11 years old (twins)
- live with their mums, Olivia and Sarah
- have got two rabbits, Double and Trouble
- like playing board games

westermann

NOTTING HILL GATE

Textbook 5

Erarbeitet von:
Theresa Künzel-Giller (Pforzheim), Gabriele Linke (Marburg), Cedric Lütgert (Marburg), Sascha Mohr (Wiesbaden), Maike Pegler (Sarstedt/Gödringen), Dr. Ivo Steininger (Wetzlar)

sowie Denise Arrandale (Neumünster), Michael Biermann (Hamburg), Hannelore Debus (Mörfelden-Walldorf), Phil Mothershaw-Rogalla (Volkmarsen-Külte), Semra Siyli (Hamburg)

Fachliche Beratung:
Sandra Bauer (Kaarst), Angela Berkenkamp (Wetzlar), Jens Bludau (Hannover), Gisela Ehlers (Schillsdorf), Imke del Federico (Kerpen), Prof. Dr. David Gerlach (Wuppertal), Dr. Matthias Munsch (Frankfurt am Main), Jun.-Prof. Dr. Julia Reckermann (Münster), Anke Riemer (Hamburg), Silvia Savelsberg (Erkelenz), Kathleen Unterspann (Halstenbek)

Story „Blaze and the Edinburgh dragons"
von Amy Frances Koerner

HoF

Notting Hill Gate 5
Textbook

Zusatzmaterialien zu Notting Hill Gate 5

Für Lehrkräfte:
- Textbook für Lehrkräfte 5 (ISBN 978-3-14-128284-9)
- Materialien für Lehrkräfte 5 (ISBN 978-3-14-128294-8)
- Lernerfolgskontrollen 5 (ISBN 978-3-14-128320-4)
- CD für Lehrkräfte 5 (ISBN 978-3-14-128304-4)
- DVD für Lehrkräfte 5 (ISBN 978-3-14-128314-3)
- Online-Diagnose zu Notting Hill Gate 5
  www.onlinediagnose.de

Für Schülerinnen und Schüler:
- Workbook 5 (inkl. Audios) (ISBN 978-3-14-128210-8)
- Interaktive Übungen 5 (WEB-14-128220)
- Arbeitsbuch Inklusion 5 (inkl. Audios)
  (ISBN 978-3-14-128230-6)
- Klassenarbeitstrainer 5 (ISBN 978-3-14-128246-7)
- Grammatiktrainer 5 (ISBN 978-3-14-128386-0)
- Wortschatztrainer 5 (ISBN 978-3-14-128240-5)
- Westermann Vokabeltrainer-App zu Notting Hill Gate 5
  www.westermann.de/vokabeltrainer

Das digitale Schulbuch und digitale Unterrichtsmaterialien für Schülerinnen und Schüler und
für Lehrkräfte finden Sie in der BiBox – dem digitalen Unterrichtssystem passend zum Lehrwerk.
Mehr Informationen über aktuelle Lizenzen finden Sie auf www.bibox.schule.

www.westermann.de/nhg

© 2022 Westermann Bildungsmedien Verlag GmbH, Georg-Westermann-Allee 66, 38104 Braunschweig
www.westermann.de

Druck A[1] / Jahr 2022
Alle Drucke der Serie A sind im Unterricht parallel verwendbar.

Redaktion: Lisa Fast, Dr. Katja Nandorf
Vokabelanhang: Doris Bos
Illustrationen: Mario Ellert, Bremen
Umschlaggestaltung: LIO Design GmbH, Braunschweig
Layout: LIO Design GmbH, Braunschweig
Druck und Bindung: Westermann Druck GmbH, Georg-Westermann-Allee 66, 38104 Braunschweig

ISBN 978-3-14-**128200**-9

So arbeitest du mit dem Buch

Über diesen QR-Code gelangst du auf die Webseite
www.westermann.de/128200
Dort findest du alle Audiotracks, Videoclips, Arbeitsblätter zur Medienbildung, zusätzliche Übungen zu den Practise-Seiten und Zusatzmaterialien zum Buch.

Im Buch findest du folgende Verweise:

1 audio   Zu dieser Aufgabe gibt es einen Audiotrack.

2 video   Zu dieser Aufgabe gibt es einen Videoclip.

3 workbook   Hier siehst du, auf welcher Seite im Workbook es weitere Übungen gibt.

4 wordbank   In den Wordbanks findest du Wörter nach Wortfeldern geordnet.

5 skill   Auf den Skills-Seiten findest du Tipps und Strategien fürs Lernen.

6 grammar   Zu dieser Aufgabe gibt es Erklärungen und Beispiele im Grammatik-Teil.

7   Dieses Symbol kennzeichnet Aufgaben, in denen du Medienkompetenz aufbaust und trainierst. Zu diesen Aufgaben gibt es Arbeitsblätter auf der Webseite.

DIGITAL+   Dieser Hinweis zeigt, dass es zusätzliches Material auf der Webseite gibt.

In den Units gibt es verschiedene Arten von Aufgaben:

8 CHOOSE YOUR LEVEL   Bei diesen Aufgaben gibt es drei unterschiedliche Schwierigkeitsgrade:
▍ leicht   ▍▍ mittel   ▍▍▍ schwierig

9 GET TOGETHER   Hier arbeitest du mit einem Partner oder einer Partnerin zusammen. Entscheidet, wer Partner A und wer Partner B ist und wählt jeweils einen Schwierigkeitsgrad. Geht dann zur entsprechenden Seite und bearbeitet die Aufgabe.

Partner A	Partner B
▍ Go to page 113.	▍ Go to page 125.
▍▍ Go to page 117.	▍▍ Go to page 129.
▍▍▍ Go to page 121.	▍▍▍ Go to page 133.

10 CHOOSE YOUR TASK   Hier gibt es drei Aufgaben, von denen du dir eine aussuchen kannst. Du kannst mit einem Partner oder einer Partnerin oder in einer Gruppe arbeiten.

TARGET TASK   In der Target Task (Zielaufgabe) wendest du an, was du gelernt hast. Du erarbeitest ein kleines Produkt, das du in der Klasse vorstellen und in deinem Portfolio aufbewahren kannst.

Kurzes Inhaltsverzeichnis für den schnellen Überblick

Ein ausführliches Inhaltsverzeichnis befindet sich auf den Seiten 233 bis 238.

In the street

1 wordbank: animals p. 150, workbook p. 4/1

What can you see? Think about:

colours · food · animals · people · ...

You can say:

I can see a skateboard.
I can see houses.
I can see a green T-shirt.
I can see one/two/three ...

An ice cream chant

2a audio 1/2

Listen to the chant.

Lots of flavours, but which is the best?
Let's get ready for the ice cream test!
If you like lemon, touch your nose.
If you like banana, touch your toes.
If you like chocolate, close one eye.
If you like mango, jump up high.
If you like vanilla, so yummy and sweet,
Then clap your hands and stamp your feet!
Lots of flavours, but which is the best?
Let's get ready for the ice cream test!

2b workbook p. 5/2

Sing the chant and do the moves.

The ice cream van

3 audio 1/4, video 1, workbook p. 6/3

Listen and point to the people.

New friends

4a audio 1/6

Listen and read along.
What do you find out about the children?

1
So, where do you go skateboarding?

I like the park. And there's an indoor skate park. It's really cool.

2
Where are you from?

I'm from Brighton but we live in Notting Hill now. What's your name?

3
My name is Ava. And that's my little brother, Joshua. He's six. What's your name?

I'm Harry. I've got a twin sister. We're eleven. How old are you?

4
I'm eleven, too. And my brother Noah is twelve. What's your sister's name?

Her name is Lily. She likes skateboarding, too.

5
That's great! Noah and my friend Tarek like skateboarding, too.
Let's go skateboarding in the park tomorrow.

OK, cool.

6
Can I have your phone number? Then I can text you.

Sure. It's 07984631205.

Great. See you tomorrow then. Bye!

4b

Who says it? Ava or Harry?

1 "I like the park."
2 "I'm from Brighton."
3 "I've got a twin sister."
4 "We're eleven."
5 "I'm eleven, too."

You can say:

Number 1: that's Ava.

Number 2: …

…

4c   workbook p. 7/4

What do Ava and Harry want to do?

You can say:

They want to go …

In the park

5a

Look at the pictures. What can you see?

5b   audio 1/8

Now listen and read along.
What do you find out about Tarek?

5c   workbook p.8/5

Get together in groups of five.
Act out the scene in the park.

Welcome

Nice to meet you

6 workbook p. 9 / 6, 7

Talk to your classmates.
Say hello, then ask questions.

You can ask:

What's your name?
Where are you from?
How old are you?
…

You can answer:

My name is …
I'm from …
I'm …
…

Hello, I'm … What's your name?

Hi, my name is …

Think and write

7 **CHOOSE YOUR TASK** A/B: wordbank: food p. 156, C: wordbank: about me p. 151

A Write an ice cream menu. You can think of special flavours, too.
B Think of more ice cream flavours and write more verses for the ice cream chant on page 7.
C Look at the picture. Write a dialogue.

A

ICE CREAM MENU

apple

broccoli

orange

B

ICE CREAM CHANT
If you like orange, touch your nose.
If you like …

Check out

1. Kannst du jemanden begrüßen und dich verabschieden?	workbook p. 10
2. Kannst du jemand anderem Fragen stellen?	workbook p. 10
3. Kannst du dich vorstellen?	workbook p. 11
4. Kannst du jemand anderen vorstellen?	workbook p. 11
5. Kannst du Telefonnummern verstehen und mitteilen?	workbook p. 11

Im Workbook findest du Aufgaben, die dir dabei helfen, diese Fragen für dich zu beantworten.

1. Look at the picture. What can you see?
2. What is "Notting Hill Gate"? A city, a station or a shop?
3. What do you think? Where is Notting Hill Gate?

People and places

Part A Me and my things

- Du erfährst mehr über die Hauptfiguren.
- Du schreibst darüber, was jemand hat.
- Du sprichst über dich selbst und was du magst.

Part B My neighbourhood

- Du erfährst etwas über Notting Hill.
- Du erzählst von deiner Wohngegend.
- Du schreibst über Lieblingsplätze in deiner Umgebung.

Meet Ava

1a

Look at the picture. What can you see? Collect words.

You can say:

There is …

There are …

1b audio 1/10

Listen to Ava and read along. What is she talking about?

You can say:

Ava is talking about her …

Ava is talking about …

Ava: Hello, I'm Ava.
Here I am in my room.

I live in a blue house in Notting Hill.
Notting Hill is in London.
I live here with my family: my mum, my dad and my brothers. Our house isn't big but I like it. We've got a small garden.

I've got two brothers, Noah and Joshua.
They are twelve and six.
I haven't got a sister.

My hobbies are playing computer games and skateboarding. These are my three skateboards. The green skateboard is new. I really like it.

This is my dog Ollie. He's four years old and he can do a lot of tricks – even on the skateboard! He hasn't got a skateboard but he has got a favourite toy. It's a red ball.

Ollie is always hungry. He even likes carrots. His favourite food is spaghetti.
I love spaghetti, too – but I hate carrots!

ACTIVATE PRACTISE DEVELOP PRACTISE APPLY

1c

Look at the text again. What is true? What is false?

1 Ava lives in a blue house.
2 Notting Hill is in Brighton.
3 Ava's house isn't big.
4 Ava has got four brothers.
5 Noah and Joshua are Ava's brothers.
6 Ava hasn't got a sister.
7 Ava's mum and dad have got two children.
8 The green skateboard is old.
9 Ollie's favourite toy is a red skateboard.

You can write:

Number 1 is true.
Number … is false.

1d workbook p. 12/1

Correct the false statements and write them down.
Work with a partner and check your statements.

About Ava

2a CHOOSE YOUR LEVEL

▌ Complete the sentences and write them down.

1 Ava has got two …
2 Ava's hobbies are …
3 Ava has got three …
4 Ava has got a …

▌▌ Complete the sentences and write them down.

1 Ava's house is …
2 She lives in Notting Hill with her …
3 The garden is …
4 Ava's brothers are …
5 She really likes …
6 Ollie is always …

▌▌▌ Write six or more sentences about Ava. Think about:

· her house
· her family
· her dog
· her hobbies
· …

You can write:

Ava lives …
She has got …
She likes …
She is …
…

2b workbook p. 13/2, 3

What about you? What do you like?
Talk to a partner.

computer games · skateboarding ·
spaghetti · carrots · …

GRAMMAR HELP   long and short forms (be p. 166, have got p. 167)

Wenn du über Personen, Tiere oder Dinge sprechen willst, kannst du die Formen *am*, *is* und *are* benutzen.
Sie sind die Formen des Verbs *be*. Im gesprochenen Englisch werden sie oft verkürzt.
Schau dir die folgenden Beispiele an: Wie wird aus der Langform die Kurzform gebildet?

I am Ava.	→ I'm Ava.
She is eleven.	→ She's eleven.
We are twins.	→ We're twins.

Auch die Formen des Verbs *have got* können verkürzt werden. Wie wird hier aus der Langform die Kurzform?

I have got two brothers.	→ I've got two brothers.
He has got a toy.	→ He's got a toy.
We have got a garden.	→ We've got a garden.

Auf den Seiten 166 und 167 kannst du weitere Beispiele finden – auch für die Kurzformen bei Verneinungen.

Long and short

3   grammar: be p. 166, have got p. 167, workbook p. 14 / 4

Find the matching forms. Write them down.

that is	he's
I am	you're
it is not	they're
they are	that's
he is	I'm
you are	it isn't

I have got	it's got
she has not got	I've got
you have got	we haven't got
they have got	they've got
it has got	she hasn't got
we have not got	you've got

What have they got?

4a   grammar: have got p. 167

Write sentences.

1 Harry: a phone
2 Ollie: a carrot
3 Ava: a dog
4 Ollie: a new toy
5 Harry and Ava: skateboards

You can write:

Harry has got a phone.

4b   grammar: have got p. 167, workbook p. 14 / 5

What have you got?
Write three or more sentences.

Friends from Notting Hill

5   grammar: be p. 166

Write five or more sentences about the friends.

Ava	is	from Notting Hill.
Joshua and Noah	is not	Ava's sisters.
Ollie	are	four years old.
Ava's house	are not	red.
...		six and twelve.

You can write:

Ava is from Notting Hill.

Joshua and Noah are ...

DIGITAL+ practise more 1

ACTIVATE   **PRACTISE**   DEVELOP   PRACTISE   APPLY

Harry and Lily

6a workbook p. 15/6

**Look at Harry and Lily's room.
What have they got?**

You can say:

Harry's got …

Lily's got …

They've got …

6b CHOOSE YOUR LEVEL audio 1/12

Listen and read along.

I **What can you say about Lily's socks?**

II **What can you say about Harry and Lily's rabbits?**

III **What can you say about Harry?**

Harry: Lily and I are new in Notting Hill.
We live here with our two mums.
This is our room. Lily's got a big bed, it's her favourite place. Lily's got a lot of things – a skateboard, books and a lot of funny socks. But she can never find them!
We love playing board games, so we've got a lot of them.

Lily: We've got two rabbits. Double is brown and Trouble is black and white. They are very sweet! They've got a blue cage.
Harry likes football. He's a big Chelsea fan and he's got a lot of posters. Harry also likes music. He's got a red guitar. He plays every evening. His favourite music is rock music and it's really loud.

6c workbook p. 15/7

Work with a partner. Ask and answer questions about the children. Take turns.

You can ask:

Who's got a red guitar?

Who's got a lot of board games?

Who's got …?

You can answer:

Harry.

Harry and Lily.

…

Tarek

7a

What can you see in the picture?

You can say:

There is …

There are …

7b audio 1/13, skill: listening p.141

Listen to Tarek.

Point to the things he is talking about.

7c

Listen again. What is true? What is false?

1 Tarek has got one book.
2 He likes hockey, football and skateboarding.
3 He is a big Arsenal fan.
4 His favourite sport is skateboarding.
5 He is in a hockey team.
6 His favourite music is pop music.
7 Tarek has got some animal posters in his room.

7d workbook p.16/8

Correct the false statements and write them down.

The children in Notting Hill

8 CHOOSE YOUR TASK

A **Choose one of the children in Notting Hill. Make a word web about him or her. Ask the class: who is it?**
B **Make an alphabetical word list of the children's things.**
C **Make a quiz. Write true/false statements about the children. Ask a partner to do your quiz.**

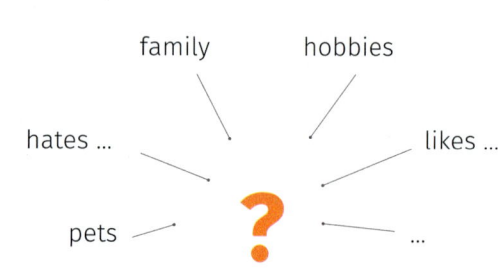

family   hobbies

hates …   likes …

pets   **?**   …

ACTIVATE PRACTISE **DEVELOP** PRACTISE APPLY

Do you know them?

9 CHOOSE YOUR LEVEL skill: writing p.143

I Look at page 12 and write four or more sentences about Ollie.

You can write:

Ollie is Ava's dog.
He is …
He likes …
He has got …

II Look at page 15 and write four or more sentences about Lily. Use the words in the box.

> big bed · favourite place ·
> funny socks · board games

III Write a short text about Harry.
Think about: family, pets, hobbies, …

The things I like

10a audio 1/14

Listen to the poem and read along.
Which of the things do you like, too?

You can say:

I like …, too.

10b

Listen again. Find the rhyming pairs and write them down.

You can write:

cake – steak
bike – …

10c workbook p.17/9

Read the poem out loud with your classmates.

Football, burgers,
chocolate cake,
computers, puppies,
rap music, steak,
loud and cool music,
riding my bike,
these are all
the things I like.

Homework, spinach,
stinky smells,
the way my sister
always yells,
shopping with my mum,
a ten-mile hike,
these are the things
I do not like.

That's me!

11a video 2

Watch the video clip. What has Kai got?

11b skill: mediation p.145, workbook p.17/10

Watch the clip again.
Tell a friend about Kai in German.

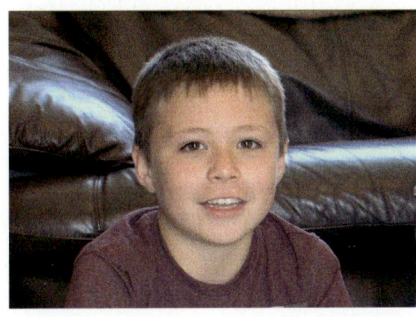

The friends

12   grammar: be p. 166, have got p. 167

Complete the sentences and write them down.

1   Harry and Lily ??? new in Notting Hill.
2   Ava's house ??? big.
3   Harry and Lily ??? twelve years old. They ??? eleven years old.
4   Ava ??? two sisters. She ??? two brothers.
5   Double and Trouble ??? a house. They ??? a cage.
6   Ollie ??? a green ball. He ??? a red ball.

> is not · are not ·
> are (2 x) ·
> has not got (2 x) ·
> has got (2 x) · have got ·
> have not got

More about the friends

13   **CHOOSE YOUR LEVEL**   grammar: be p. 166, have got p. 167, workbook p. 18/11, 12

I   **Unscramble Ava's sentences and write them down.**

1   is – My – name – Ava.
2   I – from – Notting Hill. – am
3   am – I – eleven – years old.
4   is – my – dog. – Ollie
5   playing computer games – are – My hobbies – and skateboarding.

II   **Complete Noah's sentences and write them down.**

1   I ??? a sister and a brother.
2   I ??? twelve years old.
3   I ??? from Notting Hill.
4   My sister Ava ??? a dog.
5   My brother Joshua ??? six years old.
6   Our house ??? blue. It ??? a small garden.

III   **Write down Harry's sentences. You can use the information from the word web.**

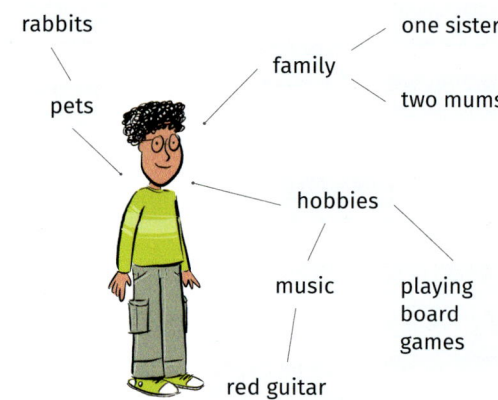

rabbits   one sister
pets   family   two mums
hobbies
music   playing board games
red guitar

You can write:

I am …
I have got …
My … are …
…

Odd one out

14

Find the odd one out.

1   sister, brother, friend, house
2   skateboarding, football, garden, hockey
3   spaghetti, book, carrot, ice cream
4   music, dog, rabbit, cat

About me and my things TARGET TASK

15 workbook p. 19/13, wordbank: about me p. 151, family p. 160, skill: presentations p. 146

Your task is to talk about yourself and your favourite things.
Before you start, look at these steps:

STEP 1

What would you like to tell your classmates? Think about:

- family
- pet(s)
- what you like
- hobbies
- favourite things
- ...

Make notes.

— *My family: mum, dad, one sister*
— *Pets: no pet*
— *I like: dogs, the park, chocolate*
— *My hobbies: football, computer games, music*
— *Favourite things: my football, my phone*

STEP 2

If you like, you can show your classmates something about yourself.
You can take a picture or draw something.

STEP 3

Get together in small groups. Use your notes and your pictures and tell your classmates about yourself.

You can say:

I live in ... with my ...
I've got ... / I haven't got ...
I like ...
My hobbies are ...
This is ...

Notting Hill

1a
workbook p. 20/1a

Lily is looking at web pages about places in Notting Hill. Talk about the photos.

You can say:

There is …

There are …

1b

Now read the information. Talk about the places.

You can say:

You can …   *There is …*

There are …   *It is …*

1

Travel to Notting Hill on the underground. It is fast and easy. You can start your tour at Notting Hill Gate Station.

READ MORE

2

One of London's best markets is in Notting Hill: Portobello Road Market. There are many cool shops and stalls. You can buy second-hand clothes and there is food from all over the world.

READ MORE

3

There are many cinemas in Notting Hill. At the Gate Picturehouse they have got special tickets for children and teenagers. At the Electric Cinema on Portobello Road there is a Kids' Club.

READ MORE

4

Are you creative?
Try something new! Decorate biscuits at Biscuiteers. It is fun and you can take your personal biscuit home.

READ MORE

ACTIVATE   PRACTISE   DEVELOP   PRACTISE   APPLY

5

Dancing in the street, music and costumes – that is Notting Hill Carnival! Every year in August over a million people come to Notting Hill. They watch the parade and listen to the music.

READ MORE

Look, Harry! So many things to do in Notting Hill!

Let's text Ava. Maybe she can take us on a tour!

1c **CHOOSE YOUR LEVEL** skill: reading p. 144, workbook p. 20/1b-4

I Complete the sentences and write them down.

1 The underground is …
2 Portobello Road Market is in …
3 The Gate Picturehouse is a …

II Complete the sentences and write them down.

1 You can travel to Notting Hill on …
2 There are … at Portobello Road Market.
3 At the Gate Picturehouse they have got …
4 At Biscuiteers you can …

III Complete the sentences and write them down. Then write two more sentences.

1 You can start your tour at …
2 You can buy … at Portobello Road Market.
3 There is a … at the Electric Cinema.

4 Kids can … at Biscuiteers.
5 Every year in August there is …

Your neighbourhood

2a audio 1/19, skill: listening p. 141, workbook p. 22/5

Listen to Ameera. What is she talking about?

2b skill: talking with people p. 142

Walk, stop and talk. Ask a partner about his or her neighbourhood.

park · market · zoo · shop · shopping centre · playground · museum · café · swimming pool · cinema · school · skate park · …

You can ask:

Is there a …?
Are there …?
Have you got a … in your neighbourhood?
Is it good / interesting / cool / …?

You can answer:

Yes, there is. / No, there isn't.
Yes, there are. / No, there aren't.
Yes, we have. / No, we haven't.
Yes, it is. / No, it isn't.

GRAMMAR HELP be: questions p. 168

Mit den Formen *am, are* und *is* kannst du Sätze bilden, um zum Beispiel Personen, Tiere, Dinge und Orte zu beschreiben. Vergleiche die Aussagesätze auf der linken Seite und die Fragen auf der rechten. Was fällt dir auf? Wie werden die Fragen gebildet?

Notting Hill is in London.	Is Notting Hill in London?
It is fun.	Is it fun?
There is a park.	Is there a park?
You are creative.	Are you creative?
Harry and Lily are from Brighton.	Are Harry and Lily from Brighton?
There are many shops in Notting Hill.	Are there many shops in Notting Hill?

Auf Seite 168 kannst du herausfinden, wie man auf diese Fragen antworten kann.
Dort gibt es auch weitere Beispiele für Fragen mit den Formen von *be*.

Questions and short answers

3a grammar: be questions p. 168

Complete the questions and write them down.

1 … Ava from London?
2 … there many cinemas in Notting Hill?
3 … Joshua and Noah Ava's sisters?
4 … Tarek Ava's friend?

3b grammar: be questions p. 168

Match the answers to the questions in 3a.

Yes, he is. · Yes, she is. ·
Yes, there are. · No, they aren't.

Asking questions

4a grammar: be questions p. 168, have got questions p. 169

Unscramble the questions and write them down.

1 Who – Noah? – is
2 How old – you? – are
3 from? – you – are – Where
4 phone number? – is – What – your
5 Ollie's ball? – Where – is
6 in Tarek's room? – is – What
7 rabbits? – got – has – Who
8 has – What – got? – Harry

4b

Choose four questions from 4a and answer them.

Question words

5 grammar: be p. 168, have got p. 169, workbook p. 23/6

Choose the correct words from the box and write down the questions.

Where (2x) · What (3x) · How · Who (2x)

1 … is Notting Hill? – In London.
2 … is your name? – Ava.
3 … has Lily got? – A lot of funny socks.
4 … old is Ollie? – He is four years old.
5 … is Lily's brother? – Harry.
6 … are Ava, Noah and Joshua from? – London.
7 … has got a red ball? – Ollie.
8 … is Portobello Road Market? – A famous market in London.

DIGITAL+ practise more 3

ACTIVATE **PRACTISE** DEVELOP PRACTISE APPLY

A tour of Notting Hill – part 1

6a

Talk about the pictures. What can you see? Where are the children?

6b audio 1/20

Listen and read along. What can you find at Ava's favourite stall?

Ava: Hi guys! Are you ready for our tour?
Lily: I can't wait!
Noah: OK, let's start. This is our favourite fish and chip shop. The best in Notting Hill.
Harry: Wow! That's great. Our mums love fish and chips.
Tarek: Your mums? You have got two mums?
Lily: Yes, Sarah and Olivia.
Tarek: Two mums – cool! I live with my dad.

Lily: So this is the famous Portobello Road Market? There are so many stalls.
Noah: Yes, there are. It's brilliant.
Ava: Over there is my favourite stall. They've got great second-hand T-shirts.
Harry: Hey Lily, look at the T-shirts.
Lily: I like that T-shirt and it's only six pounds.
Tarek: And look at this, a flyer from BaySixty6, the skate park. That's a great place, too.

6c skill: talking with people p. 142, workbook p. 24/7, 8

Get together in groups of five. Act out one of the scenes.

A flyer

7a workbook p. 25/9

Look at the flyer. What is it about?

> **BaySixty6 – A skater's paradise**
> **The only indoor skate park in London!**
> Are you an inline skater?
> A skateboarder? A BMX biker?
> BaySixty6 is fun for everyone!
>
> · lessons for beginners
> · special events for professionals
>
> Where? 56–66 Acklam Road
> When? Open daily from 12 to 9
> How much? £6 per person per session

7b skill: mediation p. 145

A friend has got questions about BaySixty6.
▮ **Answer questions 1 and 2 in German.**
▮ **Answer questions 1 – 4 in German.**
▮ **Answer all of the questions in German.**

1 Wo genau ist das?
2 Wann haben die geöffnet?
3 Wie viel kostet der Eintritt?
4 Kann man da nur Skateboard fahren?
5 Für wen gibt es da Kurse?
6 Was ist denn so besonders an BaySixty6?

A tour of Notting Hill – part 2

8a

Look at the pictures. What can you see? What can the children do there?

8b   audio 1/22

Listen and read along. What is the children's plan?

Harry: It's nice and quiet here after the market.

Tarek: Yes. This is Holland Park. A good place to relax.

Ava: There is a beautiful Japanese garden and a cafeteria.

Noah: I love the Ecology Centre. You can find out a lot about nature and you can go on bat walks there.

Harry: Ugh, I don't like bats.

Lily: Come on, Harry. Bats are not so bad!

Lily: Oh no, not a museum! Museums are boring.

Tarek: Not the Science Museum. There is a special lab called Wonderlab. Look, there's a live show at four o'clock.

Harry: Hm, maybe next time. The weather is too nice to be indoors.

Ava: Yeah, let's come back another day.

Noah: Let's go and get some ice cream.

All: Brilliant idea! Let's go!

8c   CHOOSE YOUR LEVEL   skill: reading p.144, workbook p.26/10

❙ Match the sentence parts.

1 In Holland Park,
2 At the Ecology Centre
3 At Wonderlab there are
4 In the end, the children

A live shows.
B get ice cream.
C you can find out about nature.
D it is nice and quiet.

❙❙ Complete the sentences.

1 In Holland Park, there is …
2 Noah loves the …
3 … are not Harry's favourite animals.
4 For Lily, museums …
5 There is a live show at …
6 The weather is …

❙❙❙ Write about Holland Park.

You can write:

Holland Park is …

There is … and …

You can …

…

ACTIVATE   PRACTISE   **DEVELOP**   PRACTISE   APPLY

Notting Hill words

9   **CHOOSE YOUR TASK**   wordbank places p.152

A Make a word web about Notting Hill.

B Write an acrostic. Look at the box in 2b on page 21 for ideas.

```
F A M O U S
S T A L L S
    G R E A T
B O O K S
P O S T E R S
C L O T H E S
```

C Make riddles for your classmates (words with missing letters, word searches, ...).

Word search

S	T	A	T	I	O	N	O	C
Q	I	S	L	F	R	O	L	I
B	S	H	O	P	K	P	Q	N
T	R	U	Z	A	I	B	J	E
S	G	M	J	Q	D	L	C	M
A	R	E	A	G	A	P	O	A

Two neighbourhoods

10   **GET TOGETHER**

Get together with a partner.
Talk about two different neighbourhoods.

Partner A

▌ Go to page 112.
▌▌ Go to page 116.
▌▌▌ Go to page 120.

Partner B

▌ Go to page 124.
▌▌ Go to page 128.
▌▌▌ Go to page 132.

LAND & LEUTE 1 video 3

Notting Hill

Notting Hill ist ein bei Einheimischen und Besuchern beliebter Stadtteil der Großstadt London. Notting Hill ist vor allem durch die Portobello Road und den Notting Hill Carnival bekannt.

Die Portobello Road ist berühmt für ihren Markt: Dort gibt es nicht nur Lebensmittelstände, sondern auch Antiquitätenhändler und Secondhand-Geschäfte, die viele Menschen anlocken. Jeden August wird in Notting Hill der zweitgrößte Karneval der Welt gefeiert. Das dreitägige Fest findet seit den 1960er Jahren auf den Straßen von Notting Hill statt und geht auf Einwanderer aus der Karibik zurück.

Da Notting Hill so populär ist und viele Häuser modernisiert wurden, ist das Wohnen dort mittlerweile sehr teuer. Viele Menschen mussten deshalb aus dem Stadtteil wegziehen.

Schau dir den Videoclip über Notting Hill an. Wo würdest du gerne hingehen?

A great place

11

Write down the text and fill in the gaps with words from the box.

In my city there is a famous zoo. It is very ??? and there are a lot of ???. My favourite animals are the ???. The zoo is ??? from 9 to 6 and it costs 7.50 Euro for ???. There are three ??? where you can play. There are two restaurants, a nice café and a great ???. You can buy lots of things there. I really like the zoo – it is my favourite ???!

tigers · children · animals · open · playgrounds · place · shop · big

Describing places

12   CHOOSE YOUR LEVEL   wordbank: places p. 152

I   **Collect words to describe places.**

You can write:

park: green, big, …
museum: old, …
…

II   **Describe places.**
    Write four or more sentences.

You can write:

The shopping center is new, …
…

III Describe a place you like or do not like. You can look at number 11 for ideas.

Rhyming pairs

13a   audio 1/23

Listen and repeat.

we · cat · complete · bat ·
let · take · great · get · she ·
make · bed · wait · meet · red

13b

Find the rhyming pairs and write them down.

You can write:

we – she
cat – …

DIGITAL+ practise more 4

ACTIVATE   PRACTISE   DEVELOP   **PRACTISE**   APPLY

Great places in our area TARGET TASK

14   workbook p. 27/11, wordbank: places p. 152, free time p. 157

Your task is to write a fact file about a great place in your area for children.
Before you start, look at these steps:

STEP 1

What are the best places in your area for children? Collect ideas in class.

STEP 2

Work with a partner. Choose one place and write a fact file about it.
You can add a picture or photo.

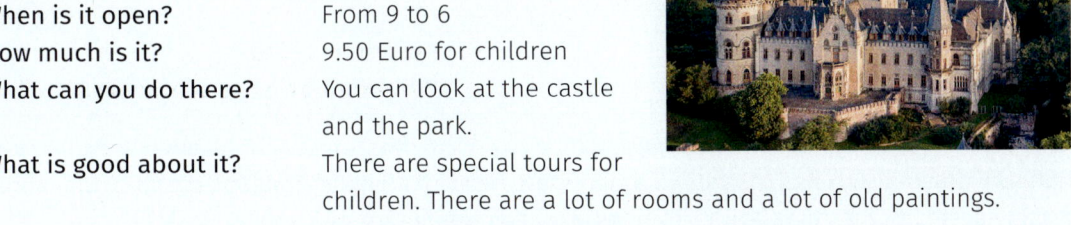

Name	Schloss Marienburg
What is it?	Castle
Where is it?	Pattensen
When is it open?	From 9 to 6
How much is it?	9.50 Euro for children
What can you do there?	You can look at the castle and the park.
What is good about it?	There are special tours for children. There are a lot of rooms and a lot of old paintings. The restaurant is really nice.

STEP 3

Display the fact files in your classroom.

Great places in our area

STEP 4

You can put all your fact files together in a brochure for someone who speaks English but no German.

Check out

1. Kannst du ausdrücken, was jemand hat oder nicht hat?	Workbook, p. 28
2. Kannst du verstehen, was jemand über sich selbst erzählt?	Workbook, p. 28
3. Kannst du etwas über dich erzählen?	Workbook, p. 28
4. Kannst du einen kurzen Text über einen Ort verstehen?	Workbook, p. 29
5. Kannst du Fragen zu Orten stellen und beantworten?	Workbook, p. 29
6. Kannst du einen Ort in deiner Nachbarschaft beschreiben?	Workbook, p. 29

A trip to Edinburgh

Hi, I'm Blaze.
I'm a dragon tamer. You don't believe me?
Well, then look at my dragon tamer's ID.
It tells you all about me.

My name is Blaze.

That's me.

I am fourteen years old.

I live in Bristol.

I have got blue eyes and brown hair.

I am really good with shy dragons and young dragons.

I have got my own dragon tamer's ID.

NAME	BLAZE
AGE	14
CITY	BRISTOL
ID NUMBER	38516
EYE COLOUR	BLUE
HAIR COLOUR	BROWN
SPECIALITY	SHY DRAGONS, YOUNG DRAGONS

DRAGON TAMER'S ID

My best friend, Kora, is a dragon tamer, too. She lives in New Zealand. That's on the other side of the world! So I don't see her a lot – but we text nearly every day. Kora is fifteen and she knows a lot about the dragons in New Zealand. All dragon tamers are teenagers. Dragons are OK with children and teenagers but they hate adults. Here we are at a dragon taming conference.

Sometimes I'm in the newspaper. It makes my mum happy, but I don't like it when everyone talks about me. People say I'm a good dragon tamer – but dragon tamers only need to be patient. And nice to the dragons.

Blaze saves English dragons

Blaze tames dragon in three days!

England's top dragon tamer is back again!

People of London thank Blaze

dragon tamer's ID = *Drachenzähmerausweis*; patient = *geduldig*; shy = *scheu, schüchtern*; speciality = *Spezialität*; tame = *zähmen*

And we need to know some tricks.
OK, and maybe we need to be brave, too.
Sometimes dragons can be scary!

Anyway, here's something COOL: It's Monday morning and all my friends are at school – but I'm in a helicopter with Stevie. I'm on my way to tame some dragons in Edinburgh. That's in Scotland. Stevie is my pilot, and she is the best pilot I know. She is my pilot on all my missions.

Dragons normally live in the mountains or in forests, but sometimes they come into cities. Then dragon tamers need to protect the people, tame the dragons and take them to a safe place.

Most dragons speak some English. And I can speak some Skkaddraa. That's the dragon language. I can say "Maa nominaadraa hes Blaze." Can you guess what that means? That's right: "My name is Blaze." How about: "Maa hobbittaa hes reddinitaa?" It means: "My hobby is reading." Oh, we're here! Hello Edinburgh! Good, a policeman is here to meet me. He can tell me all about the situation. OK, let's go …

DIGITAL+
You can listen to Blaze talking to the policeman: audio 2/51

brave = *mutig*; protect = *beschützen*; safe = *sicher, ungefährlich*; scary = *Furcht erregend*

Neighbourhoods in London

Hello, my name is Libby. I am twelve years old. I live in Brixton. Brixton is great because it has lots of shops and a street market. In Brixton you can see some great street art. We also have the Brixton Academy. Lots of famous musicians and bands perform there. It's brilliant!

Hi, I'm Lee. I am eleven years old and I live in Fulham with my mum, dad and sister. Fulham is a great place if you like football. There are two teams in Fulham: Fulham and Chelsea. I am a big Chelsea fan.
I often go to football matches with my dad. The Chelsea football team wears blue and white. There's also a swimming pool in Fulham. My friends and I like it very much.

My name is Anousa. I am thirteen years old. I live in Putney with my mum and our dog Biscuit.
I like Putney. It is a great place for sports. There are lots of parks where you can run, play and ride your bike. Every year we go to the Boat Race in Putney. There are always lots of people. You can also do sports like paddle boarding on the river. It is great fun.

I'm Fergus. I am fifteen years old and I live in Wembley with my mum, dad and grandma. Wembley is in north London. It is famous for its stadium. I like going to concerts at Wembley Stadium. I love rock music! Lots of people also come to see football matches at Wembley Stadium. When there is a big match there are always lots of people on the underground.

Which of these neighbourhoods is your favourite? Explain.

1 Look at the picture. What can you see?
2 What is the same in your classroom?
3 What is different?

School

Part A Back to school

- Du erfährst etwas über den Stundenplan der vier Freunde aus Notting Hill.
- Du sprichst über Dinge in deinem Klassenzimmer.
- Du gestaltest ein Spiel zum Thema Schule.

Part B School life

- Du sprichst über Schul-AGs.
- Du erfährst etwas über den britischen Schulalltag.
- Du stellst in einer Präsentation deine eigene Schule vor.

Don't worry, Tarek!

1a

**Look at the pictures.
What can you see?**

It's quarter past eight. Let's pack your schoolbag for tomorrow. Are you nervous about your first day at the new school?

Well, a bit …

Don't worry. You've got your friends with you.

1   8:15pm

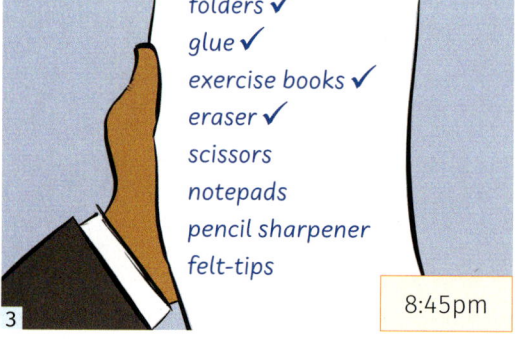

folders ✓
glue ✓
exercise books ✓
eraser ✓
scissors
notepads
pencil sharpener
felt-tips

3   8:45pm

1b   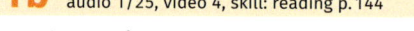 audio 1/25, video 4, skill: reading p. 144

Read and find out: what is special about the next day?

Have you got your schoolbag? Good. Take all your folders and exercise books with you. Check your pencil case, too. Have you got pens and pencils? And an eraser? Don't forget your ruler and your calculator, please.

2   8:30pm

Thanks for your help, Dad.

That's OK. Oh, it's nine o'clock! Time for bed.

4   9:00pm

1c   CHOOSE YOUR LEVEL   wordbank: school p. 154, workbook p. 30/1-3

▌ Find the words for the pictures and write them in your exercise book.

1    2    3    4   5    6

▌ Write a checklist with school things. Then check what you have got in your schoolbag.

You can write:

exercise books ✓
ruler
…

▌ Write about your schoolbag.

You can write:

This is my schoolbag.
It is …
There are … in my schoolbag.
There is …
I have got …

ACTIVATE   PRACTISE   DEVELOP   PRACTISE   APPLY

Tarek's dream

2a

**Look at the picture. What do you think:
what is Tarek's dream about?**

2b 🎬 video 5

Watch the video clip. What is not on the list?

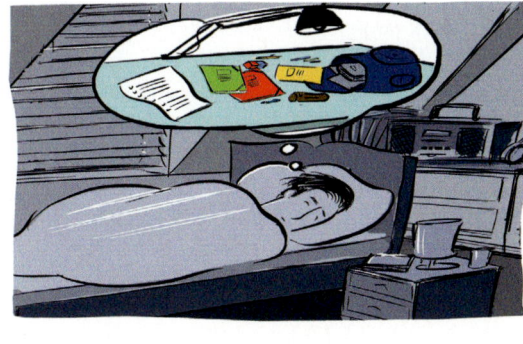

Assembly

3a workbook p. 32/4

**Look at the picture.
What is the situation?**

3b audio 1/27

**Listen and read along. What is the
headteacher talking about?**

Headteacher: Good morning boys and girls!
Welcome to Holland Park School. My name is
Mr Walker and I am your headteacher. Today
is an exciting day – but don't be nervous!

Let me tell you a bit about your new school.
Assembly is every morning at twenty to nine.
We all meet here for important information.
Always be on time, please.

After assembly you go to registration.
Registration is every morning at nine o'clock.
Lunch is at half past twelve and there are a
lot of activities in the afternoon. Look at the
noticeboard for information.

I hope you have a good first day and a great
year at Holland Park School! If you have any
problems, come and see me in my office.
Now it's time to meet your new class.
We start with class …

3c

Read again. When is assembly? When is registration? When is lunch?

Your school wordbank

4 skill: working with words p. 140

**Start your own school wordbank. You can draw pictures, too. Think about:
things in your schoolbag, people at school, what your teacher says, …**

GRAMMAR HELP   the imperative p. 170

So kannst du jemanden auffordern, etwas zu tun (Befehlsform):

Look!
Pack your schoolbag, please.
Be on time, please.
Listen to the teacher, please.

Wenn jemand etwas *nicht* tun soll, kannst du das so sagen (verneinte Befehlsform):

Don't worry!
Don't forget your pencil, please.
Don't be nervous.
Don't play football here, please.

Was fällt dir auf? Was kommt bei der verneinten Befehlsform hinzu?

Unscramble

5   grammar: the imperative p. 170

Unscramble the sentences.

1   be – Don't – nervous.
2   at – Look – noticeboard. – the
3   please. – to – Listen – the headteacher,
4   forget – your – Don't – pencil case.
5   for – please. – on time – Be – registration,
6   exercise book, – your – Open – please.

Five commands

6   grammar: the imperative p. 170, workbook p. 33/5, 6

Write down five commands. Then read them to a partner. Your partner mimes the actions. Take turns.

You can write:

Open your …
Close …
Play …

What's the time, please?

7   wordbank: time p. 155, numbers p. 232, workbook p. 34/7

Look at the wordbank "time" on page 155. Then look at the clocks and ask and answer questions with a partner. Take turns.

| 07:00 | 11:00 |

| 05:15 | 07:30 |

| 08:40 | 09:50 |

| 10:05 | 11:25 |

You can ask:

What's the time, please?
What time is it, please?

You can answer:

It's … o'clock.

It's quarter past … / It's … fifteen.
It's half past … / It's … thirty.
It's quarter to … / It's … forty-five.

It's ten past … / It's … ten.
It's twenty past … / It's … twenty.
It's twenty to … / It's … forty.

It's five past … / It's … oh five.
It's twenty-five past … / It's … twenty-five.
It's twenty-five to … / It's … thirty-five.

DIGITAL+ practise more 5

ACTIVATE   **PRACTISE**   DEVELOP   PRACTISE   APPLY

Registration

8 audio 1/30, skill: listening p.141, mediation p.145

Look at the picture and listen. What is happening? Talk to a partner in German.

Mr Patel

The new timetable

9a

Look at the timetable.
Which subjects can you name in German?

9b audio 1/31, skill: listening p.141

Listen to the children.
What are they talking about?

	Time	Lesson	Monday	Tuesday	Wednesday	Thursday	Friday
am	8:40 – 9:00				assembly		
	9:00-9:40				registration and form time		
	9:40 – 10:30	1	maths	French	ICT	maths	English
	10:30 – 10:50				break		
	10:50 – 11:40	2	English	maths	science	art	French
	11:40 – 12:30	3	English	maths	science	art	maths
pm	12:30 – 1:30				lunch		
	1:30 – 2:20	4	geography	history	English	history	geography
	2:20 – 3:10	5	geography	music	English	history	PE
	3:10 – 4:00	6	French	music	RE	science	PE

9c CHOOSE YOUR LEVEL skill: listening p.141

▌ Listen again. What is true? What is false? Write down the true statements.

1 It's half past ten.
2 Harry likes Mr Patel.
3 Tarek's favourite day is Friday.

▌▌ Listen again. What is true? What is false? Correct the false statements and write them down.

1 It's ten o'clock.
2 Noah says Mr Patel is not a good teacher.
3 Harry says Tuesdays are great.
4 Ava's favourite day is Thursday.

▌▌▌ Listen again. Answer the questions and write down your answers.

1 What time is it?
2 What does Harry say about Mr Patel?
3 What does Noah say about Mr Patel?
4 What does Tarek say about the timetable?
5 What is Harry's favourite subject?

9d skill: talking with people p.142, workbook p.35/8

What is your favourite subject? What is your favourite school day? Talk about it with a partner.

In the classroom

10a

What can you see in the picture? Collect words in class.

10b   audio 1/32

Listen and point to the things in the picture.

a board · chairs · desks · a noticeboard · a bin · a map · a poster · bookshelves · a clock · school uniforms · a lunchbox · a bottle · schoolbags · an exercise book

10c   audio 1/33, video 6, skill: listening p. 141

Look at the picture again. Who is talking? Listen and point.

ACTIVATE   PRACTISE   **DEVELOP**   PRACTISE   APPLY

Your classroom

11a   grammar: the article p.171, plural p.172, numbers p.232

Talk about your classroom.

You can say:

There is a …

There is an …

There are …

There are two / three / …

11b   CHOOSE YOUR LEVEL

I **Label things in your classroom.**

II **Make an alphabetical list of things in your classroom.**

III **Write true/false statements about your classroom. Let a partner correct the false statements.**

At school

12   CHOOSE YOUR TASK   A: wordbank: time p.155, B: wordbank: school p.154, C: classroom phrases p.162

A **Make a game of dominoes with clocks and times for a partner.**

B **Write your dream timetable.**

C **Write mini classroom dialogues. Look at 10a for ideas.**
   You can record your dialogues.

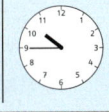

The alphabet song

13a   audio 1/34

Listen to the song. Then sing along and clap your hands.

Come on children, sing it out.
Come on children, sing it loud.
Come on children, sing with me.
This is the song of the ABC.

(Chorus:)
A B C D
E F and a G
H I J K
Oh, so far it is OK.

L M N O P
Q R S and T
U V W X Y Z
That's the alphabet.

Hey everybody, sing once more.
Sing it as we've done before.
Come on, everybody now, don't forget
this rock song of the alphabet.
(Chorus)

13b   workbook p.35/9, 10

Work with a partner. Your partner spells a word. You write it down.
Then check the word together. Take turns.

Nouns

14a   grammar: the article p. 171

Read the words in the box. Match them with the correct article, "a" or "an". Make two lists.

board · English book · chair · desk ·
apple · child · map · lunchbox ·
orange · pencil case · uniform ·
schoolbag · exercise book · bookshelf

You can write:

a	an
a board	an English book
…	…

14b   audio 1/35

Listen and check your lists.

14c   grammar: plural of nouns p. 172

Write down the plural forms of the nouns.

Classroom phrases

15   CHOOSE YOUR LEVEL   workbook p. 36/11

❙ Match the sentence parts and write down the classroom phrases.

1 Can I
2 Sit
3 What is "Buch"
4 Have you got

A your homework?
B in English?
C open the window, please?
D down, please.

❙❙ Complete the classroom phrases with the words from the box. Write them down.

be · borrow · Have · Open · forget · spell

1 Always ??? on time, please.
2 Can I ??? a pencil, please?
3 ??? you got your ruler?
4 ??? your books, please.
5 Don't ??? your homework.
6 Can you ??? your name, please?

❙❙❙ Unscramble the classroom phrases and write them down.

1 window, – I – open – Can – the – please?
2 Sorry – I – late. – am
3 the – at – Look – picture.
4 borrow – please? – Can – pen, – I – a
5 homework? – Where – your – is
6 the toilet, – please? – go – Can – I – to
7 your – Write – timetable. – down
8 spell – you – Can – the word "science"?

Spelling

16   audio 1/37, workbook p. 36/12

Listen and write down the words. Then check them with a partner.

DIGITAL+ practise more 6

ACTIVATE   PRACTISE   DEVELOP   **PRACTISE**   APPLY

A classroom board game TARGET TASK

17 workbook p. 37/13, wordbank: school p. 154, grammar: the imperative p. 170

Your task is to write challenge cards for a board game. Before you start, look at these steps:

STEP 1

Get together with a partner or in a small group.
Go to www.westermann.de/128200 to find a board for the game.

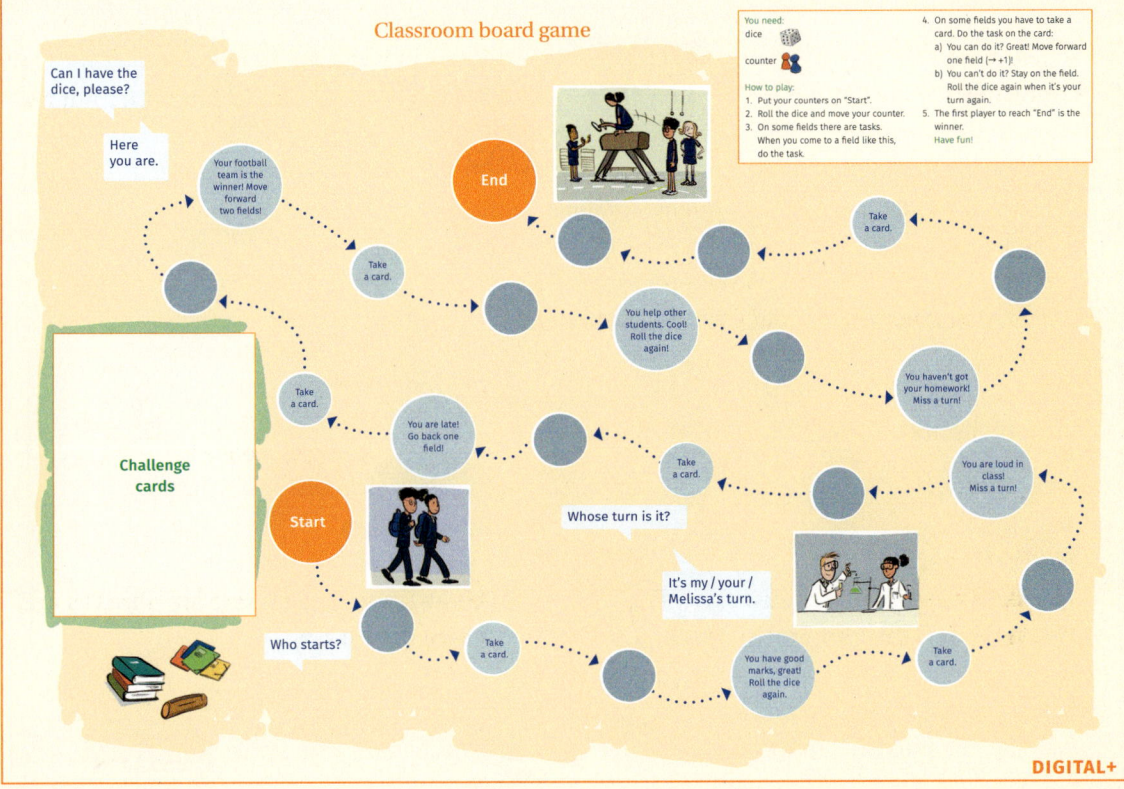

STEP 2

Be creative: write down tasks or questions for the players on cards.
Here are some ideas:

Name three things in your classroom.	*What is your favourite subject?*	*What is … in German / English?*	*What time is it?* 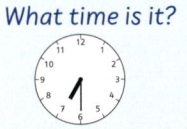

STEP 3

Place the cards on the board. Play the game.

What's on at Holland Park School?

1a workbook p. 38/1

Look at the posters. What do you think:
· Where can you find them?
· Who are they for?
· What are they about?

You can say:
They are …
There is a poster about …

SCHOOL CLUBS

Book club
Do you like books?
Come to the book club!
Where: in the library
When: Mondays at
lunchtime
We read one new book
every month.
This month it's "Favourite
School Stories".

Drama club
Be a star at the
drama club!
When: Mondays,
4:00pm – 6:00pm
Where: assembly hall
Who: everybody is
welcome
For more information talk
to Mrs Baker.

Cooking club
Do you like cooking?
Then join our cooking club!
Who: all students are
welcome!
Where: school kitchen
When: Tuesdays,
4:15pm – 5:45pm

Football team
The football team needs you!
We practise at the gym on
Wednesdays from 4:00pm to
5:30pm.
We play matches on Saturdays.

Go Tigers

Science club
Come to the science club!
Where: science lab
When: Thursdays,
4:15pm – 5:00pm
What: exciting
experiments and more

School band
Do you play an instrument?
We need you!
The band meets every Friday
in the music room from 4:00pm to
6:00pm.
Bring your instrument.

LUNCH MENU

Monday: Cafeteria lunch menu
Main course: chilli con carne
Vegetarian: vegetarian chilli
Side: chips or rice
Dessert: apple pie

ACTIVATE   PRACTISE   DEVELOP   PRACTISE   APPLY

1b CHOOSE YOUR LEVEL skill: reading p.144, workbook p.38/2-4

Read the posters on the noticeboard. What do you find out? Write about it.

█ Complete the sentences.

1 The book club meets in …
2 The drama club meets on Mondays from … to …
3 The cooking club meets in the …
4 The football team practises on …

██ Correct the sentences.

1 The science club meets on Mondays.
2 The book club reads one book every week.
3 The football team plays matches on Sundays.
4 The cooking club meets on Thursdays from 4:15pm to 5:00pm.

███ Write five or more sentences.

The school band The … club …	meets practises plays …	in … on … from … to … …

A club for Lily

2a audio 1/43

Listen and read along.

Ava: Do you want to join a club?
Lily: Hmm, I don't know. I don't play an instrument, I don't like team sports, …
Ava: Noah says the science club is great.
Lily: Yeah, that doesn't sound bad. What do they do?
Ava: Noah says they do a lot of experiments. Sometimes there are even small explosions.
Lily: That sounds great! Science club on Thursdays for me! What do you like?
Ava: I like the book club. What do you think?
Lily: But they meet today at lunchtime. Do you think there is enough time for lunch, too? I really like apple pie …
Ava: That's not a problem. Noah always goes to lunch before his lunchtime clubs.
Lily: OK, let's get some lunch first and then try the book club.

2b skill: listening p.141, workbook p.40/5

Listen again. What do the girls like? What don't they like?
You can say:

Lily doesn't like … Lily likes …
Ava likes …
…

The best clubs

3 workbook p.41/6

Look at the noticeboard again. Write down your top three clubs. Tell a partner about them.
You can say:

My number one is …
I like …
…

GRAMMAR HELP

simple present: statements p. 173

Wenn du ausdrücken willst, dass jemand etwas regelmäßig tut, dass etwas regelmäßig stattfindet oder dass etwas über längere Zeit gültig ist, verwendest du das *simple present*:

I meet my friends every Friday.
You like the science club.
We play matches on Saturdays.
They practise on Wednesdays.

The school band meets every Friday.
Lily likes the science club.
Harry plays the guitar.
The football team practises on Wednesdays.

Vergleiche die Verbformen. Was fällt dir auf?

Auf Seite 173 kannst du weitere Beispiele finden – auch für die verneinten Formen im *simple present*.

School

 4 grammar: simple present statements p. 173, workbook p. 41/7, 8

Complete the sentences and write them down. Use the correct forms of the words from the box.

join · meet · do · play · go · start

1 Tarek, Ava, Lily and Harry ??? to Holland Park School.
2 School ??? at 8:40.
3 Ava and Lily ??? the book club.

4 The book club ??? in the library.
5 The students ??? a lot of experiments at the science club.
6 The football team ??? matches on Saturdays.

About Harry

 5 grammar: simple present statements p. 173

What does Harry like or do (+)? What doesn't he like or do (-)? Write sentences.

+ like football · like music · play the guitar in the school band

You can write:
Harry likes …

- like maths · like Tuesdays · go to the science club

You can write:
He doesn't …

About you

 6 grammar: simple present statements p. 173

What about you? What do you like or do?
What don't you like or do?
Write five or more sentences.

You can write:
I …
I don't …

DIGITAL+ practise more 7

ACTIVATE **PRACTISE** DEVELOP PRACTISE APPLY

Tarek and his new school

7a

**Tarek meets his uncle Sami every Thursday after school. Look at the pictures.
What do you think? What is Tarek talking about with his uncle? Make notes.**

7b audio 1/46

Listen and read along. Check your ideas from 7a.

Uncle: Hi Tarek. Good to see you.

Tarek: Hi, Uncle Sami.

Uncle: So, how do you like your new school? What subjects do you like best?

Tarek: School is good. I really like science. There's a big science lab where we do experiments.

Uncle: Sounds interesting. What else do you like?

Tarek: I go to the cooking club on Tuesdays.

Uncle: Wow. That's useful. You can cook for me next Thursday. And who's your favourite teacher?

Tarek: Mr Patel, my form tutor. He teaches English and music. He sometimes plays the guitar in his lessons. I also like Mrs Fisher, my PE teacher. We've got football this term.

Uncle: Oh cool – my favourite game! Where do you play?

Tarek: At the sports ground. There's also a gym where we practise when it rains.

Uncle: Brilliant! What about a game in the park right now?

Tarek: Great idea. Homework can wait!

7c CHOOSE YOUR LEVEL grammar: simple present statements p. 173, skill: writing p. 143, workbook p. 42/9

▍ Match the sentence parts and write down the sentences.

1 Tarek's new school is
2 Tarek really likes
3 Tarek goes
4 Mr Patel

A to the cooking club on Tuesdays.
B is Tarek's favourite teacher.
C science.
D good.

▍▍ Write five or more sentences about Tarek.

You can write:

Tarek likes …

He goes to …

His favourite … is …

▍▍▍ Write a short text about Tarek and his new school. Write six sentences or more.

You can write:

Tarek goes to Holland Park School.

He thinks school is … He likes …

…

LAND & LEUTE 2 video 7, workbook 42/10

Schulalltag in Großbritannien

An den meisten britischen Schulen tragen die Kinder Schuluniform. Ein Schultag dauert etwa von 9 bis 16 Uhr. Häufig beginnt der Tag mit der Überprüfung der Anwesenheit *(registration)*. Oft gibt es auch eine Schulversammlung *(assembly)*. Die Lehrkräfte haben eigene Räume, in denen sie unterrichten. Nachmittags nehmen viele Kinder an AGs *(clubs)* teil. Viele Schulen haben ein Haus-System. Dabei bildet eine Gruppe von Schülerinnen und Schülern aus verschiedenen Klassen jeweils ein *house,* für das sie zum Beispiel bei Wettkämpfen antreten.

Sieh dir den Videoclip an. Was ist an deiner Schule ähnlich? Was ist anders?

A video chat

8a

Look at the picture. What can you see?

8b   audio 1/47

Listen and read along. What are the children talking about?

Lily is talking to her old friends in Brighton.
Lily: Hi guys!
Jonah: Hey Lily! How are you?
Lily: I'm good, thanks.
Ellen: How do you like London?
Lily: I like it a lot. But I miss you!
Ellen: We miss you, too. School is a bit boring without you.
Jonah: Do you like your new school?
Lily: Yes, I do. The teachers are good and there are cool clubs. Do you still go to the drama club, Ellen?
Ellen: No, I don't. I'm in the school band now. Does Harry still play the guitar?

Lily: Yes, he does. He plays in the school band, too. He goes there every Friday.
Oh, here he comes. Say hello to Ellen and Jonah, Harry.
Harry: Hi Ellen, hi Jonah. Is that your new school uniform? It looks so … red.
Do you like it?
Ellen and Jonah: No, we don't!
Ellen: The colour is really bad.
Jonah: Do you wear a uniform at school?
Lily: Yes, we do. I wear a black blazer, a black skirt or a pair of trousers and a blue shirt.
Harry: I wear the same. Well, not the skirt … And the boys wear ties.

8c   grammar: simple present questions p. 174, workbook p. 43/11

Match the questions and answers.

1 Does Lily like her new school?
2 Does Ellen still go to the drama club?
3 Do Jonah and Ellen like their uniform?
4 Do Harry and Lily wear uniforms at school?

A No, they don't.
B Yes, they do.
C No, she doesn't.
D Yes, she does.

ACTIVATE   PRACTISE   **DEVELOP**   PRACTISE   APPLY

The children at school

9a

Talk about the pictures. Where are the children?

Ava reads in the library on Mondays at lunchtime.

The students do sports in the gym on Fridays.

Noah and Lily do experiments in the science lab every Thursday.

Tarek cooks in the kitchen on Tuesdays from 4:15pm to 5:45pm.

9b

Answer the questions.

1 Who reads in the library?
2 What do the students do on Fridays?
3 Where do Noah and Lily do experiments?
4 When does Tarek cook?

9c   workbook p. 44/12

Write down more questions for a partner. Then ask and answer the questions.

You can write:

When do Noah and Lily …?

Where does … ?

School life

10   CHOOSE YOUR TASK   A: wordbank: clothes p. 153, B/C: wordbank: school p. 154

A **Design your own school uniform. Draw a picture and label it.**
B **Create a poster for a (dream) school club.**
C **Write a short text about your dream school. Think about rooms, places, things, activities, …**

Rohan's school

11   audio 1/48, skill: mediation p. 145

Listen to Rohan, an exchange student. Your little sister does not understand everything. Answer her questions in German.

1 Wann fängt Rohans Schule morgens an?
2 Was sagt er über seine Schuluniform?
3 Was ist sein Lieblingsfach?
4 Welche AGs besucht er?

David and Julia

12   GET TOGETHER

Get together with a partner. Read and talk about David and Julia.

Partner A

▌ **Go to page 113.**
▌ **Go to page 117.**
▌ **Go to page 121.**

Partner B

▌ **Go to page 125.**
▌ **Go to page 129.**
▌ **Go to page 133.**

Questions

13 **CHOOSE YOUR LEVEL** grammar: simple present questions p. 174

I **Copy the questions into your exercise book. Find the matching answers and write them down.**

1 Where do the students eat lunch?
2 When does the book club meet?
3 What do the students do in the lab?
4 Who teaches PE?

A They do experiments.
B Mrs Fisher.
C In the cafeteria.
D On Mondays at lunchtime.

II **Unscramble the questions and write them down.**
Find the matching answers in the box. Write them down, too.

1 does – like? – Lily – What dessert
2 music? – teaches – Who – English – and
3 do – What – wear – the children – at school?
4 the students – do sports – on Fridays? – Where – do
5 to – does – Tarek – cooking club? – When – the – go

On Tuesdays.
School uniforms.
Mr Patel.
Apple pie.
In the gym.

III **Unscramble the questions.**
Then look at number 8b on page 44 and write answers to the questions.

1 are – Ellen and Jonah? – Who
2 Ellen and Jonah – Where – live? – do
3 How – Lily – London? – like – does
4 does – Harry – school band? – When – practise – with – the
5 is – Ellen and Jonah's – What colour – school uniform?

This is our school

14a video 8

Watch the video clip.
What do the girls present?

14b

Watch the video clip again.
Match the statements to the rooms.

library · sports hall · classroom

1
"We have assemblies in here.
We do PE in here or outside."

2
"It's my favourite place.
It's open break times,
lunchtimes and after school."

3
"We have registration
at the start of each day
to see who's here."

14c wordbank: school p. 154, workbook p. 44/13

Work with a partner. Describe a room or place at your school.
Your partner says which room or place it is. Take turns.

Our school TARGET TASK

15 workbook p. 45/14, wordbank: school p. 154, skill: presentations p. 146

Your task is to prepare a presentation about your school, for example for new students.
Before you start, look at these steps:

STEP 1

In class decide how you want to present your school.
You could make:
• a poster presentation
• a brochure
• a slide show
• a video
• …

STEP 2

What do you want to show? Collect ideas.
Think about:
• rooms
• teachers
• subjects
• clubs
• places outdoors
• what is special about your school?
• …

STEP 3

Get together in groups. Decide which group presents which topic.

STEP 4

Prepare your presentation in your group. Collect ideas and make a plan.

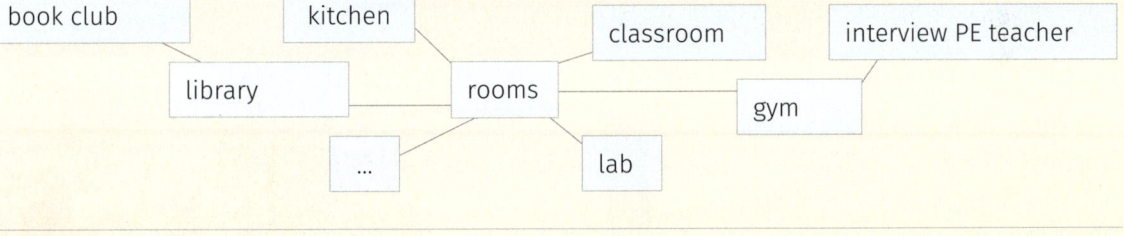

book club | kitchen | classroom | interview PE teacher | library | rooms | gym | … | lab

STEP 5

Create your poster, slide show, video, …
Check it.

STEP 6

Present your work.

Check out

1. Kannst du jemanden auffordern, etwas zu tun oder nicht zu tun? Workbook, p. 46
2. Kannst du Dinge in deiner Schultasche und in deinem Klassenzimmer benennen? Workbook, p. 46
3. Kannst du die Uhrzeit auf Englisch nennen? Workbook, p. 46
4. Kannst du darüber berichten, was regelmäßig stattfindet oder was jemand regelmäßig tut? Workbook, p. 47
5. Kannst du verstehen, was jemand über den Schulalltag berichtet? Workbook, p. 47
6. Kannst du jemandem Fragen zur Schule stellen? Workbook, p. 47

Meeting the dragons

Oh, hello again. So, now I know where the dragons are. The policeman says they're at Edinburgh Castle. It's a family of dragons: a mum dragon, a dad dragon and a young dragon. Right, let's see … Where is the castle? OK, here it is. Look:

It's dragon taming time – let's go!
Look, there's the National Museum of Scotland.
I like museums. Oh, and the National Library of Scotland.
Maybe they have got some good dragon books.
And there's the castle! Come on!

We're here! Now, where are the dragons?
Oh, over there. Shhhh. I see them. Two purple dragons. I think they are the parents. And there's the young one. It's a girl. She's blue and oh, isn't she sweet? Look how small she is! Oh wow, there's a dragon egg, too. There, the light purple thing in the nest. Purple parents, blue child, light purple egg? These must be Feli-Rhymus dragons. Oooh, they're very difficult. And they are from New Zealand. Maybe Kora can give me some tips.

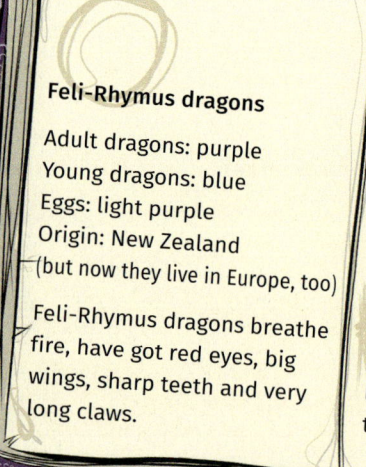

Feli-Rhymus dragons

Adult dragons: purple
Young dragons: blue
Eggs: light purple
Origin: New Zealand
(but now they live in Europe, too)

Feli-Rhymus dragons breathe fire, have got red eyes, big wings, sharp teeth and very long claws.

They like rhymes, poems, gold and presents and they love hot and spicy food. They do not like sudden movements and they absolutely hate cats.

breathe fire = *Feuer speien*; difficult = *schwierig*; hot and spicy = *scharf und würzig*;
present = *Geschenk*; sudden movement = *plötzliche Bewegung*

Right. It's time to say hello. OK, that's it, slowly, slowly. And now … Bow. Slowly, slowly. I hope they don't attack me. I bow for a looooooong time. Then I look up and say: "Hello. My name is Blaze. Maa nominaadraa hes Blaze. What about you?"
I look at the dragons. The parents say nothing. But the little one points at herself and says: "Tazzy." Then she points to her mum and says: "Volta," and to her dad and says: "Ignus."

Wait, is that a … Yes, it's a cat! Oh no!
Feli-Rhymus dragons hate cats. The cat lies down next to the dragons' nest. I look up at the dragons.
They look angry. That cat needs to go – now!
I slowly move towards the cat and then – oh no!
I stumble and fall over. The cat jumps up and runs away. I look at the dragons.
Uh oh. They really, really don't like cats. And they really, really don't like fast movements.

Suddenly, Ignus – the dad dragon – flies up into the air. I see his eyes. They are big and red and angry.
I get up and look up. I see Ignus begin to fly at me.
I see the huge flames of his hot, fiery breath.
Uh oh. Here he comes!

angry = *verärgert*; attack = *angreifen*; bow = *(sich) verbeugen*; fiery breath = *glühender Atem*; stumble = *stolpern*

Different schools in the UK

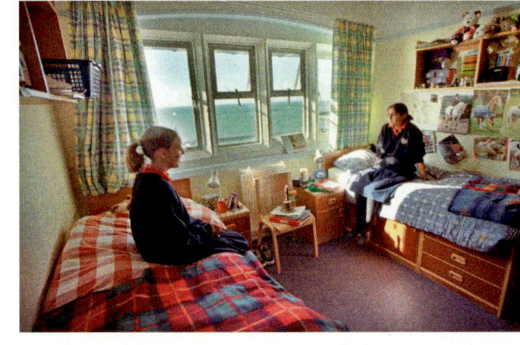

My name is Aisha. I go to a boarding school in Scotland. I don't go home after school. I stay in the boarding house and share a room with my friend. My boarding school is only for girls. Our school uniform is blue and grey. There are four houses at my school. A house is a group of students and each house has a name. My house is called "Queens". When we have school competitions, like sports day, Queens plays against the other houses.

My name is Callum. I go to a comprehensive school in England. You don't have to pay to go to my school. It's a mixed school which means both boys and girls can go there. Our school colours are green and blue. The school day starts at 8:30am when we have registration. Then we have assembly where a teacher stands in front of the school and tells a story or talks about something inspiring. Lessons start at 9am, lunch is at 12:30pm and we finish school at 4pm.
My favourite subject is art and my favourite days are Fridays because we have PE and because it's almost the weekend!

My name is Kate. I go to Summerhill School in England. It's a boarding school and you have to pay to go there. It's very famous because it's different to other schools. The special thing about Summerhill is that we students can decide a lot of things. For example we can decide which lessons we go to. At the beginning of every term we make our own timetables. I really like languages so I always go to French and German lessons. Lessons at Summerhill start at 9am and finish at about 3pm. There is no school uniform. After school there are a lot of activities and projects. I write for the school website, for example.

Which school do you like best? What is special about it?

1. Look at the picture. What can you see?
2. What do you think: what day is it in the picture?
3. What is your favourite activity outdoors?

Free time

Part A At the weekend

- Du unterhältst dich über Frühstücks-gewohnheiten und Wochenendaktivitäten.
- Du verfasst ein kurzes Gedicht.
- Du präsentierst deine Ideen für einen perfekten Tag am Wochenende.

Part B Sports and hobbies

- Du unterhältst dich über Hobbys und Sportarten.
- Du erstellst ein *fact file* zu einer Sportart.
- Du präsentierst deiner Klasse ein Hobby oder eine Sportart.

Saturday family breakfast

1a

Look at the pictures. Talk about them.

You can say:

There is a/an …
There are …

> Let's see … We need bacon, eggs and sausages. Noah eats vegetarian sausages. Mum likes tomatoes with her breakfast. So let's have two or three. The children don't eat tomatoes. Then we need baked beans, toast and butter, orange juice, coffee, tea and milk. Oh, and some cereal.

1b audio 1/50, video 9

Listen and read along.
What does Ava's family have for breakfast?
Which of the things do you like or not like?

> Children! It's time for breakfast! Could you set the table? We need plates, cups, knives, forks and spoons.

> Ava, put the jam and the chocolate spread on the table, please. Joshua, could you take the fruit?

1 9:00am

Baked beans

> Good morning, guys.

> You're always late for breakfast, Noah. And you never help.

> Well, Noah can help clean up after breakfast. Ava, could you pass the jam, please?

3

Jam

1c CHOOSE YOUR LEVEL skill: reading p. 144, workbook p. 48/1

❙ Read again, then write about the family's breakfast. Copy the text and fill in the gaps.

It is Saturday morning. Ava's dad is in the k???. He needs bacon, e??? and s???. Ava's mum likes t??? with her breakfast. The family also needs baked beans, t??? and b???. They drink o???, c??? and t???.

❙❙ Read again, then write about the family's breakfast. Copy the text and fill in the gaps.

It is 9 o'clock on ??? morning. Ava's dad is in the ???. It is time for ???. He asks the children to set the ???. They need ???, ???, ???, ??? and ???. Dad asks Joshua: "Could you take the ??? ?" Noah is ??? for breakfast.

ACTIVATE PRACTISE DEVELOP PRACTISE APPLY

III **Read again and write a short text about the family's breakfast.**
Answer these questions in your text:

1. What time and day is it?
2. Where is Ava's dad?
3. What does he need for the family's breakfast?
4. What does Noah eat?
5. What do the children not eat?

6. Who is late for breakfast?
7. What does Ava say about Noah?

You can write:

It is 9 o'clock on … Ava's dad is …

…

What about you?

2 skill: talking with people p. 142, workbook p. 49/2, 3

Think about breakfast with your family.
Talk about it with a partner.

You can say:

I like … for breakfast. What about you?
I don't like …, but I like …
At the weekend my dad eats …
My sister doesn't eat …

…

Breakfast

3   **CHOOSE YOUR TASK** wordbank: food p. 156

A **Make a word search with breakfast words for a partner.**
B **Create a domino game with breakfast words. You can play it with a partner.**

 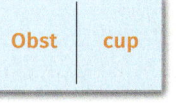

C **What do you need for a perfect breakfast? Write about it.**

LAND & LEUTE 3 video 10, workbook 50/4-7

Englisches Frühstück

Zu einem traditionellen englischen Frühstück *(full English breakfast)* gehören zum Beispiel gebratener Speck *(bacon)* mit Ei, Bratwürstchen, Bohnen in Tomatensauce *(baked beans)* und Grilltomaten. Außerdem gibt es oft Toast mit Butter und Marmelade. Nur Marmelade aus Zitrusfrüchten heißt *marmalade*. Marmelade aus anderen Früchten nennt man *jam*. Für ein *full English breakfast* ist allerdings meist nur am Wochenende Zeit. Viele Menschen in Großbritannien essen es nur zu besonderen

Gelegenheiten, andere nie. Während der Woche isst man oft nur Müsli, Cornflakes, Haferbrei *(porridge)* oder Toast. Du kannst dir im Videoclip anschauen, wie ein *full English breakfast* zubereitet wird.

Was weißt du über Frühstücksgewohnheiten in anderen Ländern?

GRAMMAR HELP word order in statements p.175

Subjekt, Verb und Objekt stehen in englischen Aussagesätzen immer in dieser Reihenfolge:
Subjekt – Verb – Objekt (S – V – O).
Im Anschluss können noch Ergänzungen folgen.

Subjekt	Verb	Objekt	Ergänzung
Ava's mum	likes	tomatoes.	
Ava	eats	eggs and bacon	for breakfast.
Ava's dad	drinks	tea	in the morning.
Ava and Noah	meet	their friends	in the park.
Tarek	plays	hockey	on Saturdays.

Wie ist es im Deutschen oder in einer anderen Sprache, die du sprichst?

Weitere Beispiele und Erklärungen zur Wortstellung im Englischen findest du auf Seite 175.

Joshua

4a grammar: word order in statements p.175

Unscramble the sentences and write them down.

1 cereal. – Joshua – likes
2 every morning. – it – eats – He
3 plays – Joshua – video games – on Sundays.
4 He – TV – watches – in the evening.
5 He – about animals. – likes – books
6 does – He – his homework – after school.
7 He – his friends – on Tuesdays. – meets
8 chips. – fish – and – He – loves

4b grammar: word order in statements p.175

Write four or more sentences about someone in your family. Look at 4a for help.

Odd one out

5

Find the odd one out.

1 bacon, baked beans, sausages, juice
2 fork, knife, cereal, spoon
3 toast, coffee, tea, milk
4 cup, table, chair, shelf
5 Sunday, Saturday, English, Friday
6 apple, jam, orange, banana

How to say *j* and *ch*

6a 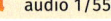 audio 1/55

Listen and repeat.

jam · chair · teacher · juice · child · check · Joshua · subject

6b

Listen again. Make two lists: words with /dʒ/ as in *jam* and words with /tʃ/ as in *chair*. What can you say about the spelling?

DIGITAL+ practise more 9

ACTIVATE **PRACTISE** DEVELOP PRACTISE APPLY

Hurry up, Noah!

7a wordbank: body parts p. 153

Look at the picture.
Point to the body parts and say the words.

7b audio 1/56

Listen and read along.
What is the problem?

Saturday at 11:40. Noah is still in the bathroom.
Ava: Noah! Hurry up! It's twenty to twelve. We leave in ten minutes!
Noah: Just a second. I need to take a shower ...
Ava: ... and clean your ears and style your hair. Yes, I know ... And don't forget to wash your smelly feet!

Ten minutes later.
Family: Noaaaaah! Are you ready?
Noah: Relax, guys. Perfection takes time! I just need to brush my teeth and comb my hair!
Mum: Come on! We're late!
Ava: And Ollie needs to go out!
Noah: OK, OK.

Ten minutes later.
Noah: Here I am!
Mum: Good, let's go!

7c **CHOOSE YOUR LEVEL**

I **Which of the statements are true? Copy them into your exercise book.**
II **Which of the statements are false? Correct them and write them in your exercise book.**
III **Which of the statements are false? Correct them and write them in your exercise book.**
Make up three or more true/false statements for a partner.

1 It is Wednesday.
2 Noah is still in the bathroom at 11:40.
3 Noah needs to take a shower.
4 Noah needs to style his hair.
5 Ava says: "Wash your smelly ears!"
6 Noah is ready at 12:40.

7d workbook p. 52/8-11

What do you think? What is the family's plan? Collect ideas for weekend activities.

The family weekend planner

8a

Get together with a partner.
Partner A: Look at Saturday.
Partner B: Look at Sunday.
Tell each other about the family's plans.

You can say:

The family wants to have …

Noah plans to …

…

	Saturday	Sunday
Morning	have a big breakfast	sleep in!!!!! (Noah) play video games (Joshua) 30 minutes!!!
Lunchtime	12pm: meet Granny at Portobello Road Market	get an Indian takeaway for lunch
Afternoon	4pm: meet Tarek, Harry and Lily in the park (Ava and Noah)	go swimming (Dad and Joshua) 3pm: yoga class (Mum) 4:30pm: pick up Mum, have ice cream
Evening	watch a film together	

8b workbook p. 53 / 12

Look at the planner again. Answer the questions and write down your answers.

1 Who goes to yoga class?
2 What does Noah do on Sunday morning?
3 Where do they meet Granny?
4 When does Joshua play video games?
5 What do they do on Saturday evening?
6 When do they get an Indian takeaway?

You can write:

… goes to yoga class.

Noah …

…

A message for Noah

9a audio 1/58, skill: listening p. 141

Listen to the message for Noah.
Answer the questions.

· What does Tim want to do?
· When does he want to meet Noah?

9b

Listen to the message again. Check the planner in 8a. Has Noah got time?

Saturdays

10 skill: talking with people p. 142

What do you do on Saturdays? Ask and answer questions with a partner. Take turns.

You can ask:

What do you do in the morning?

What do you do at lunchtime?

…

You can answer:

In the morning I …

At lunchtime I …

…

ACTIVATE   PRACTISE   **DEVELOP**   PRACTISE   APPLY

What a perfect day!

11a workbook p. 54 / 13

Look at the picture and check the planner on page 56. What day is it?

11b audio 1/59

Listen and read along. What are the friends talking about?

Ava: Sunshine, friends and watermelon – what a perfect day!

Harry: Yeah, you're right, Ava. This is pretty perfect. Tarek, what's your idea of a perfect day?

Tarek: Hmm, let me think. Oh yes, on my perfect day I make lunch for my dad and my uncle. I make their favourite meal – and they clean up! In the afternoon I play hockey with my friends. And in the evening I stay up really late. What about you, Lily?

Lily: On my perfect day I stay in bed all morning and read a lot. I also play with my rabbits. In the afternoon I go to a flea market with a friend. For dinner we go to the fish and chip shop and then we play board games in the evening.

Noah: On my perfect day I sleep in. For breakfast I have pancakes. Then I meet my friends in the park. First we play football and then, at lunchtime, we eat pizza. In the afternoon my friends and I watch a film together.

Harry: And don't forget ice cream! It's not a perfect day without ice cream!

Lily: That's true, Harry! And on your perfect day you play the guitar, listen to loud music and play computer games, right?

Harry: Yeah, on my perfect day I do what I want.

11c CHOOSE YOUR LEVEL skill: reading p. 144

I Take notes on Tarek's perfect day.

II Take notes on Lily's perfect day. Then use your notes and write four or more sentences about her perfect day.

III Take notes on Noah's perfect day. Then use your notes and write a short text about his perfect day. Use "first", "then", "at lunchtime" and "in the afternoon".

Tarek
– makes lunch for …
– …

A poem of eleven words

12 skill: writing p. 143

Write a weekend poem. Only use eleven words. Read your poem out to the class.

Saturday
no school
really yummy breakfast
time for my friends
perfect

Weekend plans

13 **CHOOSE YOUR LEVEL** skill: mediation p. 145

Imagine you are Alex. Ben, your friend from England, is at your house. You are looking at the family planner together. Ben has got questions about the plans for the weekend.

	Samstag	Sonntag
Morgen	10:00 Fußballspiel (Alex, Ben) einkaufen (Papa)	ausschlafen großes Familienfrühstück
Mittag	schwimmen (Mama und Johanna)	Museum für Naturwissenschaften (Live-Experimente um 13:00!!!)
Nachmittag	16:00 Kino (Alex, Ben, Johanna)	15:00 Kunstworkshop (Mama) 17:00 Oma besuchen (alle)
Abend	Pizza machen	Spieleabend

I **Look at the plans for Saturday. Answer Ben's questions in English.**
1 What is our plan for Saturday morning?
2 What about the afternoon?
3 What about the evening?

II **Look at the plans for Sunday. Answer Ben's questions in English.**
1 What is the plan for Sunday morning?
2 What can we do at the museum?
3 What is the plan for Sunday afternoon?
4 And what about the evening?

III **Look at the planner. Answer Ben's questions in English.**
1 What are our plans for the mornings?
2 What about Saturday afternoon?
3 What's for dinner on Saturday?
4 What's this about a museum?
5 Where is your mum at three o'clock on Sunday?
6 What are the plans for Sunday evening?

Scrambled words

14a

Unscramble the words and sort them: activities, food, people and places.

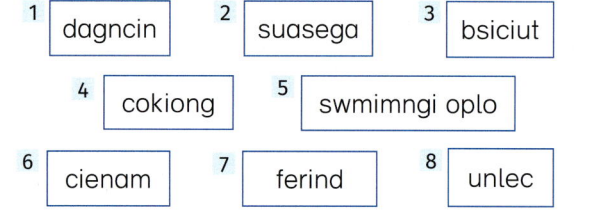

1 dagncin
2 suasega
3 bsiciut
4 cokiong
5 swmimngi oplo
6 cienam
7 ferind
8 unlec

You can write:
activities: dancing, …
food: …
…

14b

Scramble more words for a partner.
He or she unscrambles them and writes them down.

DIGITAL+ practise more 10

ACTIVATE   PRACTISE   DEVELOP   **PRACTISE**   APPLY

My perfect day at the weekend TARGET TASK

15   workbook p.55/14, wordbank: time p.155, skill: writing p.143

Your task is to present ideas for your perfect day at the weekend.
Before you start, look at these steps:

STEP 1

What is important for a perfect day at the weekend? Collect ideas in class.
Think about: activities, food, people, places, weather, …

STEP 2

What is important for your perfect day? Make notes.

STEP 3

How do you want to present your ideas?
You could:
· label pictures
· make a word web
· design a page from a planner
· write a short text
· …

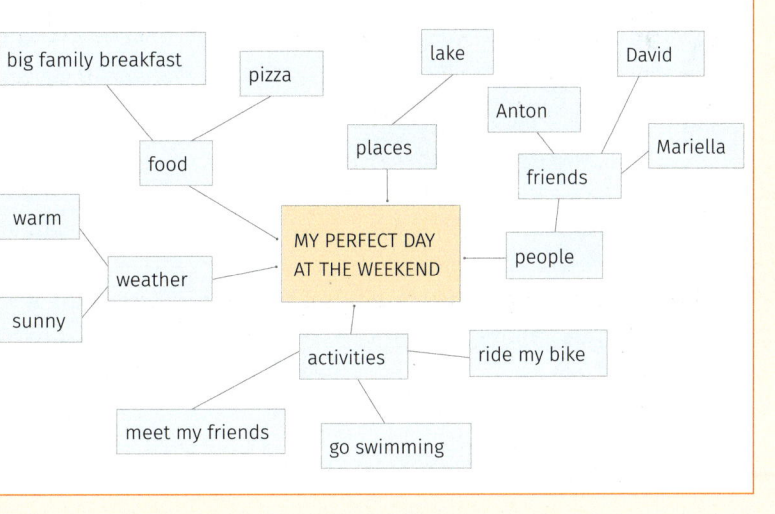

STEP 4

Create a first version and check it.
You can ask a classmate or your teacher for feedback.

STEP 5

Now create your final version.

STEP 6

Display your works in your classroom.

Free time

1   workbook p. 56/1

What do you do in your free time?
Talk about it with a partner.

You can say:

In my free time I …

I go to …

Talking about hobbies

2a   audio 2/1

Look at the pictures and listen to the children. What information is new to you?

2b   skill: listening p. 141

Read the statements, then listen again. Who says what?

1   "I can cook lots of different things."
2   "I can do some tricks."
3   "I can't sing."
4   "I can't play an instrument."
5   "I can dance."

2c   **CHOOSE YOUR LEVEL**   workbook p. 56/2

Listen again. What can the children do? What can't they do?

❚ **Write three or more statements.**

Tarek		cook.
Ava	can	play …
Harry	can't	do …
Lily		…

❚❚ **True or false? Correct the false statements and write them down.**

1   Tarek can cook lots of different things.
2   Ava can't cook.
3   Ava can't do skateboard tricks.
4   Harry can play the guitar.
5   Lily can play an instrument.
6   Lily can't dance.

❚❚❚ **Write five or more statements about the children.**

You can write:

Tarek can cook lots of different …

Ava can't …

ACTIVATE   PRACTISE   DEVELOP   PRACTISE   APPLY

Sports and hobbies

3a   audio 2/2

Listen and point to the sport or hobby.

1
do arts and crafts

2
do karate

3
ride a bike

4
sing

5
do gymnastics

6
make videos

7
play table tennis

8
climb

9
do athletics

10
ride a horse

11
play the piano

12
ice-skate

3b

Play a guessing game with your class. Mime and guess sports and hobbies.

3c   wordbank: free time p. 157

**Write four or more sentences about
what you can and can't do.
You can look at the pictures for help.**

You can write:
I can …, but I can't …
I can't …, but I can …

3d   workbook p. 57/3, 4

Ask and answer questions with a partner.

You can ask:
Can you do karate?
Can you …?

You can answer:
Yes, I can.
No, I can't.

GRAMMAR HELP can: statements p. 176

Mit *can* bzw. *can't* kannst du ausdrücken, was jemand tun kann bzw. nicht tun kann.
Sieh dir die Beispiele an. Was fällt dir auf?

I can dance, but I can't sing.
You can play football, but you can't play hockey.
Harry can play the guitar, but he can't play the piano.
Lily can sing, but she can't play an instrument.
The dog can swim, but it can't do skateboard tricks.

We can play table tennis, but we can't play tennis.
You can speak English, but you can't speak French.
The children can swim, but they can't ice-skate.

Auf Seite 176 findest du weitere Erläuterungen zu *can* und *can't*.

Can they or can't they?

4 grammar: can statements p. 176, workbook p. 58/5

**Look at the pictures and write about them.
What can the children do? What can't they do?**

You can write:
The boy can't swim.
The girls can …

Play, do or ride?

5

Match the verbs to the words in the box. Then find three more examples with play, do or ride.

play
do
ride

a horse · the piano · athletics ·
gymnastics · table tennis · a bike ·
computer games · arts and crafts

You can write:
play the piano, play …
do …
ride …

DIGITAL+ practise more 11

ACTIVATE **PRACTISE** DEVELOP PRACTISE APPLY

What's their sport?

6a

Look at the photos. What do you think: what sports do the children do?

6b video 11

Now watch the video clip and find out.

6c CHOOSE YOUR LEVEL skill: mediation p.145, workbook p.58/6

A friend, who does not speak English, wants to know what the children are saying. Read his or her questions. Then watch the video clip again, take notes and answer your friend's questions in German.

I Was braucht Gracie für ihren Sport?

II Was mögen Gracie und Amy an ihren Sportarten?

III Wie oft betreibt Gracie ihren Sport?
Was braucht Amy für ihren Sport?
Was mag Sophia an ihrem Sport?

What's in the pictures?

7a

Can you find out what is in the pictures? Name the places. You can look at the box for help.

swimming pool · racetrack · ice rink · tennis court · football ground · climbing wall · mini golf course

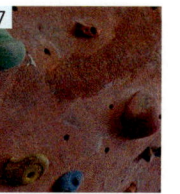

7b workbook p.59/7

Tell your classmates what you can do at these places.

You can say:

Number 1 is a … You can … there.

Two sports

8   GET TOGETHER audio 2/5, 2/6

Work with a partner.
Talk about two different sports.

Partner A	**Partner B**
I Go to page 114.	I Go to page 126.
II Go to page 118.	II Go to page 130.
III Go to page 122.	III Go to page 134.

LAND & LEUTE 4 video 12

Fußball

Die meisten Regeln, nach denen heute auf der ganzen Welt Fußball gespielt wird, wurden im vorletzten Jahrhundert von der 1863 in England gegründeten *Football Association*, dem englischen Fußballverband, festgelegt.
Die englische Nationalmannschaft der Herren, die den Spitznamen *Three Lions* trägt, gehört zu den international erfolgreichsten. Bei den Damen heißt die Nationalmannschaft *The Lionesses* (die Löwinnen). Auch Schottland, Wales und Nordirland haben eigene Nationalmannschaften. Die *Premier League* ist die höchste englische Liga. Einige der Vereine *(clubs)*, die in der *Premier League* spielen, sind weltbekannt und haben Topspieler unter Vertrag.

Viele Mannschaften haben begeisterte Fans, die ausgestattet mit Trikot *(jersey)* und Schal *(scarf)* zu den Spielen fahren. Das Wort Fan kommt ursprünglich von dem Wort *fanatic* – jemand, der sich sehr für etwas begeistert. Wenn US-Amerikaner von *football* sprechen, dann meinen sie damit *American football*. Das Fußballspiel nach englischem Vorbild heißt in den USA *soccer*.

Sieh dir den Videoclip an und finde heraus, wie gut du dich mit Fußball auskennst.

Find out …

9   CHOOSE YOUR TASK A+C: skill: searching the Internet p. 148, workbook p. 59/8

A ▨ **Find out about German players in the Premier League.**
Tell your class about them.

B **Make a fact file about your favourite sportsperson.**
Tell your class about him or her.

C ▨ **Find out about unusual hobbies.**
Tell your class about them.

B
MY FAVOURITE SPORTSPERSON
Name: Rheed McCracken
Sport: wheelchair racing
Birthday:
20 January 1997
Home:
Bundaberg, Australia
Biggest success:
world record

ACTIVATE   PRACTISE   **DEVELOP**   PRACTISE   APPLY

Getting into the game

10a workbook p. 60/9

Look at the pictures. What do you think: what is each text about? Talk about your ideas in class.

10b audio 2/7, 2/8, 2/9

Now read the texts and check your ideas from 10a.

1 A lot of people play video games in their free time. You can play alone or with other players and you can play offline or  online. You need a computer, a console, a tablet or a smartphone. There are lots of different kinds of video games, for example sports games or simulations.

2 Tennis is a ball game for two or four players. Every player needs a tennis racket. You play tennis on a tennis court. There is a net in the middle of the court. One player hits the ball over the net with his or her racket. The other player tries to hit it back over the net. It is important to keep the ball inside the lines. You get a point if the other player can't hit the ball back or hits the ball out.

3 Rugby is a team sport. There are different versions of rugby. In standard rugby, there are two teams of 15 players. You play rugby on a rugby field. There are two field goals that look like the letter "H". You also need a rugby ball. A rugby ball is not round like a football – it looks like an egg. Each team tries to get the ball behind the other team's field goal. The players can kick, throw and catch the ball. They can tackle other players to 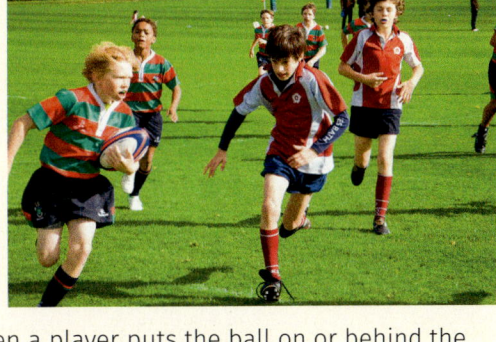 take the ball from them. The team scores points when a player puts the ball on or behind the other team's goal line or when the player kicks the ball over the field goal.

10c skill: reading p. 144

Choose at least one text. Read it again and write a fact file. Think about:
· name of the activity
· number of players
· what you need
· where you play it
· other information

10d workbook p. 61/10

Tell a partner facts from your fact file but do not say the name of the activity.
Say one fact after the other. He or she has to guess which activity it is.

Sports

11 CHOOSE YOUR LEVEL

I Match the sentence parts and write down the sentences.

1 I really like
2 I am
3 We practise
4 My team plays
5 My mum and dad watch

A all my matches.
B football.
C on Mondays and Wednesdays.
D in a team with my friends.
E matches on Saturdays.

II Match the questions 1–5 to the answers and write them down. Then answer question number 6.

1 What do you need?
2 How many players are there in a team?
3 Where do you play it?
4 What do the players do?
5 How do you score?
6 What sport is it?

A You play it on a sports ground.
B They kick the ball.
C There are eleven players in a team.
D It's …
E You need a ball and two goals.
F You score when you get the ball into the other team's goal.

III Write a short text about handball. Look at the fact file for help.

You can write:

You play handball in … There are …

…

WHAT:	handball
WHERE:	in a gym
HOW MANY:	two teams, seven players in a team
WHAT YOU NEED:	a ball, two goals, sports clothes
WHAT YOU DO:	…

Opposites

12 workbook p.61/11–14

Match the opposites. Write them down.

love · catch · long ·
open · old ·
boring · small · good

bad · throw · short ·
exciting · hate ·
new · close · big

You can write:

love ↔ hate

catch ↔ …

…

DIGITAL+ practise more 12

ACTIVATE   PRACTISE   DEVELOP   **PRACTISE**   APPLY

Present a sport or a hobby TARGET TASK

13 ▨ workbook p. 63/15, wordbank: free time p. 157, skill: presentations p. 146, searching the Internet p. 148

Your task is to present a hobby or a sport to your class. Before you start, look at these steps:

STEP 1

What sport or hobby could you present? Collect ideas in class.

STEP 2

Choose a topic. Decide if you want to work in a group or on your own.

STEP 3

Collect information and make notes. Think about:
· Do you do it alone or with others?
· Where can you do it?
· What do you need for the sport or hobby?
· If it is a sport with rules: can you explain them?
· ...

For BMX-ing you need
· *BMX bike*
· *helmet*
· *pads*
· *gloves*

STEP 4

Prepare your presentation. Decide:
· How do you want to present the information?
· If you work in a group: who presents what?
· Do you need any pictures?
· Have you got things you can show the class (clothes, equipment, instrument, ...)?

STEP 5

Practise your presentation.

STEP 6

Give your presentation.

Check out

Time for some presents

Ah, you're back. Hi! Oh, and yes, that is an angry dragon. And yes, those are flames! But it's OK. I've got a plan. I'll tell Ignus how scary he is. That helps, you see. Dragons like to feel big and scary. Right, here we go. "Ignus, listen to me!" I shout at the angry dragon. You are a really, really scary dragon! Your wings are so big, and your eyes are so red – like fire – and you are so fast. I'm so scared of you."

Uh oh. It's not working. Ugh, his breath is so hot. And STINKY! Yuck. I need a new plan. "You win, Ignus. You are too scary!" I shout. And then I run – really, really fast! Even dragon tamers need to run away sometimes. That's what Kora always says.

Kora! Maybe she can help me … I'll call her later. But now I have to run!

DIGITAL+ You can listen to Blaze's phone call to Kora: audio 2/52

The next day

Hey there! I've got some fantastic new ideas! Thanks, Kora! The plan is to give the dragons presents.

Feli-Rhymus dragons love presents. They also like gold. Let's see what I can find.

Oh look, in that shop window … That's a nice golden box! Perfect.

Now, I only need my wallet – oh, where is it? My official dragon tamer's credit card is in there – I need it!

I look everywhere, but I can't find it.

Oh no … Now I have no money. And no official dragon tamer's credit card. I can't buy presents. Now what?

be scared (of) = *Angst haben (vor)*; call = *anrufen*; I'll (= I will) = *ich werde*; money = *Geld*; wallet = *Brieftasche*

Twenty minutes later

Right, I've got the earring and lots of yellow flowers. I hope the dragons like my presents!
I walk up to the dragons. Slowly, slowly. I put the earring and the flowers down. Volta and Ignus kick the presents away. Oh no, they don't like them. But wait …
Look, Tazzy is sniffing the flowers. She's got her whole nose in them. SNIFF. She's so funny. I think she likes them!
Oh no, I think she's going to … SNEEZE!
Uh oh! The egg! No, oh no …

The dragon parents are angry again! Uh oh, here comes Volta. Look at her eyes! Help!

I walk down the street. Suddenly I see something golden on the ground. It's an earring. I pick it up. Ooh … I have an idea!
I look around for other things that are gold or yellow. I can't *buy* gold presents – but maybe I can *find* some!

be going to do something = *etwas tun werden;* ground = *Boden;* sneeze = *niesen;* sniff = *riechen an*

Breakfast recipes

Breakfast smoothie

(For 1)

Slice one banana and put it in a blender with 150g
of berries (for example strawberries, blackberries or
raspberries), 100ml of milk and a teaspoon of honey.
Blend the mixture until smooth.

Apple and cinnamon porridge

(For 2)

You need: 400ml milk, 60g porridge oats, 1 apple,
½ teaspoon cinnamon

Peel and grate the apple. Mix the milk, porridge
oats, apple and cinnamon. Heat the mixture for
about 10 minutes. Add sugar if you like.

Scrambled eggs

(For 2)

Mix four eggs with a bit of salt and pepper.
Heat a pan. Melt a little bit of butter in the pan.
Pour in the eggs and let them cook. Scramble the eggs
with a wooden spoon. Cook for about 2 minutes.
Serve the eggs with toast.

Pancakes

(For 4)

Mix two eggs, 250g of flour and 500ml milk.
Heat a pan. Melt a little bit of butter in the pan.
Pour just enough pancake mixture into the pan to cover its
base. Cook the pancake until golden brown and then flip it.
Do the same on the other side.
Repeat these steps with the rest of the mixture.
Serve the pancakes with maple syrup.

**Which recipe would you like to try? Do you know more breakfast recipes?
Tell your class about them.**

4

1. What can you see in the picture? Collect words.
2. What do you think? What time of the day is it?
3. Which room do you like best?

At home

Part A At home with friends

- Du sprichst darüber, wo sich Dinge in einem Raum befinden.
- Du schreibst über dein (Traum)Zimmer.
- Du erstellst einen Podcast mit Tipps für Aktivitäten zu Hause.

Part B Chores

- Du sprichst über Aufgaben, die regelmäßig erledigt werden müssen.
- Du lernst, wie man ausdrücken kann, wie oft man etwas tut.
- Du präsentierst eine typische Woche.

At Harry and Lily's place

1a workbook p. 66/1

Look at the picture. What do you think the children are thinking or saying? Write down your ideas and share them in class.

You can write:

Lily: *"The weather is so bad."*

Ava: *"…"*

1b audio 2/14

Listen and read along. What are the children talking about?

1

> The weather is so bad. What can we do? Have you got any ideas?

> I don't know. Maybe we could watch a film … Hey, who wants to watch a film?

2

> I think that's boring … We could paint some T-shirts! What do you think?

> But we haven't got any extra T-shirts. Let's make something to eat – a pizza or some cupcakes!

3

> I don't know … What do you think about a contest? We could all wear funny clothes and do a talent show or a modelling contest.

> Hm, I'm not sure … I've got an idea! We've got a cool new board game. It's an escape game.

4

> Good idea! Let's check it out.

> Yeah, why not?

> And let's get some snacks and drinks from the corner shop. I can ask Mum if that's OK.

> Excellent plan! Let's escape!

ACTIVATE PRACTISE DEVELOP PRACTISE APPLY

1c

List all of the children's ideas.
What do they decide to do in the end?

You can write:

1. watch a film

…

1d workbook p.66/2

Tell a partner which three of the children's ideas you like best.

You can say:

I like these ideas best:

…

Asking Mum

2a audio 2/15, skill: listening p.141

Listen to Lily and her mum.
What are they talking about?

2b CHOOSE YOUR LEVEL workbook p.67/3

❚ Listen again. Match the sentence parts. Then write down the sentences.

1 Mum asks, "Where do …
2 The children want …
3 Lily asks, "When is …
4 Dinner is …

A … to buy the snacks at the corner shop.
B … dinner?"
C … at seven o'clock.
D … you want to get the snacks?"

❚❚ Listen again. Then correct these false statements and write them down.

1 Mum thinks it's a bad idea to try the new escape game.
2 Mum needs some lemonade and five apples.
3 Mum gives Lily ten pounds.
4 Lily asks, "Where is my bag?"

❚❚❚ Listen again. Then write down the answers to these questions.

1 Does Mum like the children's idea to play the new game?
2 Where do the children want to get the snacks and drinks?
3 What does Mum need?
4 How much money does Mum give Lily?
5 When is dinner?

Rainy afternoons

3 wordbank: free time p.157, workbook p.67/4

What do you do on rainy afternoons? Talk to a partner. Ask and answer questions.

You can ask:

What do you do on rainy afternoons?
What is your favourite …?
Where do you …?

You can answer:

I often … (watch … / read … / listen to …)
My favourite … is …
…

GRAMMAR HELP questions with question words (revision) p. 178

Du hast schon gesehen, wie man im Englischen Fragen bildet.
Schau dir die Fragen unten an und vergleiche sie miteinander. Was fällt dir auf?

What do I need?
What does Tarek think?
Where do the children play the game?

What have I got?
What has Lily got in her schoolbag?
What have the children got?

What can I do?
When can the children start the game?
Where can we play?

Where am I?
Who is Tarek's favourite teacher?
Where are the children in the afternoon?

Auf Seite 178 findest du eine Übersicht zur Bildung von Fragen mit Fragewort.

Question words

4 grammar: questions with question words p. 178

Write down the correct questions for the answers.

What (2x)	1 … does Ava meet her friends? – Ava meets her friends on Fridays.
When	2 … do they meet? – They meet in the park.
Who (2x)	3 … do the children buy? – The children buy snacks and drinks.
How	4 … can play the guitar? – Harry can play the guitar.
Where	5 … has got two rabbits? – Harry and Lily have got two rabbits.
	6 … old is Tarek? – Tarek is twelve years old.
	7 … is Ollie's favourite toy? – Ollie's favourite toy is a red ball.

Scrambled questions

5a grammar: questions with question words p. 178

Unscramble the questions and write them down.

1 old – are – you? – How
2 What – number? – phone – is – your
3 teacher? – is – Who – favourite – your
4 got? – books – have – How many – you
5 do – What – you – on Saturdays? – do

6 does – Where – live? – Ava
7 got? – has – Ollie – What
8 does – go – When – Tarek – to bed?
9 What – play? – the – children – can
10 can – the – go? – Where – children

5b

Choose three or more of the questions and answer them. Write down your answers.

You can write:

How old are you? – I am …

…

5c workbook p. 68/5

Write three or more quiz questions about the friends from Notting Hill. You can look in the front of your book for help. Then ask and answer questions with a partner.

DIGITAL+ practise more 13

ACTIVATE **PRACTISE** DEVELOP PRACTISE APPLY

In the corner shop

6a workbook p. 68/6

Work with a partner. Look at the picture and play "I spy with my little eye …".

a lemon · a sandwich · a cake ·
a box of cornflakes · a bag of crisps ·
an orange · an apple · a banana ·
a packet of biscuits · a bottle of milk

6b audio 2/16

Listen and read along. What do the children buy?

Harry: Ava, can you get three bottles of lemonade, please? They're at the back behind the water bottles.

Ava: Yes, of course.

Harry: Let's get some crisps, Tarek. We always get salt and vinegar. What flavour would you like?

Tarek: Cheese and onion, please.

Harry: OK. They're here, between the chocolate and the biscuits.

Lily: Let's get some ice cream, too!

Tarek: Ice cream is over there in the freezer next to the fridge.

Is chocolate OK?

Ava: Oh, yes, please. I love chocolate ice cream!

Lily: Good. And there's the milk, too. We also need lemons – but I can only see bananas. Excuse me, Mr Hu, where are the lemons, please?

Mr Hu: Oh, they're here on the shelf, above the melons. In front of the oranges.

Lily: Thanks a lot!

Harry: Hey guys, have you got everything?

Ava: Yes, we have.

Lily: OK, let's pay then.

6c ▨ **CHOOSE YOUR LEVEL** skill: talking with people p. 142, wordbank: shopping p. 159, workbook p. 69/7-9

Get together in groups.

I **Read out the dialogue. You can record your reading.**

II **Act out the dialogue. You can record your role play.**

III **Make up your own shopping dialogue. Act it out. You can record your role play.**

In Harry and Lily's room

7a

Look at the picture. Then close your book. Write down all the things you remember.

7b audio 2/20, video 13

Listen and read along. What is the problem?

Lily: Sorry, our bedroom is a mess.
Harry: We need room to play the game. This is my cap on the floor. Tarek, can you put it on my bed on the right, please?
Tarek: No problem, and whose T-shirt is this under the chair?
Lily: It's Harry's, too. He is so messy, his stuff is everywhere!
Harry: That's rubbish. Lily is the messy one, just look at her desk. Her school things are all over the place!
Ava: Erm – where can I put the drinks?

Harry: Oh, sorry, just put them on Lily's table on the left.
Ava: I like your red lamp, Lily. It looks cool.
Lily: Oh, thank you. It's my own design.
Tarek: Your rabbits are so cute. What are their names again?
Lily: Their names are Double and Trouble. You can put their cage under the desk. We need lots of room.
Tarek: OK. Wow, that's a heavy cage.
Harry: All done, guys! Our room is tidy and now we can play!

7c CHOOSE YOUR LEVEL skill: reading p.144, workbook p.71/10

I Which of the statements are true? Copy them into your exercise book.

II Which of the statements are false? Correct them and write them in your exercise book.

III Which of the statements are false? Correct them and write them in your exercise book. Make up three or more true/false statements for a partner.

1 Lily's cap is on the floor.
2 Harry's bed is on the right.
3 Harry's T-shirt is on the chair.
4 Lily's school things are in her schoolbag.
5 Ava likes Lily's lamp.
6 The rabbits' names are Double and Trouble.
7 In the end the children's room is messy.

ACTIVATE PRACTISE **DEVELOP** PRACTISE APPLY

Things in a room

8 CHOOSE YOUR TASK wordbank: at home p. 158

A **Draw furniture words.**

B **Make a word snake for a classmate. Use words for things you can find in a bedroom. Think about toys, furniture, …**

C **Create a word search for a classmate. Use words for things you can find in a bedroom. Think about toys, furniture, …**

A	D	F	P	M	X	S	T	G	C
L	E	B	F	E	O	R	V	V	O
W	S	E	J	O	L	F	Q	V	M
G	K	K	B	E	D	R	T	S	P
F	H	E	K	L	P	P	E	O	U
S	W	E	S	T	Z	U	I	C	T
O	T	P	A	S	D	F	G	K	E
G	O	H	K	L	T	X	C	S	R
V	Y	N	B	M	G	E	D	R	U
K	S	E	P	O	S	T	E	R	O

This is my room

9a 🟫 video 14

Watch the video clip. Where does Gracie keep her sweets?

9b workbook p. 72/11-12

Watch the video clip again. What is there in Gracie's room? Take notes.

9c wordbank: at home p. 158, skill: writing p. 143

Write a short text about your (dream) room.

Let's play

10a audio 2/21

Work with a partner. Listen to the podcast. Partner A: focus on part 1 "quiz games". Partner B: focus on part 2 "escape games". Take notes.

10b skill: mediation p. 145, workbook p. 72/13

Partner A: tell your partner about quiz games in German. Partner B: tell your partner about escape games in German.

Team work

11a grammar: genitive -s p. 179

Whose things are these? Write about them.

1
Finn

2
the students

3
Israh

4
Thomas

5
Mia

6
the teacher

You can write:

1. *This is Finn's notepad.*
2. *These are …*

11b grammar: possessive determiners p. 179

Choose the correct word. Write down the sentences.

1 Get together with ??? (you/your) group members.
2 What is ??? (we/our) topic?
3 What do ??? (we/our) want to say?
4 What about ??? (I/my) group members?
5 What are ??? (they/their) jobs?
6 Do some research on ??? (you/your) topic.
7 What about ??? (you/your) teacher?
   Can ??? (he/his) or ??? (she/her) help you?
8 Collect ??? (you/your) ideas in a word web.

Podcast language

12 CHOOSE YOUR LEVEL

I Match the German and the English sentences. Write them down.

1 Hallo zusammen.
2 Willkommen zum heutigen Podcast.
3 Lasst uns über … sprechen.
4 Danke und auf Wiedersehen.

A Thank you and goodbye.
B Hello everyone.
C Welcome to today's podcast.
D Let's talk about …

II Match the sentence parts. Write down the sentences.

1 Welcome to our
2 Our topic today is
3 Let's start with a
4 Now let's talk
5 Thank you and

A quiz games.
B about our next topic.
C goodbye. Don't miss next week's podcast.
D podcast today.
E cool activity.

III Match the sentence parts. Write down the sentences.

1 Hello and welcome to this
2 Our first topic today
3 Let's start with a really
4 Next, we want to talk
5 That's it for
6 Don't miss our next podcast! Thanks

A today.
B week's podcast.
C a lot and goodbye.
D is escape games.
E cool game. Its name is …
F about quiz games.

DIGITAL+ practise more 14

ACTIVATE   PRACTISE   DEVELOP   **PRACTISE**   APPLY

Fun activities at home TARGET TASK

13 workbook p. 73/14, wordbank: free time p. 157, skill: searching the Internet p. 148, writing p. 143

Your task is to make a podcast about one or more fun activities that you can do at home.
You can work alone or with a partner.
Before you start, look at these steps:

STEP 1

Think about fun activities that you can do at home on a boring rainy day.
You can also search the Internet.
Use search terms, for example:

· fun things to do at home
· fun activities at home
· activities at home for rainy days
· ...

STEP 2

Decide which activity or activities you want to present. Then plan your podcast.

INTRODUCTION
· How can you say hello?
· How can you introduce your topic?

MAIN PART
· What details do you want to talk about?
· Why is it a good activity to do at home?

END
· How can you say goodbye?

STEP 3

Write a script for your podcast. You can ask
a classmate or your teacher to give you feedback.

STEP 4

Practise your podcast, then record it. Edit it if necessary.

STEP 5

Present your podcast.

(Music)
Hi everyone, this is Tommy from "Fun Activities at Home". Today we'd like to talk a bit about activities that get you moving. Let's start with an easy game — all you need are some old boxes and table tennis balls. You can play it alone or with friends.
Put all the boxes in different places on the floor. Then throw the ball — can you hit the box you want to hit? Can you hit the box farthest away from you? How many balls can you get into the same box? Think of more ideas and make a really boring afternoon more interesting!
Next we'd like to look at ...

That's it for today! Thanks a lot for listening and don't miss next week's podcast about reading games! Bye, guys.
(Music)

Dad's message

1a workbook p. 74/1, skill: reading p. 144

Read the text messages. What are they about?

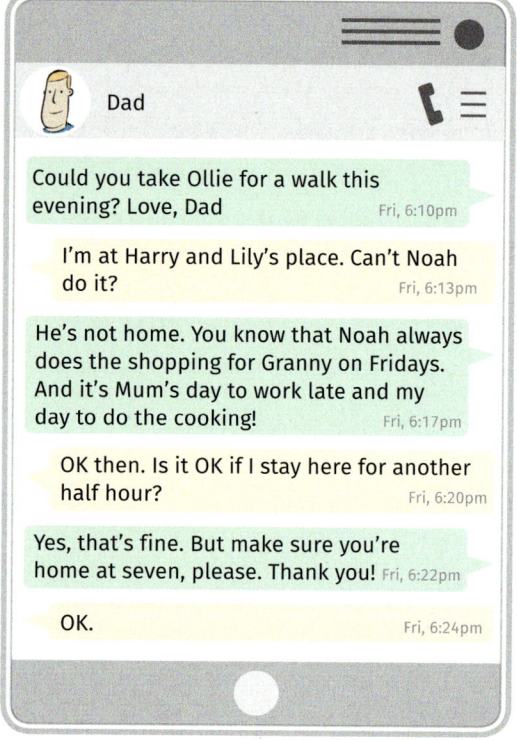

> **Dad**
>
> Could you take Ollie for a walk this evening? Love, Dad
> Fri, 6:10pm
>
> I'm at Harry and Lily's place. Can't Noah do it?
> Fri, 6:13pm
>
> He's not home. You know that Noah always does the shopping for Granny on Fridays. And it's Mum's day to work late and my day to do the cooking!
> Fri, 6:17pm
>
> OK then. Is it OK if I stay here for another half hour?
> Fri, 6:20pm
>
> Yes, that's fine. But make sure you're home at seven, please. Thank you! Fri, 6:22pm
>
> OK.
> Fri, 6:24pm

1b workbook p. 74/2, 3

Read again and answer these questions:

1 Where is Ava?
2 What does Noah always do on Fridays?
3 What do Ava's parents do on Fridays?
4 Who is taking Ollie for a walk this evening?

Talking about chores

2a audio 2/23

Listen and read along. What are "chores"?

Ava: Oh. It's ten to seven already. It's my turn to take Ollie for a walk this evening. I need to leave in five minutes.

Lily: Oh yes, and Harry needs to clean Double and Trouble's cage.

Harry: I always clean the cage. It's your turn!

Lily: That's not true! I clean it, too! And I always vacuum our bedroom! And I usually set the table for breakfast.

Ava: It's always like that with Noah and me. I often empty the dishwasher and I always tidy the living room. But Noah says that I never do anything because he never sees it!

Tarek: My dad and I always share the chores.

I sometimes take out the rubbish and tidy up. My dad usually cleans the bathroom and he always does the shopping.

Ava: My dad always cleans the kitchen and often loads the dishwasher. But my mum usually does the cooking. Joshua hasn't got many chores because he's only six.

Harry: I want to be six again! – Now what about the rabbit cage?

Lily: Maybe we could clean it together this time?

Harry: OK. But next time it's your turn!

Ava: Oh, it's five to seven. I really need to go.

Tarek: Yeah, me too. Thanks for the great afternoon. And have fun cleaning the cage!

ACTIVATE PRACTISE DEVELOP PRACTISE APPLY

2b

❙❙ **Who does what? Match the sentence parts.**

1 Lily usually ...
2 Ava often ...
3 Tarek and his dad always ...
4 Tarek's dad usually ...

A ... share the chores.
B ... cleans the bathroom.
C ... empties the dishwasher.
D ... sets the breakfast table.

❙❙ **What do Tarek's dad and Ava's parents do? Write down their chores.**

You can write:

Tarek's dad: usually cleans ...

Ava's mum: usually ...

Ava's dad: ...

...

❙❙❙ **Write about the children, their parents and their chores.**

You can write:

Lily always vacuums ...

Ava often ...

...

...

Mime the chores

3

Tell a partner what to do.
Your partner mimes the chore. Take turns.

You can say:

Set the table, please.

My chores

4a wordbank: at home p. 158

Write about your chores.

I	always usually often sometimes never	vacuum my bedroom. make my bed. tidy the living room. empty the dishwasher. clean the kitchen. take out the rubbish. ...

You can write:

I always make my bed.

I never clean the kitchen.

...

4b

Work with a partner. Ask and answer questions.

You can ask:

Do you empty the dishwasher?

Do you clean the kitchen?

...

You can answer:

Yes, sometimes.

No, never.

...

GRAMMAR HELP   adverbs of frequency p. 180

Mit *always* (immer), *usually* (normalerweise), *often* (oft), *sometimes* (manchmal) und *never* (nie) kannst du ausdrücken, wie oft etwas geschieht. Sieh dir die Beispielsätze an. Was fällt dir auf?

I always tidy the living room.
Lily sometimes cleans the rabbit cage.
We always share the chores.
My parents usually do the cooking.

I am often in the park.
He is usually at home.
We are never late.
He is always hungry.

Auf Seite 180 findest du weitere Beispiele und Erklärungen zur Position der Häufigkeitsadverbien im Satz.

Chores in the house

5   grammar: adverbs of frequency p. 180, workbook p. 75/4, 5

Unscramble the sentences and write them down.

1 the kitchen. – Ava's dad – cleans – always
2 Ava's mum – the cooking. – does – usually
3 tidies – the living room. – always – Ava
4 up. – tidies – Tarek – sometimes

5 often – Ava's dad – loads – the dishwasher.
6 the shopping. – Tarek's dad – does – always

Who does what?

6a   grammar: adverbs of frequency p. 180

Look at 2a on page 80 again and write five or more quiz questions for a partner.

You can write:

Who often empties the dishwasher?

Who sometimes … ?

…

6b   workbook p. 76/6, 7

Work with a partner. Ask and answer your questions.

You can answer:

That's Ava.

Lily sometimes …

…

How to say *ch* and *sh*

7a   audio 2/26

Listen and repeat.

chant · fish · show · touch · share ·
chore · chocolate · shop · children ·
she · choose · chips · sunshine

7b

Listen again. Make two lists: words with /tʃ/ as in *chore* and words with /ʃ/ as in *share*. What can you say about the spelling?

DIGITAL+ practise more 15

ACTIVATE   **PRACTISE**   DEVELOP   PRACTISE   APPLY

Don McClean

8 CHOOSE YOUR LEVEL workbook p. 77/8

Your little sister sees an ad on the Internet, but it is in English. Can you help her? Read the ad and answer her questions in German.

Ⅰ 1 Wer oder was ist Don McClean?
  2 Was steht denn da über Schulsachen?

Ⅱ 1 Wer oder was ist Don McClean?
  2 Was steht denn da übers Wäschewaschen?
  3 Funktioniert Don McClean auch, wenn ich nicht da bin?

Ⅲ 1 Wer oder was ist Don McClean?
  2 Kannst du mir genau erklären, was der kann und wie er funktioniert?
  3 Wie teuer ist Don McClean und wo kann man ihn kaufen?

You don't like chores? Here is your solution!

Don McClean is a robot, and it can do all your chores for you! It can vacuum your floor! It has sensors so it can find your dirty clothes. It collects them and puts them in the washing machine.

Don McClean can put your school things back on your desk and your books back on the bookshelves. It picks up your toys and puts them in the box where they belong.

If you need to find something, you can ask your **Don McClean**. It knows where everything is!

Just switch on the **Don McClean** when you go to school in the morning and find your room clean and tidy when you come back.

Only £999 in a shop near you or online!

Doing the chores

9 CHOOSE YOUR TASK A+B: wordbank: at home p. 158, B: skill: presentations p. 146

A **Make notes about chores in your family. Tell a partner who does what.**
B **Do you have ideas for a robot? What can your robot do? Present your ideas to the class.**
C **Write a list of activities that make chores fun. Think about a competition, music, …**

LAND & LEUTE 5 video 15

Wohnen in Großbritannien

Viele Menschen in Großbritannien wohnen in Einfamilienhäusern. Wohnungen *(flats)* gibt es vor allem in größeren Städten. In manchen – oft älteren – Häusern in Großbritannien ist einiges anders als in deutschen Häusern. Zum Beispiel haben viele Waschbecken dort immer noch zwei getrennte Wasserhähne, einen für heißes und einen für kaltes Wasser.

Die Steckdosen in Großbritannien haben manchmal Schalter zum Ein- und Ausschalten. Sie sehen auch

anders aus als in vielen anderen Ländern. Viele Reisende brauchen deshalb Adapter für ihre Elektrogeräte.

Schau dir den Videoclip an. Was findest du interessant?

Ollie's week

10a   workbook p. 78/9

Look at the pictures. Talk about Ollie's week.

Monday

Tuesday

Wednesday

Thursday

Friday

10b   audio 2/28

Read about Ollie's week.

Hello, I'm Ollie! I'm a dog and I live with Ava and her family. I want to tell you about my week and all my chores.
On Monday afternoon my chores begin when the children come back from school. I take Ava for a walk to the park. We usually practise skateboarding. I teach her tricks on the skateboard.

Tuesday is a good day for me. I go to dog school and meet my friends there.
We always do a lot of fun activities together and I usually get lots of treats. That's a good chore because it's a lot of fun. But I have to look after Ava because sometimes she is too nice to the other dogs!

Wednesday is spaghetti day! It's great! When Ava comes home, we always eat spaghetti. On Wednesdays Ava often has a lot of homework and I'm in the garden. I have to dig holes and look for squirrels. That's very important!

On Thursdays I usually look after Ava and her little brother, Joshua. In the evening Ava sometimes helps her mum with the cooking but Joshua never helps. Ava says that's OK because he's only six but that's no excuse. I'm only four and I've got a lot of chores!

Ava is often away on Friday afternoons. But I've got my chores! I have to look after Joshua and the rest of the family. Ava's dad usually does the cooking and cleans the kitchen. After dinner Ava's mum often makes plans for the weekend and I help her and tell her my ideas for family time.

ACTIVATE   PRACTISE   **DEVELOP**   PRACTISE   APPLY

Saturday

I really like the weekend! Everyone is usually at home and we have a great time together! On Saturdays Ava cleans her room and I always have to check it! If she does it right, I take her to the park and we play ball.

Sunday

On Sunday mornings we usually have a nice long breakfast. I sometimes find bacon under the table. I haven't got many chores on Sundays. That's cool because I am very busy on all the other days!

10c   CHOOSE YOUR LEVEL   skill: writing p. 143, workbook p. 79/10

❚ Copy Ollie's planner and complete it.

Monday	*take Ava for a walk, …*
Tuesday	
Wednesday	
Thursday	
Friday	*help mum, …*

❚❚ Choose five days from Ollie's week and write a short text about them. Write one or more sentences for each day.

You can write:

On Monday afternoons Ollie usually practises skateboarding with Ava. He teaches her tricks. Ollie likes Tuesdays because …

❚❚❚ Imagine you are Ava. Choose five days from Ollie's week and write a short text about them. Write one or more sentences for each day.

You can write:

On Mondays I take Ollie to the park. I usually practise skateboarding. Ollie sometimes tries it, too. On Tuesdays …

A terrible day

11a   audio 2/31, skill: listening p. 141

Listen to Ollie.
What day of the week is he talking about?

11b   workbook p. 80/11

Listen again.
Why is it a terrible day for Ollie?

Chores

12   GET TOGETHER

Get together with a partner.
Talk about chores.

Partner A	**Partner B**
❚ Go to page 114.	**❚** Go to page 126.
❚❚ Go to page 118.	**❚❚** Go to page 130.
❚❚❚ Go to page 122.	**❚❚❚** Go to page 134.

From Monday to Sunday

13   **CHOOSE YOUR LEVEL** grammar: simple present statements p. 173

▌ Write about Harry and Lily's week.
Copy the text and fill in the gaps with
the words from the box.

vacuum · goes · cleans · help · meet

At the weekend Harry and Lily often ??? their mothers with the cooking. On Mondays Harry usually ??? the rabbit cage. Lily does not ??? the bedroom on Tuesdays because there is no time. She ??? to her dancing class on Tuesdays. On Fridays Harry and Lily always ??? their friends.

▌▌ **Unscramble the two texts about Harry and Lily's week. Write one text about Lily and one text about Harry.**

Lily goes to the book club with Ava on Mondays. On Mondays Harry usually cleans the rabbit cage. On Tuesdays she goes to dancing class. She doesn't like team sports so dancing is perfect for her. He likes Tuesday afternoons because he has lots of time to play the guitar. He does not like Thursday mornings. On Sundays he often plays board games with his family. She sets the breakfast table at the weekend.

▌▌▌ **Look at the pictures. Write about Lily and Harry's week.**

You can write:
On Mondays Harry usually …
On Tuesdays Lily …
…

on Mondays – usually   on Tuesdays – always   on Wednesdays

on Thursdays   on Fridays – always   on Saturdays – never   on Sundays – often

Word groups

14   workbook p. 80/12

Sort the words from the box into these groups:
days, pets, sports, chores.

dog · Friday · tidy the room ·
football · vacuum the floor ·
rabbit · Tuesday · empty the dishwasher ·
hockey · karate · Thursday · cat

DIGITAL+ practise more 16

A typical week TARGET TASK

15 ⬛ workbook p. 81/13, wordbank: time p. 155, at home p. 158, free time p. 157, skill: presentations p. 146

Your task is to present your or someone else's typical week.
Before you start, look at these steps:

STEP 1

Decide whose week you want to present.
Your own? Someone else's? Make notes for
Monday, Tuesday, …
Think about chores and activities.

Tarek's week
Monday: vacuums the living room, cleans
*   kitchen floor (sometimes)*
Tuesday: goes to the cooking club
Wednesday: has a free afternoon
Thursday: meets Uncle Sami (usually)
Friday: meets friends
Saturday: does homework
Sunday: sets the breakfast table

STEP 2

Decide how you want to present the week.
You can:
· make a collage and label it
· draw pictures and label them
· write a text
· make a recording
· make a video
· …

Tarek's week
On Mondays Tarek vacuums the living room
after school. He sometimes cleans the kitchen
floor, too.
He has cooking club after school on Tuesdays.
Wednesdays are free of chores and on
Thursdays Tarek usually meets his uncle. They
often go for a walk together.
On Fridays Tarek often meets his friends and
they go to the park or play board games.
He does the rest of his homework on Saturdays.
On Sundays Tarek usually sets the breakfast
table.
In the evening he packs his schoolbag for
Monday.

STEP 3

Present the week in class.

Check out

1. Kannst du in einem Gespräch Vorschläge machen?	Workbook, p. 82
2. Kannst du Fragen mit Fragewort stellen?	Workbook, p. 82
3. Kannst du sagen, wem etwas gehört?	Workbook, p. 82
4. Kannst du kurze Textnachrichten verstehen?	Workbook, p. 83
5. Kannst du verstehen, wenn jemand von seiner Woche berichtet?	Workbook, p. 83
6. Kannst du sagen, was jemand wie häufig macht?	Workbook, p. 83

A poem

Er, hi there. So, the good news: the egg is OK.
But the bad news: Volta is really angry, and
I need to think of something quickly! I can't
run into town. There are lots of people there
– it's too dangerous! Oh, what can I do?
I look up and see Volta right above me. Look
at those big flames and red eyes. I need to try
something different. But what?
Think, Blaze, think!
Ooh, I know – I can tell her a poem!
Feli-Rhymus dragons love poems.
I stop and look up at the dragon. "Hey Volta!"
I shout. "Here's a poem for you! " I think for a
moment, and then I begin:

> You're a very big dragon – it's true!
> And everyone's so scared of you.
> You breathe fire so hot, which hurts quite a lot
> When it burns a big hole in my shoe.

Ouch! That was my shoe. But I think Volta is
listening to me. Even if she is still angry.
I quickly think of another verse.

> You're a large, scary dragon – it's true!
> And everyone's so scared of you.
> Your claws are so long, and your jaws are so strong,
> You could eat me in one bite – or two!

DIGITAL+ You can listen to Blaze's poem: audio 2/53

Hey, look! Volta is flying back to the castle. Yes!
That's good. REALLY good! Oh, and there's my wallet.
Fantastic! Ah, now I'm happy.

bite = *Bissen;* burn = *(ver)brennen;* dangerous = *gefährlich;* news = *Neuigkeit, Nachricht;* quickly = *schnell*

Ooh, I need to tell Kora about everything.
Let's just take a photo … Good …

Dear Kora, this is Edinburgh
Castle. Look, you can see one
of the dragons. That's Volta.
She likes my poems — but not
my presents … Speak soon!
Blaze :)

And … Send! Right, that's enough for today.

The next day

Welcome back to the castle! It's day three,
and I think the dragons like me a bit more. Maybe.
My next trick is … A delicious dragon dinner!
Dragons love hot and spicy food, like chillies.
So I'm serving a starter, a main course and a dessert.

Suddenly I hear a CRACK! Wow, look at the egg …
I think the baby is coming …

delicious = köstlich, lecker

My home is my castle

There are lots of different kinds of houses, and people live in lots of different ways. Here are some examples from the UK.

Aaron lives on a houseboat in Bristol with his dad and his little sister. They usually don't move the boat – it stays where it is. Aaron, his sister and his dad really love life on their houseboat. Aaron's dad says it is also cheaper than a house.
Aaron thinks it's really cool to have a home on the water.

Leo lives in a rented flat in a big house in London. The flat isn't big, but it's big enough for Leo, his two younger brothers and his parents. Leo has got his own bedroom. He is really happy about that because his brothers have to share a room. Leo's family hasn't got a garden, but they have got a balcony.
There are many children in the neighbourhood, so there is always someone he can play with. Leo thinks that's great!

Maya's family has got a farm in Wales. Maya lives with her mum, her dad and her sister in the farmhouse. The family has got 100 cows, six horses and some sheep. They sell milk and make their own cheese.
Life on a farm can be really hard work, but it is also a lot of fun. Maya and her sister sometimes help their parents on the farm.
Maya's family also has a small Bed and Breakfast on their farm, so they can earn some extra money.
Maya likes living on a farm because there are lots of animals and she can spend a lot of time outside.

Which of these places is your favourite? Where would you like to live? Explain.

1 **What can you say about the people in the picture?**
2 **What can you say about the situation?**
3 **What do you usually do on a day like this?**

Have a great day!

Part A Happy birthday!

· Du sprichst über Geburtstage und Familie.
· Du beschäftigst dich mit Vorschlägen für Geburtstagsfeiern.
· Du präsentierst eigene Ideen für eine außergewöhnliche Geburtstagsparty.

Part B A day out

· Du erfährst etwas über die Stadt Brighton.
· Du sprichst über mögliche Ziele für Tagesausflüge in deiner Umgebung.
· Du übst Einkaufsdialoge.
· Du schreibst eine Postkarte.

Birthday fun

1a   workbook p.84/1a

**What do you like about birthdays?
Talk to your classmates.**

1b   video 16, workbook p.84/1b

**Watch the video clip. What do the children
like about birthdays?**

The party

3a   video 17, skill: reading p.144

**Ava's mum is sending messages to Grandma Edyta in Poland. Look at the pictures and read the
texts. Write down one or two keywords from each message.**

Making plans

2a   audio 2/33, skill: listening p.141

**Listen to Ava and her parents. Which of
these things are they talking about?
Take notes.**

> pizza · selfie box · pool · birthday cake ·
> having a barbecue

2b   workbook p.85/2

**Listen again. What are their plans for Ava's
birthday party?**

Saturday, 4th June

It's a great party! Ava is opening her presents now.

5

Saturday, 4th June

Oops, Ollie is jumping into the pool!

6

3b workbook p.86/3

Work with a partner. Tell him or her your keyword(s) for one message. Can he or she guess which message it is? Take turns.

What is happening?

4 CHOOSE YOUR LEVEL

I **Look at the messages in 3a again. Match the sentence parts and write down the sentences.**

1 Ava and her dad
2 Noah and Ava
3 Ollie and Joshua
4 Noah

A are playing.
B is buying some more balloons.
C are writing invitations.
D are baking biscuits.

II **Look at the messages in 3a again. Complete the sentences and write them down.**

1 Ava and her dad are writing ???.
2 ??? isn't writing, he is drawing ???.
3 ??? aren't helping in the kitchen.
4 ??? are arriving with presents.
5 ??? is jumping into the ???.

III **What is happening or not happening? Look at the messages in 3a again and write six or more sentences.**

Joshua		writing.
Ollie and Joshua	is	helping.
Grandpa and	are	eating cake.
Grandma	isn't	...
Ava	aren't	
...		

GRAMMAR HELP   present progressive: statements p. 181

Wenn du ausdrücken möchtest, dass jemand etwas jetzt gerade tut oder dass etwas in diesem Moment stattfindet, verwendest du das *present progressive*. Sieh dir die Beispiele an. Was fällt dir an den Verben auf?

I am opening my presents now.
You are writing messages.
Noah is buying balloons at the moment.
She is decorating the garden.

We are baking biscuits.
Noah and Ava are putting the biscuits on a plate.
They are arriving at the party.

Auf Seite 181 findest du weitere Beispiele für das *present progressive*.
Dort findest du auch Erklärungen zu verneinten Sätzen.

After the party

5   grammar: present progressive statements p. 181, wordbank: at home p. 158

After the party Ava and her family are still busy. Look at the pictures. What are they doing?

say goodbye ·
empty the
dishwasher ·
sleep · take out
the rubbish ·
play · read ·
clean the kitchen

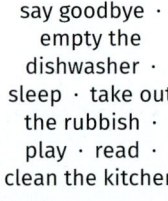   

You can write:

Ava is saying goodbye to her guests.
Joshua and Ollie are …
…

What are they doing?

6   grammar: present progressive statements p. 181

Complete the sentences and write them down. Use the present progressive.

1 Harry ??? (do) his homework.
2 Lily and Ava ??? (not read) books,
   they ??? (watch) TV.
3 Double and Trouble ??? (eat) carrots.
4 Tarek and Uncle Sami ??? (play) football.

5 Tarek's dad ??? (make) dinner.
6 Ollie ??? (not eat) cake,
   he ??? (play) with balloons.
7 Ava's mum ??? (buy) presents.
8 Ava's dad ??? (talk) to Grandma Edyta.

DIGITAL+ practise more 17

ACTIVATE   **PRACTISE**   DEVELOP   PRACTISE   APPLY

Calendar rap

7a audio 2/34

Listen to the rap and rap along. Stand up when you hear your birthday month.

January · February · March · April · May · June · July · August · September · October · November · December

7b numbers p.232, workbook p.87/4

Walk, stop and talk. Talk about birthdays.

You can say:

When is your birthday? – My birthday is on the twenty-first of June.

You say:	You write:
the first of March	1st March *or* 1 March
the second of April	2nd April *or* 2 April
the third of May	3rd May *or* 3 May
the fourth of June	4th June *or* 4 June
the fifth of July	5th July *or* 5 July
…	…

Family tree

8a

Look at this part of the family tree. Point to Ava's mum, Ava's grandmother, Helen's husband and Fiona's sister.

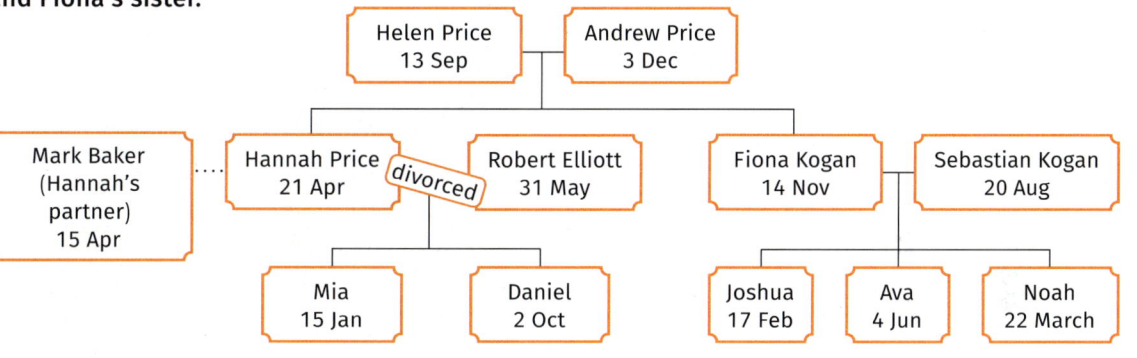

8b CHOOSE YOUR LEVEL wordbank: time p.155, family p.160, workbook p.88/5-7

I **Work with a partner. Write about three or more members of Ava's family.**

You can write:

Daniel is Ava's cousin. His birthday is on 2 October.

II **Write four or more false statements about Ava's family. Ask a partner to correct them.**

You can write:

Fiona is Ava's sister. Her birthday is on …

III **Write down five or more questions about Ava's family. Ask a partner to answer them.**

You can write:

Whose birthday is on 15 January?

Who is Andrew's wife?

girls and women:
· mother
· daughter
· sister
· grandmother
· granddaughter
· aunt
· cousin
· wife
· partner

boys and men:
· father
· son
· brother
· grandfather
· grandson
· uncle
· cousin
· husband
· partner

Tarek's birthday party

9a

Read the dialogue. What is Tarek doing?

Uncle Sami: What are you doing?
Tarek: I'm looking for some ideas for my birthday.
Uncle Sami: Oh right. Your birthday is in three weeks. Are you planning a big party? Something special?
Tarek: Yes, I am! I'm planning a cool party with all my friends. But what can we do?
Uncle Sami: Well, let me help you!

9b

Look at the pictures on the web pages. What are the children doing? Talk to a partner.

9c   skill: reading p. 144, workbook p. 89/8

Now read about the party ideas. Which idea is your favourite? Why?

---

1   × −

A sleepover party
If an afternoon is not enough – have a sleepover party!

What you need	mattresses or sleeping mats pillows and sleeping bags
Activities	have a pillow fight with your friends build a fort out of mattresses and pillows watch a film tell ghost stories
Food	pizza popcorn

---

2   × −

An alien themed party
Dress up as aliens, astronauts and planets and have an "aliens and space" party!

What you need	First, you need a great costume. To look like something out of this world, create your own costume, for example a space suit with a funny helmet. Or paint your face to look like an alien!
Activities	You can do karaoke to songs about the sun, the moon, the stars and the planets.
Food	You can eat astronaut ice cream! Astronauts eat this kind of ice cream in space and you can buy it in special shops.
Decorations	You can put up small lights that look like stars and use glitter.

ACTIVATE   PRACTISE   **DEVELOP**   PRACTISE   APPLY

3 ——— × –

Photo treasure hunt party

Take to the streets and have a great group experience!
Get into teams. Each team gets a checklist of things and activities.
They use their smartphones to take photos of the things and activities.
The things could be: a street light, a cat or a dog, something blue, …
The activities could be: hug a tree, hold a pet in your arms,
take a group selfie in front of a house with a 7 in the number, …
The fastest team is the winner and gets a prize!

9d CHOOSE YOUR LEVEL skill: mediation p. 145

▌ Your sister is planning a party. Tell her about the ideas for a sleepover party from text 1 in German.

▌▌ Your sister is planning a party. Tell her about the ideas for a themed party from text 2 in German.

▌▌▌ Your sister is planning a party. Tell her about all three ideas in German.

9e grammar: present progressive questions p. 182

Mime a party activity. Your partner has to guess what you are doing.

You can ask:	You can answer:
Are you dancing?	*Yes, I am.*
Are you …?	*No, I'm not.*

Tarek's invitation

10 workbook p. 89/9

**Look at Tarek's invitation.
What can you find out?**

You can say:

Tarek's party is from … to …

It starts at …

It is at …

…

> **Invitation to my
> SPACE SLEEPOVER PARTY!**
>
> Dear Ava,
> I would like to invite you to my birthday party.
> **When:** 23rd July, 6pm till 24th July, 10am (after breakfast)
> **Where:** at my house
> **What to bring:** costume and equipment, sleeping bag, toothbrush
> **What to expect:** space adventures
>
> Please tell me if you can come.
> Tarek

Birthdays

11 CHOOSE YOUR TASK wordbank: party time p. 161

A **Bring a picture of a birthday party. Write about what the people in the picture are doing.**

B **Write about your birthday.**

C **Make your own family tree. Add birthday dates if you can.**

B

My birthday is on 4th January. I always have a party with my friends and I get a lot of presents. We usually play games and have crisps and lemonade. I love birthdays!

On the phone

12a   audio 2/39, skill: listening p. 141

Listen to Tarek on the phone. Who is he talking to?

12b   CHOOSE YOUR LEVEL   workbook p. 90/10

I **Listen again. Write down the answers to the questions.**

1 Where are the children?
2 What are they doing?
3 What are they eating?

II **Listen again. Write down the answers to the questions.**

1 Where are the children?
2 What are they doing?
3 What are they eating?
4 What is Harry wearing?
5 Who is wearing a robot-alien costume?

III **Listen again. Write down the answers to the questions.**

1 Which room are the children in?
2 What are they doing?
3 What are they eating?
4 Who is playing the guitar?
5 What is Harry wearing?
6 Where do the children go on a treasure hunt?
7 Who is cleaning the kitchen?

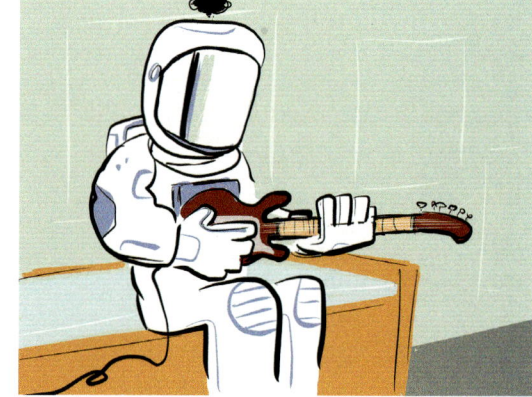

Words

13a

Put words from box A and words from box B together to make new words.

You can write:

treasure hunt

...

A

treasure · board · chocolate · living ·
ice · orange · sleepover · swimming · free

B

cream · hunt · room · juice · party ·
pool · time · game · cake

13b

Write three or more sentences with your new words from 13a.

DIGITAL+ practise more 18

ACTIVATE   PRACTISE   DEVELOP   **PRACTISE**   APPLY

Planning a cool birthday party TARGET TASK

14 workbook p. 91/11, wordbank: party time p. 161, skill: presentations p. 146

Your task is to plan the coolest birthday party ever and present your ideas in a (digital) collage. Before you start, look at these steps:

STEP 1

**Get together in groups and decide what kind of party you want to plan – there are no limits!
Is it a pool party, a superhero-party, a travel-around-the-world-party, a … party?**

STEP 2

Make notes on:

Place

in a spooky castle, on a spaceship,
on the moon, …

Guests

superheroes, all your friends,
a character from a book, a music star, …

Activities

go on a treasure hunt,
sleep in a tree house, …

Food and drinks

hamburgers and chips,
pink and green lemonade, …

Music

pop, rock, hip hop, …

Decorations

lights, glitter, …

STEP 3

Create everything you need for your collage: write lists, draw pictures, design the invitation, …

STEP 4

Put together your collage.

STEP 5

Use your collage to present your party plans.

GUEST LIST
• Bruno
• Oliver
• Summer
• Ajsel
• Ida
• Nora
• Lennart
• Noah

TO-DO LIST
• go shopping
• decorate living room
• download songs
• bake muffins
• make costumes (Rana: mermaid, Silvia: marine biologist, Markus : aquanaut.)

Dear Henri,
We would like to invite you to our UNDER THE SEA SUPER SPLASH PARTY!!
When: 15th August, 3pm
Where: Sarah's house
What to bring: costume
What to expect: a surprise
Please tell us if you can come,
Silvia, Rana, Markus

PLAYLIST
• the mermaid song
• the sailor's alphabet

SHOPPING LIST
• material for costumes
• decorations (blue and green balloons, glitter)
• lemonade
• crisps
• icing for the cake
• sweets

GAMES
• pin the leg on the octopus
• paddling pool fishing
• pass the parcel

Photos of Brighton

1a

**Look at the heading and the picture.
What are the children doing?**

1b   audio 2/41

Listen and read along. What can you see or do in Brighton?

Lily: Look. That was a really crazy seagull at Brighton beach last year. Harry and I were there with some friends.
Ava: Weren't you scared of the seagull?
Lily: Oh yes, we were! It was very hungry! There are more photos of Brighton on my phone. Look at the next one.

Tarek: Oh, who's that? She looks nice.
Lily: That's Ellen. She was in our year at school in Brighton.
Ava: Was that at Brighton beach, too?
Harry: Yes, it was. This was at the pier. It's great fun there!
Lily: Let me show you another cool picture …

Tarek: Wow, how cool is that – a fatbike!
Lily: Yes. Harry wasn't very good at riding it …
Harry: Oh thanks. It was my first time.
Ava: That really looks fun. Can't we go on a day trip to Brighton next weekend?
Lily: Great idea! What do you think?
Tarek: A day out in Brighton. That sounds cool. I'd love to go to the beach!
Harry: Yeah. Let's see if Mum can take us.

1c

**Look at the map in the back of your book or check online.
Where is Brighton? How far is it from London?**

ACTIVATE   PRACTISE   DEVELOP   PRACTISE   APPLY

1d CHOOSE YOUR LEVEL   skill: reading p. 144, workbook p. 92/1, 2

I Match the questions to the answers and write them down.

1 Where were Harry and Lily last year?
2 Who was very hungry?
3 Who is Ellen?
4 What does Harry say about the pier?

A She is a friend from Brighton.
B He says that it is great fun.
C The seagull was very hungry.
D They were at Brighton beach last year.

II True or false? Correct the false statements and write them down.

1 The friends are sending text messages.
2 Lily and Harry were at the beach in Brighton with some friends.
3 The seagull was very hungry.
4 Ellen was at Lily and Harry's school.
5 Harry thinks that the pier is boring.
6 Ava wants to go to Brighton next month.

III Answer the questions. Write down full sentences.

1 When were Harry and Lily at Brighton beach?
2 What animal was there at the beach?
3 What does Tarek say about Ellen?
4 Where do Harry and Lily know Ellen from?
5 What does Harry think about the pier?
6 Where do the children want to go next weekend?
7 What would Tarek love to do in Brighton?

A day trip

2a   audio 2/43, skill: listening p. 141

Listen to Harry and his mum. What do they check?

2b

Listen again and answer the questions.

1 What does Harry's mum want to do in Brighton?
2 On which day do they want to go to Brighton? Why?
3 How do they want to go to Brighton? By train, by boat, by bus or by car?
4 What are Noah's plans for Saturday?
5 How many tickets do they need?

2c   wordbank: places p. 152, workbook p. 93/3, 4

Where can you go on a day trip? Think about interesting places near your home town (lakes, mountains, cities, …). What can you do there? Talk to a partner.

You can say:
There's a/an … It's called …
You can … there.

GRAMMAR HELP

be: simple past p. 183

Wenn du über Dinge sprechen möchtest, die in der Vergangenheit passiert und jetzt vorbei sind, verwendest du das *simple past*. Sieh dir die Sätze an. Was fällt dir an den Vergangenheitsformen des Verbs *be* auf?

I was in Brighton last year.
You were great, Harry!
He was at the beach, too.
Ellen was in Lily's year.
It was brilliant.

We were at home.
You were all scared of the seagull.
The children were at the beach.
They were all really happy.

Auf Seite 183 findest du eine Übersicht der Formen von *be* im *simple past* und weitere Erklärungen – auch zu Verneinungen und Fragen.

Ellen's diary

3 grammar: be simple past p. 183, workbook p. 94/5

This is Ellen's diary from last year. Copy it and fill in the gaps with *was* or *were*.

Today ??? a great day. I ??? at the beach with Harry and Lily. Philipp, Jonah and Sophie ??? there, too. It ??? warm and sunny and there ??? a lot of people at the beach. There ??? a really crazy seagull. We ??? all a bit scared but it ??? funny, too. It ??? so hungry. Later we ??? at the pier. It ??? good fun.

Where were they?

4 grammar: be simple past p. 183, workbook p. 95/6

Look at the pictures. Where were or weren't the people last summer? Write about them.

Helen
~~New York~~ Paris

Mark and Hannah
~~Brighton~~ London

Andrew
~~Italy~~ France

Mia
~~Hamburg~~ Berlin

Sebastian and Fiona
~~Germany~~ Poland

Daniel ~~England~~
Scotland

You can write:

Helen wasn't in New York, she was in Paris.
Mark and Hannah weren't in …
…

DIGITAL+ practise more 19

ACTIVATE **PRACTISE** DEVELOP PRACTISE APPLY

A message from Brighton

5a

Harry, Lily, Tarek and Ava are sending a video message from Brighton to Noah.
Look at these pictures from the message. Talk about them with a partner.

5b 🔲 CHOOSE YOUR LEVEL video 18, workbook p. 95/7, 8

Watch the friends' video message and take notes. Then talk about your notes in class.
I Write down the names of three or more sights.
II Take notes on three or more of the sights.
III Take notes on four or more of the sights.

5c audio 2/44, skill: mediation, p. 145

You are at the i360 observation tower. A German family does not understand the announcement. Listen to the announcement and answer their questions in German.

1 Was kosten die Tickets für Kinder?
2 Gibt es einen Flug am Montag um 9 Uhr?
3 Wie lange dauert der Flug?

4 Woher bekommen wir die Tickets?
5 Kann man im i360 etwas zu trinken kaufen?

LAND & LEUTE 6 video 19, workbook p. 96/9, 10
Britische Küstenstädte

Brighton liegt wie viele Städte in Großbritannien am Meer.
In vielen Küstenstädten (seaside towns) gibt es Piers, die früher als Anlegestellen für große Schiffe dienten. Heute werden die Piers oft für Vergnügungszwecke genutzt.
Auf dem *Brighton Palace Pier* in Brighton gibt es sogar einen Freizeitpark (amusement park) und eine Spielhalle (amusement arcade). Amusement arcades gibt es auch in vielen anderen Küstenstädten. Bei einem Ausflug ans Meer darf eins nicht fehlen:

fish and chips. Der panierte und frittierte Fisch wird mit den Pommes (chips) zusammen

traditionellerweise in einer Papiertüte verkauft. Es ist sehr beliebt, auf die Pommes noch einen Schuss Essig (vinegar) zu geben.

Sieh dir den Videoclip an. Was findest du interessant? Wo würdest du gerne einmal hinfahren?

Shopping in Brighton

6a workbook p.97/11

Look at the pictures. Where are the children? What are they doing?

6b audio 2/45, 2/46, 2/47

Listen and read along. What do the children buy?

Tarek: Hello. Could I have three of those Brighton Rock candy sticks, please?
Shopkeeper: Yes, of course! That's 3 pounds, please.
Tarek: Here you are – 10 pounds.
Shopkeeper: Thank you. That's 7 pounds change. Enjoy and have a nice day!
Tarek: Have a nice day, too. Bye.

Ava: Excuse me. I'm looking for a postcard of Brighton Pier.
Shopkeeper: The postcards are over there, next to the comic books.
Ava: Oh thanks. – I'd like this one, please.
Shopkeeper: That's 95p, please. Would you like a stamp, too?
Ava: Yes, please. One for a postcard to Poland, please. How much is it then?
Shopkeeper: That's 1 pound 80, please.
Ava: Here you are.
Shopkeeper: And 3 pounds 20 change.
Ava: Thank you. Have a nice day.
Shopkeeper: Thanks, you too. Bye.

Shopkeeper: Hi, can I help you?
Harry: Yes, please. Have you got this T-shirt in red?
Shopkeeper: Just a minute. Let me have a look ... Here is one. What size do you need?
Harry: Size M, please.
Shopkeeper: Here you are.
Harry: Oh great. I think it fits. How much is it?
Shopkeeper: It's 15 pounds 99.
Harry: Cool. I'll take it. Where can I pay?
Shopkeeper: The till is over there.
Harry: Thanks for your help. Bye.
Shopkeeper: No problem. Bye.

ACTIVATE   PRACTISE   **DEVELOP**   PRACTISE   APPLY

6c skill: reading p.144

Read the dialogues again. How many candy sticks does Tarek buy? How much is the stamp that Ava buys? What is Harry's size?

6d 🖼 **CHOOSE YOUR LEVEL** skill: talking with people p.142, wordbank: shopping p.159

Work with a partner.

I Practise reading dialogue 1. Then do a role play. You can record your role play.

II Make up your own shopping dialogue in a souvenir shop. Look at dialogue 2 for help. Act it out. You can record your role play.

III Make up your own shopping dialogue in a clothes shop. Look at the dialogues for help. Act it out. You can record your role play.

Shopping

7 **GET TOGETHER**

Get together with a partner. Go shopping.

Partner A	Partner B
I Go to page 115.	**I** Go to page 127.
II Go to page 119.	**II** Go to page 131.
III Go to page 123.	**III** Go to page 135.

It was a great day!

9a

**Look at the picture.
Where are the children?**

Sightseeing

8 **CHOOSE YOUR TASK**

A **Plan a visit to Brighton. What would you like to see and do there?**

B **What are the special places in your home town? What can you see and do there?**

C 🖼 **Check out another British seaside town on the Internet. What would you like to see and do there?**

9b audio 2/49, workbook p.98/12

Listen and read along. What were the children's favourite things?

Mum: So, how was your day?

Ava: It was great – the Upside Down House was so cool! Thanks for taking us.

Tarek: Yes, that was fantastic. My favourite thing was the view from the i360! And the fish and chips at the seaside!

Mum: Were there any hungry seagulls?

Ava: No, there weren't. We were lucky, there weren't any hungry animals.

Lily: My favourite thing was the beach. I really miss it in London.

Mum: And what was your favourite thing of the day, Harry?

Harry: My new T-shirt!

A day trip

10   **CHOOSE YOUR LEVEL** grammar: be simple past p. 183

▌ Find the correct answers to the questions.

1 Was Ava at the souvenir shop?	A Yes, it was.
2 Was Noah in Brighton?	B Yes, they were.
3 Were the children at the beach?	C Yes, she was.
4 Was it a great day?	D No, he wasn't.

▌▌ Copy the questions and fill in the gaps with *was* and *were*.
Then find the correct answers to the questions.

1 ??? the weather good?	A It was 15 pounds and 99 pence.
2 ??? the children at the i360?	B Yes, it was.
3 How much ??? Harry's T-shirt?	C Harry and Lily's mum.
4 When ??? the children in Brighton?	D Yes, they were.
5 Who ??? in Brighton with the children?	E The beach.
6 What ??? Lily's favourite thing of the day?	F On Saturday.

▌▌▌ Copy the questions and fill in the gaps with *was* and *were*.
Think about a day trip or holiday in the past and answer the questions.

1   When ??? your day trip or holiday?
2   Where ??? you?
3   How ??? the weather?
4   Who ??? with you?
5   ??? the trip or holiday good?
6   What ??? your favourite thing?

Odd one out

11

Find the odd one out.

1   bye, hello, hi, good morning
2   warm, famous, sunny, rainy
3   pizza, lemonade, baked beans, ice cream
4   swimming pool, beach, friends, hotel
5   Germany, New York, Italy, France
6   uncle, aunt, cousin, student

Good or bad?

12

Sort the words from the box into two groups: good and bad.

> great · boring · nice · cool · beautiful ·
> brilliant · terrible · excellent · fantastic

You can write:

good: great, …
bad: …

DIGITAL+ practise more 20

ACTIVATE   PRACTISE   DEVELOP   **PRACTISE**   APPLY

Writing a postcard TARGET TASK

13 workbook p. 99/13, wordbank: places p. 152, food p. 156, free time p. 157, skill: writing p. 143

Your task is to write a postcard. Before you start, look at these steps:

STEP 1
Imagine you are on a day trip or on holiday. Where are you?

STEP 2
Who are you writing to?
Find a good way to say hello.

Hi Grandma,
I was in Brighton with my friends today.
Now we're on the train back to London.
Brighton was really cool! The weather
was warm and sunny. First we were
at the beach. There is a famous pier in
Brighton — you can see it on this postcard.
It was cool and the fish and chips there
were really good, but the best thing was
the observation tower. You can see all
over Brighton from up there!
I hope to see you again soon!
Love, Ava

Edyta Kogan
ul. Targowa 248/5
03-733 Warszawa
Poland

STEP 3
Write about:
· where you are,
· what it is like,
· the food,
· the weather,
· ...

STEP 4
Find a good way to say goodbye
and write the address.
Draw a stamp if you like.

STEP 5
Display your postcards in your classroom.
If you like, you can send a postcard to your class from your summer holidays.

Check out

1. Kannst du beschreiben, was jemand gerade tut?	Workbook, p. 100
2. Kennst du Wörter, um über Familienmitglieder und deren Geburtstage zu sprechen?	Workbook, p. 100
3. Kannst du Tipps für eine besondere Geburtstagsfeier verstehen?	Workbook, p. 100
4. Kannst du sagen, wo jemand in der Vergangenheit war oder nicht war?	Workbook, p. 101
5. Kannst du den Inhalt einer Durchsage verstehen und das Wichtigste auf Deutsch wiedergeben?	Workbook, p. 101
6. Kannst du einen Einkaufsdialog führen?	Workbook, p. 101

The delicious dragon dinner

Hello again! There's still no baby dragon, but you're just in time for our delicious dragon dinner. Our starter is ready … Let's see if the dragons like it. I give the salad to the dragons.
They look at me, but they don't eat. I eat some of the salad to show the dragons that it's nice. Phew, it's spicy! My cheeks are warm. But still, the dragons do not eat. Hmm. Let's try the main course: hot and spicy pizza with extra red and green chillies. Yum, that looks good! I give the pizza to the dragons. Ignus and Volta just look at it. Oh no … But wait! Look at Tazzy. She's trying it. She's eating lots of it. WOOHOO, she likes it! Wait, what's happening? Oh dear, the poor little dragon. Look at her face! Oh Tazzy – she looks like a tomato! And then … MIAOWWWW! Oh no, the castle cat!

Suddenly, Tazzy lets out a really big BURP! Wow, look at those flames! Another BURP. And more flames!
Look … I think the cat is a bit shocked by Tazzy's flames. Look at its tail – it's so big! Hahaha.
Oh, Tazzy thinks it's funny, too. She's laughing with me now!
Tazzy and I laugh and laugh. The poor cat with her big tail!

CRUNCH! I look up. Wow, Volta and Ignus are eating some pizza, too! AND some salad. Yes! Tazzy finds the dessert and starts eating that.
I'm hungry, too. Pizza for me! For a moment we are all quiet. We eat our delicious dragon dinner. And then … Oh no, the chillies! They are so spicy! My face goes red and feels HOT, HOT, HOT.
Ignus and Volta start to laugh.

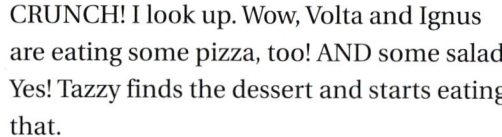
burp = *Rülpser*; cheek = *Wange*; go red = *rot werden*; poor = *arm*

And then: CRAAAAACKKK! CR … A … CK!
We all stop eating and turn around to look at the egg.
Finally, the egg cracks open and – POP! – out comes
a blue baby dragon. Oh, it's so sweet!

Suddenly, I feel something on my shoulder.
It's Tazzy! She is sitting on my shoulder and
eating some chilli chocolate! I look at Ignus
and Volta. They look at me. And Volta nods
her head.
Up and down.
That's it! They trust me. Fantastic! I'm so
happy.

Two hours later

"Ignus? Can I talk to you?" I ask. I have some questions. The huge dragon looks at me and nods his
head. Remember, dragons can speak some English, but not much.
So I ask a simple question: "Why are you here?"
"Our home, it was in a forest. Near here," he begins. "But now, there is a hotel there. A big hotel.
Many people came. There was no space for us. It is not our home now. We have no home.
We are sad."
I feel sad, too. The poor dragons. I look at Ignus and say just one word, in Skkaddraa, the dragon
language: "Helppiffaa." It means: "I will help."

came = *kam(en)*; nod = *nicken*; sad = *traurig*;
space = *Raum, Platz*; trust = *vertrauen*; will = *werden*

A new home

Hello again! How are you? I'm really happy because the dragons are tame! But I need to find a new home for them – a place where they are safe. So I'm just checking the dragon tamers' map app. The app is really cool. It's a map that shows you safe places for dragons. Oh good, there's a group of Feli-Rhymus dragons not far from here. Perfect!

"Ready?" I ask Ignus and Volta. "Ready!" they reply. Tazzy runs up to me and jumps up on my shoulder. She's my favourite dragon – she's so sweet and fun.

Ignus lies down, and I climb up onto his back with Tazzy still on my shoulder. Volta takes her baby and soon we are up, Up, UP in the air! We fly for an hour, and then I tell Ignus: "Go down here. Look … That field there!" We land in a field near a forest. "This is it," I tell the dragons. "Your new home. It's safe here, and there are lots of other Feli-Rhymus dragons, just like you. Look!"

Tazzy jumps down and runs over to the other dragon children. Volta looks at me. "Thank you," she says. "Taa welcommaada," I reply. "You're welcome."

It's time for me to go home. I find my phone and call Stevie, my pilot. I ask her to come and get me. Then I take a final photo of the dragons and send the photo and a text message to Kora.

Soon the helicopter arrives. I say goodbye to the dragons, and then I get into the helicopter and say hi to Stevie. I'm sad to leave the dragons, but I'm happy, too. Now I've got only one thing to worry about: what will my mum say when she sees that one of my new shoes has a big hole in it?
You know what? Dragons aren't that scary, but my mum really is! Wish me luck! Goodbye!

DIGITAL+ You can listen to Blaze talking to his mum: audio 2/54

air = *Luft*; onto his back = *auf seinen Rücken*; reply = *antworten, erwidern*; You're welcome. = *Gern geschehen., Keine Ursache.*

Water sports and activities in the UK

Do you think holidays where you just sit on the beach are boring? Do you love adventures? Then try one of the many exciting water sports and activities you can do in the UK!

What about white water rafting? You can go white water rafting in County Tyrone in Northern Ireland on the River Blackwater. You, your friends and a guide need a special boat and paddles. It's an exciting activity, but it can be dangerous — so you have to work together on the boat. Always listen to your guide and be prepared to get very wet!

Maybe white water rafting isn't your thing? You can try paddle boarding instead. You can go paddle boarding on lakes, rivers or on the sea.
A great place to go paddle boarding is North Wales. Enjoy a day out in nature while you're paddling. You need a board and a paddle. There are lots of different places where you can rent equipment. Enjoy Wales on a paddle board and have a good workout at the same time!

Do you like sea creatures? Then rock pooling is the perfect activity for you. You can go rock pooling almost everywhere at the seaside.
One great place is Fistral Bay in Cornwall. When the tide is out, you can find interesting things in the rock pools.
You need good shoes to go rock pooling. If you're feeling brave, you can turn over small rocks and see what lives under them. But don't forget to put the rocks back afterwards!

Which of these activities would you like to try? Why?

Two different neighbourhoods

10a UNIT 1, p. 25 PARTNER A

Look at the picture.
What can you see?
Write down words.

10b UNIT 1, p. 25 PARTNER A

Tell your partner about your picture.

You can say:

There's a ... in my picture.

There are ... in my picture.

I've got ... in my picture.

...

10c UNIT 1, p. 25 PARTNER A

Listen to your partner. What places are there in his or her picture?
Take notes.

10d UNIT 1, p. 25 PARTNER A, wordbank: places p. 152

Ask your partner three or more questions about his or her picture.
Then answer your partner's questions.

You can ask:

Is there a ... in your picture?

Are there ... in your picture?

Have you got ... in your picture?

You can answer:

Yes, there is. / No, there isn't.

Yes, there are. / No, there aren't.

Yes, I have. / No, I haven't.

10e UNIT 1, p. 25 PARTNER A

What is your favourite place
where you live? Tell your partner about it.
Then listen to your partner.
What is his or her favourite place?

You can say:

My favourite place is ...

I like the ...

...

David and Julia

12a   UNIT 2, p. 45   PARTNER A, skill: reading p. 144

▌ **Read what David says about his school.**
Find answers to the following questions
and take notes.

1 Where is his school?
2 When does school start in the morning?
3 What is David's favourite subject?
4 Which school club does he go to?

Hi everyone!
My name is David.
I go to West Derby School
in Liverpool. Liverpool is
a big city.
School starts at 8:30 in
the morning.
My favourite subject is art.
The art teacher is very nice, she is my
favourite teacher. Her name is Mrs Miller.
I go to the drama club after school. I don't
like maths and history.

12b   UNIT 2, p. 45   PARTNER A, wordbank: school p. 154

▌ **Now find out about Julia. Ask your partner three or more questions about her.**
Then answer your partner's questions about David.

Julia

You can ask:

Where is …?

When does …?

What …?

Which …?

Does Julia like …?

…

You can answer:

His school is in …

His school starts at …

It's …

He goes to …

I don't know. It's not in the text.

Yes, he does. / No, he doesn't.

12c   UNIT 2, p. 45   PARTNER A

▌ **What about you? Tell your partner three or more things about your school life.**

You can say:

My favourite … is …

I like …

I go to …

…

Two sports

8a UNIT 3, p. 64 PARTNER A, audio 2/5, skill: listening p. 141

Look at the picture and listen to Eric talking about his sport – lacrosse. Then listen again and take notes on these questions:

1 How many players are there in a lacrosse team?
2 Where does Eric play lacrosse?
3 When does Eric practise?

8b UNIT 3, p. 64 PARTNER A

Tell your partner two or more things about Eric and his sport.
Then listen to your partner. He or she tells you about Cho and her sport. Take notes.

You can say:

There are …
Eric plays …
He practises …

8c UNIT 3, p. 64 PARTNER A

Which sport do you like better? Tell your partner about it.

You can say:

I like … better.
I think it's …
…

Chores

12a UNIT 4, p. 85 PARTNER A, skill: reading p. 144

Ava's parents have got a lot of chores. Who does what and how often?
Copy the table. Then read about Ava's mum and write her chores in the table.

	mum	dad
always	*makes breakfast on weekdays, …*	
usually	✕	
often	✕	
sometimes		
never		

Ava's mum: There are three children and a dog in our family – that's a lot of work. But we share the chores. I always make breakfast on weekdays and I always vacuum the living room. I work late on Fridays, so I haven't got much time for chores on Fridays. I sometimes empty the dishwasher but that is usually Ava's job. And I never tidy the children's rooms. That's their job!

12b UNIT 4, p. 85 PARTNER A

What about Ava's dad?
Ask your partner about Ava's dad's chores and complete the table.
Draw an X when there is no answer.
Then answer your partner's questions about Ava's mum.

You can ask:

What does Ava's dad always / never / … do?

You can answer:

She always / never / … tidies / makes / …
I don't know. / It's not in the text.

12c UNIT 4, p. 85 PARTNER A

Work with your partner. Look at your tables and check them. Is everything correct?

12d UNIT 4, p. 85 PARTNER A

Which of the jobs from the table would you choose? Tell your partner.

Shopping

7 UNIT 5, p. 105 PARTNER A, wordbank: shopping p. 159

You are the shopkeeper in a clothes shop. Your partner would like to buy a T-shirt.
Look at the boxes and do a role play. You start.

1 Begrüße deinen Kunden / deine Kundin und frage, ob du helfen kannst.
You can say:
Hi. Can I help you?

2 Partner B fragt nach etwas.

3 Sage, dass du T-Shirts hast und dass sie da drüben sind.
You can say:
Sure. They're over there.

4 Partner B hat noch eine Frage.

5 Sage, dass es das T-Shirt auch in Rot gibt. Frage, welche Größe Partner B braucht.
You can say:
Yes, I …
What size do you need?

6 Partner B antwortet.

7 Bringe ein rotes T-Shirt in Größe M. Gib es Partner B und frage, ob es passt.
You can say:
Here it is. A red T-shirt in size M.
Does it fit?

8 Partner B antwortet.

9 Sage, dass das super ist und dass das T-Shirt £14.90 kostet.
You can say:
Great. It's £14.90.

10 Partner B reagiert.

11 Bedanke dich, gib 10p Wechselgeld und verabschiede dich.
You can say:
Thank you. And 10p change.
Bye then.

12 Partner B reagiert.

Two different neighbourhoods

10a UNIT 1, p. 25 PARTNER A

▌ Look at the picture.
What can you see?
Write down words.

MARKET
second-hand clothes
MUSEUM
live experiments
ZOO
shop

10b UNIT 1, p. 25 PARTNER A

▌ Tell your partner about your picture.

You can say:

There's a ... in my picture.

There are ... in my picture.

I've got ... in my picture.

You can ... there.

10c UNIT 1, p. 25 PARTNER A

▌ Listen to your partner. What places are
there in his or her picture?
Take notes.

10d UNIT 1, p. 25 PARTNER A, wordbank: places p. 152

▌ Ask your partner four or more questions about his or her picture.
Then answer your partner's questions.

You can ask:

Is there a ... in your picture?

Are there ... in your picture?

Have you got ... in your picture?

You can answer:

Yes, there is. / No, there isn't.

Yes, there are. / No, there aren't.

Yes, I have. / No, I haven't.

10e UNIT 1, p. 25 PARTNER A

▌ What is your favourite place
where you live? Tell your partner about it.
Then listen to your partner.
What is his or her favourite place?

You can say:

My favourite place is ...

I like the ...

You can ... there.

David and Julia

12a UNIT 2, p. 45 PARTNER A, skill: reading p. 144

Read what David says about his school. Take notes on:

1 where it is
2 start of school day
3 David's favourite subject
4 his favourite teacher
5 school clubs

Hi everyone!
My name is David. I go to West Derby School in Liverpool.
School starts at 8:30 in the morning with assembly.
At assembly the teachers give us important information. Then at 8:45, we go to our classrooms for registration.
My favourite subject is art and our art teacher is my favourite teacher. Her name is Mrs Miller.
On Wednesdays I go to the drama club and on Fridays I go to the science club.
I don't like maths or history. I think they are really boring subjects!

12b UNIT 2, p. 45 PARTNER A, wordbank: school p. 154

Now find out about Julia. Ask your partner four or more questions about her. Then answer your partner's questions about David.

Julia

You can ask:

Where is …?
When does …?
What …?
Which …?
Does Julia like …?

You can answer:

It's …
His school starts at …
He …
I don't know. It's not in the text.
Yes, he does. / No, he doesn't.

12c UNIT 2, p. 45 PARTNER A

What about you? Tell your partner four or more things about your school life.

You can say:

My favourite … is …
I like …
I go to …
…

Two sports

8a   UNIT 3, p. 64 PARTNER A, audio 2/5, skill: listening p. 141

❙❙ **Look at the picture and listen to Eric talking about his sport – lacrosse. Then listen again and take notes on:**

1 how many players there are in a team
2 where Eric plays
3 when Eric practises
4 what he says about the other players in his team

8b   UNIT 3, p. 64 PARTNER A

❙❙ **Tell your partner three or more things about Eric and his sport.
Then listen to your partner. He or she tells you about Cho and her sport.
Take notes.**

You can say:

There are …
Eric plays …
…

8c   UNIT 3, p. 64 PARTNER A

❙❙ **Which sport do you like better?
Tell your partner about it.**

You can say:

I like … better.
I think it's …
…

Chores

12a   UNIT 4, p. 85 PARTNER A, skill: reading p 144

❙❙ **Ava's parents have got a lot of chores. Who does what and how often?
Copy the table. Then read about Ava's mum and write her chores in the table.**

	mum	dad
always	*makes breakfast on weekdays, …*	
usually	✕	
often		
sometimes		
never		

Ava's mum: We've got three children and a dog in our family. There's so much to do around the house. But we all help with the chores.
I always make breakfast on weekdays and I always vacuum the living room. I work late on Fridays, so I haven't got much time for chores on Fridays. But I often make the plans for the weekend and I always clean the bathroom. I often take Ollie for his walks, too. I sometimes empty the dishwasher but that is usually Ava's job. And I never tidy the children's rooms. That's their job!

12b UNIT 4, p. 85 PARTNER A

What about Ava's dad?
Ask your partner about Ava's dad's
chores and complete the table.
Draw an *X* when there is no answer.
Then answer your partner's questions
about Ava's mum.

You can ask:

What does Ava's dad always / never / … do?

You can answer:

She always / never / … tidies / makes / …
I don't know. / It's not in the text.

12c UNIT 4, p. 85 PARTNER A

Work with your partner. Look at your tables and check them. Is everything correct?

12d UNIT 4, p. 85 PARTNER A

Which of the jobs from the table would you choose? Tell your partner.

Shopping

7 UNIT 5, p. 105 PARTNER A, wordbank: shopping p. 159

You are the shopkeeper in a clothes shop. Your partner would like to buy a T-shirt.
Look at the boxes and do a role play. You start.

1 Begrüße deinen Kunden / deine Kundin
und frage, ob du helfen kannst.
You can say:
Hi. Can I …?

2 Partner B fragt nach etwas.

3 Sage, dass du T-Shirts hast und dass
sie da drüben sind.
You can say:
Sure. They're …

4 Partner B hat noch eine Frage.

5 Sage, dass es das T-Shirt auch in Rot
gibt. Frage, welche Größe Partner B
braucht.
You can say:
Yes, …
What size …?

6 Partner B antwortet.

7 Bringe ein rotes T-Shirt in Größe M.
Gib es Partner B und frage, ob es passt.
You can say:
Here it is. A … in size M.
Does it fit?

8 Partner B antwortet.

9 Sage, dass das super ist und dass das
T-Shirt £14.90 kostet.
You can say:
Great. It's …

10 Partner B reagiert.

11 Bedanke dich, gib 10p Wechselgeld und
verabschiede dich.
You can say:
Thank you. And … change.
Bye then.

12 Partner B reagiert.

Two different neighbourhoods

10a   UNIT 1, p. 25 PARTNER A

||| Look at the picture.
What can you see?
Write down words.

MARKET
second-hand clothes,
food
MUSEUM
live experiments, shop
ZOO
shop, playground

10b   UNIT 1, p. 25 PARTNER A

||| Tell your partner about your picture.

You can say:

There's a … in my picture.

There are … in my picture.

I've got … in my picture.

You can … there.

10c   UNIT 1, p. 25 PARTNER A

||| Listen to your partner. What places are
there in his or her picture?
Take notes.

10d   UNIT 1, p. 25 PARTNER A, wordbank: places p. 152

||| Ask your partner five or more questions about his or her picture.
Then answer your partner's questions.

You can ask:

Is there a … in your picture?

Are there … in your picture?

Have you got … in your picture?

You can answer:

Yes, there is. / No, there isn't.

…

10e   UNIT 1, p. 25 PARTNER A

||| What is your favourite place where
you live? Tell your partner about it.
Then listen to your partner.
What is his or her favourite place?

You can say:

My favourite place is …

I like the …

You can … there.

David and Julia

12a UNIT 2, p. 45 PARTNER A, skill: reading p. 144

Read what David says about his school. Take notes on:

1 where it is
2 start of school day
3 assembly
4 favourite subject
5 favourite teacher
6 school clubs

Hi everyone!
My name is David and I live in Liverpool. I go to West Derby School. School starts at 8:30 in the morning.
At 8:30, we go to assembly, where the teachers give us important information. Then at 8:45 we go to our classrooms for registration with our teachers.
My favourite subject is art. I like being creative. Our art teacher is my favourite teacher. Her name is Mrs Miller and she is a really good teacher.
After school on Wednesdays I go to the drama club. It's so much fun!
On Fridays I go to the science club. We do experiments and sometimes there are small explosions. That is fun, too. I don't like maths or history. I think they are really boring subjects!

12b UNIT 2, p. 45 PARTNER A, wordbank: school p. 154

**Now find out about Julia. Ask your partner five or more questions about her.
Then answer your partner's questions about David.**

Julia

You can ask:
Where …?
When …?
What …?
Which …?
Does …?

You can answer:
It's …
It starts at …
He …
I don't know. It's not in the text.
Yes, he does. / No, he doesn't.

12c UNIT 2, p. 45 PARTNER A

What about you? Tell your partner five or more things about your school life.

Two sports

8a   UNIT 3, p. 64 PARTNER A, audio 2/5, skill: listening p. 141

||| Look at the picture and listen to Eric talking about his sport – lacrosse. Then listen again and take notes:

1 how many players there are in a team
2 where Eric plays
3 when Eric practises
4 what he likes about lacrosse

8b   UNIT 3, p. 64 PARTNER A

||| Tell your partner four or more things about Eric and his sport.
Then listen to your partner. He or she tells you about Cho and her sport. Take notes.

You can say:

There are …

…

8c   UNIT 3, p. 64 PARTNER A

||| Which sport do you like better?
Tell your partner about it.

You can say:

I like … better.

I think it's …

…

Chores

12a   UNIT 4, p. 85 PARTNER A, skill: reading p 144

||| Ava's parents have got a lot of chores. Who does what and how often?
Copy the table. Then read about Ava's mum and write her chores in the table.

	mum	dad
always	*makes breakfast on weekdays, …*	
usually		
often		
sometimes		
never		

Ava's mum: We share the chores in our family – our family that's my husband, our three children and, of course, our dog, Ollie.
I always make breakfast on weekdays and I always vacuum the living room. I usually work late on Fridays, so I haven't got much time on Fridays. But I often make the plans for the weekend and I always clean the bathroom.
I usually tidy the living room. I often take Ollie for his walks, too. I sometimes empty the dishwasher but that is usually Ava's job.
And I never tidy the children's rooms. That's their job!

12b
UNIT 4, p. 85 PARTNER A

What about Ava's dad?
Ask your partner about Ava's dad's chores and complete the table.
Draw an *X* when there is no answer.
Then answer your partner's questions about Ava's mum.

You can ask:

What does Ava's dad always / never / … do?

You can answer:

She always / never / … tidies / makes / …
I don't know. / It's not in the text.

12c
UNIT 4, p. 85 PARTNER A

Work with your partner. Look at your tables and check them. Is everything correct?

12d
UNIT 4, p. 85 PARTNER A

Which of the jobs from the table would you choose? Tell your partner.

Shopping

7
UNIT 5, p. 105 PARTNER A, wordbank: shopping p. 159

You are the shopkeeper in a clothes shop. Your partner would like to buy a T-shirt. Look at the boxes and do a role play. You start.

1 Begrüße deinen Kunden / deine Kundin und frage, ob du helfen kannst.	7 Bringe ein rotes T-Shirt in Größe M. Gib es Partner B und frage, ob es passt.
2 Partner B fragt nach etwas.	8 Partner B antwortet.
3 Sage, dass du T-Shirts hast und dass sie da drüben sind.	9 Sage, dass das super ist und dass das T-Shirt £14.90 kostet.
4 Partner B hat noch eine Frage.	10 Partner B reagiert.
5 Sage, dass es das T-Shirt auch in Rot gibt. Frage, welche Größe Partner B braucht.	11 Bedanke dich, gib 10p Wechselgeld und verabschiede dich.
6 Partner B antwortet.	12 Partner B reagiert.

Two different neighbourhoods

10a UNIT 1, p. 25 PARTNER B

Look at the picture.
What can you see?
Write down words.

10b UNIT 1, p. 25 PARTNER B

Listen to your partner. What places are there in his or her picture?
Take notes.

10c UNIT 1, p. 25 PARTNER B

Tell your partner about your picture.

You can say:

There's a … in my picture.

There are … in my picture.

I've got … in my picture.

…

10d UNIT 1, p. 25 PARTNER B, wordbank: places p. 152

Answer your partner's questions about your picture.
Then ask three or more questions about his or her picture.

You can answer:

Yes, there is. / No, there isn't.

Yes, there are. / No, there aren't.

Yes, I have. / No, I haven't.

You can ask:

Is there a … in your picture?

Are there … in your picture?

Have you got … in your picture?

10e UNIT 1, p. 25 PARTNER B

Listen to your partner. What is his or her favourite place?
What is your favourite place where you live? Tell your partner about it.

You can say:

My favourite place is …

I like the …

…

David and Julia

12a UNIT 2, p. 45 PARTNER B, skill: reading p. 144

Read what Julia says about her school. Find answers to the following questions and take notes.

1 Where is her school?
2 When does school start in the morning?
3 What is Julia's favourite subject?
4 Which school club does she go to?

Hi there!
My name is Julia.
I go to the Queen's College in Cardiff. School starts at 8:45 every day. My favourite subject is history. I think it is really interesting. I also really like our history teacher, Mr Walker. He is my favourite teacher. Mr Walker's lessons are really fun. I don't like ICT or geography. I go to the book club on Thursdays.

12b UNIT 2, p. 45 PARTNER B, wordbank: school p. 154

Answer your partner's questions about Julia. Then find out about David. Ask your partner three or more questions about him.

You can answer:

Her school is in ...
Her school starts at ...
It's ...
She goes to ...
I don't know. It's not in the text.
Yes, she does. / No, she doesn't.

David

You can ask:

Where is ...?
When does ...?
What ...?
Which ...?
Does David like ...?
...

12c UNIT 2, p. 45 PARTNER B

What about you? Tell your partner three or more things about your school life.

You can say:

My favourite ... is ...
I like ...
I go to ...
...

Two sports

8a   UNIT 3, p.64 PARTNER B, audio 2/6, skill: listening p.141

▌ **Look at the picture and listen to Cho talking about her sport – climbing. Then listen again and take notes on these questions:**

1 Where can you go climbing?
2 What do you need for climbing?
3 When does Cho go climbing?

8b   UNIT 3, p.64 PARTNER B

▌ **Listen to your partner. He or she tells you about Eric and his sport. Take notes.**
Then tell your partner two or more things about Cho and her sport.

You can say:

You can go climbing …
You need …
…

8c   UNIT 3, p.64 PARTNER B

▌ **Which sport do you like better? Tell your partner about it.**

You can say:

I like …better.
I think it's …
…

Chores

12a   UNIT 4, p.85 PARTNER B, skill: reading p.144

▌ **Ava's parents have got a lot of chores. Who does what and how often?**
Copy the table. Then read about Ava's dad and write his chores in the table.

	mum	dad
always		*makes breakfast on Saturdays, …*
usually		✕
often		✕
sometimes		
never		

Ava's dad: There are three children and a dog in our family – that's a lot of work. But we share the chores. I always make breakfast on Saturdays and I always clean the kitchen. I sometimes empty the dishwasher but that is usually Ava's job. And I never tidy the children's rooms. That's their job!

12b   UNIT 4, p. 85 PARTNER B

▌ **Answer your partner's questions about Ava's dad.**
Then ask your partner about Ava's mum's chores and complete the table. Draw an X when there is no answer.

You can answer:

He always / never / … makes / cleans / …
I don't know. / It's not in the text.

You can ask:

What does Ava's mum always / never / … do?

12c   UNIT 4, p. 85 PARTNER B

▌ **Work with your partner. Look at your tables and check them. Is everything correct?**

12d   UNIT 4, p. 85 PARTNER B

▌ **Which of the jobs from the table would you choose? Tell your partner.**

Shopping

7   UNIT 5, p. 105 PARTNER B, wordbank: shopping p. 159

▌ **You are in a clothes shop and would like to buy a T-shirt. Look at the boxes and do a role play. Your partner starts.**

1 Partner A beginnt.	7 Partner A reagiert.
2 Begrüße den Verkäufer / die Verkäuferin und sage, dass du nach einem T-Shirt suchst. **You can say:** *Hi. I'm looking for a T-shirt.*	8 Sage, dass es passt und du es kaufen möchtest. Frage nach dem Preis. **You can say:** *It fits. Great. I'll take it.* *How much is it?*
3 Partner A antwortet.	9 Partner A antwortet.
4 Du findest ein T-Shirt, hättest es aber lieber in Rot. **You can say:** *Have you got this T-shirt in red?*	10 Bezahle mit £15. **You can say:** *Here you are. £15.*
5 Partner A reagiert.	11 Partner A reagiert.
6 Sage, dass du das T-Shirt in Größe M brauchst. **You can say:** *Size M, please.*	12 Bedanke und verabschiede dich. **You can say:** *Thank you. Bye.*

Two different neighbourhoods

10a   UNIT 1, p. 25 PARTNER B

Look at the picture.
What can you see?
Write down words.

CINEMA
film parties
PARK
playground
SWIMMING POOL
café

10b   UNIT 1, p. 25 PARTNER B

Listen to your partner. What places are
there in his or her picture?
Take notes.

10c   UNIT 1, p. 25 PARTNER B

Tell your partner about your picture.

You can say:

There's a … in my picture.

There are … in my picture.

I've got … in my picture.

You can … there.

10d   UNIT 1, p. 25 PARTNER B, wordbank: places p. 152

Answer your partner's questions about your picture.
Then ask four or more questions about his or her picture.

You can answer:

Yes, there is. / No, there isn't.

Yes, there are. / No, there aren't.

Yes, I have. / No, I haven't.

You can ask:

Is there a … in your picture?

Are there … in your picture?

Have you got … in your picture?

10e   UNIT 1, p. 25 PARTNER B

Listen to your partner. What is his or
her favourite place?
What is your favourite place
where you live? Tell your partner
about it.

You can say:

My favourite place is …

I like the …

You can … there.

David and Julia

❙❙ **Read what Julia says about her school.**
Take notes on:

1 where it is
2 start of school day
3 Julia's favourite subject
4 her favourite teacher
5 school clubs

Hi there!
My name is Julia. I go to the Queen's College in Cardiff.
School starts with registration at 8:45 every day. We only have assemblies on Tuesdays.
My favourite subject is history. I think it is really interesting. Our history teacher, Mr Walker, is my favourite teacher. His lessons are never boring.
I don't like ICT or geography. The teachers always give us a lot of homework.
I go to the book club on Thursdays with my friend Eila. On Fridays, I practise with the football team after school.

❙❙ **Answer your partner's questions about Julia. Then find out about David.**
Ask your partner four or more questions about him.

You can answer:

It's …
Her school starts at …
She …
I don't know. It's not in the text.
Yes, she does. / No, she doesn't.

David

You can ask:

Where is …?
When does …?
What …?
Which …?
Does David like …?

❙❙ **What about you? Tell your partner four or more things about your school life.**
You can say:

My favourite … is …
I like …
I go to …
…

Two sports

8a UNIT 3, p. 64 PARTNER B, audio 2/6, skill: listening p. 141

▌ Look at the picture and listen to Cho talking about her sport – climbing. Then listen again and take notes on:

1 where you can go climbing
2 what you need
3 when Cho goes climbing
4 what she likes about climbing

8b UNIT 3, p. 64 PARTNER B

▌ Listen to your partner. He or she tells you about Eric and his sport. Take notes.
Then tell your partner three or more things about Cho and her sport.

You can say:

You can go climbing …
You need … for climbing.
…

8c UNIT 3, p. 64 PARTNER B

▌ Which sport do you like better? Tell your partner about it.

You can say:

I like … better.
I think it's …
…

Chores

12a UNIT 4, p. 85 PARTNER B, skill: reading p. 144

▌ Ava's parents have got a lot of chores. Who does what and how often?
Copy the table. Then read about Ava's dad and write his chores in the table.

	mum	dad
always		*makes breakfast on Saturdays, …*
usually		✕
often		
sometimes		
never		

Ava's dad: I have a great family and we share everything – the chores, too.
I always make breakfast on Saturdays and I always clean the kitchen. I always take out the rubbish, too. I often do the shopping and I often do the cooking on Fridays because Ava's mum works late.
I sometimes empty the dishwasher but that is usually Ava's job. And I never tidy the children's rooms. That's their job!

12b UNIT 4, p. 85 PARTNER B

▌ **Answer your partner's questions about Ava's dad.**
Then ask your partner about Ava's mum's chores and complete the table. Draw an X when there is no answer.

You can answer:

He always / never / … makes / cleans / …
I don't know. / It's not in the text.

You can ask:

What does Ava's mum always / never / … do?

12c UNIT 4, p. 85 PARTNER B

▌ **Work with your partner. Look at your tables and check them. Is everything correct?**

12d UNIT 4, p. 85 PARTNER B

▌ **Which of the jobs from the table would you choose? Tell your partner.**

Shopping

7 UNIT 5, p. 105 PARTNER B, wordbank: shopping p. 159

▌ **You are in a clothes shop and would like to buy a T-shirt. Look at the boxes and do a role play. Your partner starts.**

1 Partner A beginnt.	7 Partner A reagiert.
2 Begrüße den Verkäufer / die Verkäuferin und sage, dass du nach einem T-Shirt suchst. **You can say:** *Hi. I'm looking …*	8 Sage, dass es passt und du es kaufen möchtest. Frage nach dem Preis. **You can say:** *It fits. Great. I'll …* *How …?*
3 Partner A antwortet.	9 Partner A antwortet.
4 Du findest ein T-Shirt, hättest es aber lieber in Rot. **You can say:** *Have you got …?*	10 Bezahle mit £15. **You can say:** *Here …*
5 Partner A reagiert.	11 Partner A reagiert.
6 Sage, dass du das T-Shirt in Größe M brauchst. **You can say:** *Size …*	12 Bedanke und verabschiede dich. **You can say:** *Thank you …*

Two different neighbourhoods

10a UNIT 1, p. 25 PARTNER B

III **Look at the picture. What can you see? Write down words.**

CINEMA
film parties,
really good popcorn
PARK
playground,
skater's paradise
SWIMMING POOL
open daily, café

10b UNIT 1, p. 25 PARTNER B

III **Listen to your partner. What places are there in his or her picture? Take notes.**

10c UNIT 1, p. 25 PARTNER B

III **Tell your partner about your picture.**

You can say:

There's a … in my picture.

There are … in my picture.

I've got … in my picture.

You can … there.

10d UNIT 1, p. 25 PARTNER B, wordbank: places p. 152

III **Answer your partner's questions about your picture. Then ask five or more questions about his or her picture.**

You can answer:

Yes, there is. / No, there isn't.

…

You can ask:

Is there a … in your picture?

Are there … in your picture?

Have you got … in your picture?

10e UNIT 1, p. 25 PARTNER B

III **Listen to your partner. What is his or her favourite place? What is your favourite place where you live? Tell your partner about it.**

You can say:

My favourite place is …

I like the …

You can … there.

David and Julia

12a UNIT 2, p. 45 PARTNER B, skill: reading p. 144

**▌▌▌ Read what Julia says about her school.
Take notes on:**

1 where it is
2 start of school day
3 assembly
4 favourite subject
5 favourite teacher
6 school clubs

Hi there!
My name is Julia. I go to the Queen's College in Cardiff. Cardiff is a big city in Wales.
School starts with registration at 8:45 every day.
We only have assemblies on Tuesdays. I don't like assembly, it is never interesting.
My favourite subject at school is history. Our history teacher, Mr Walker, is my favourite teacher. His lessons are never boring.
I don't like ICT or geography because the teachers give us a lot of homework. And in geography we always have to do a lot of tests.
I go to the book club at lunchtime on Thursday with my friend Eila. On Fridays I practise with the football team after school. We practise in the gym or outside at the sports ground.

12b UNIT 2, p. 45 PARTNER B, wordbank: school p. 154

**▌▌▌ Answer your partner's questions about Julia. Then find out about David.
Ask your partner five or more questions about him.**

You can answer:

It's …
It starts at …
She …
I don't know. It's not in the text.
Yes, she does. / No, she doesn't.

David

You can ask:

Where …?
When …?
What …?
Which …?
Does …?

12c UNIT 2, p. 45 PARTNER B

▌▌▌ What about you? Tell your partner five or more things about your school life.

Two sports

8a   UNIT 3, p. 64 PARTNER B, audio 2/6, skill: listening p. 141

Look at the picture and listen to Cho talking about her sport – climbing. Then listen again and take notes on:

1 where you can go climbing
2 what you need
3 when Cho goes climbing
4 what Cho's favourite place for climbing is
5 what she likes about climbing

8b   UNIT 3, p. 64 PARTNER B

Listen to your partner. He or she tells you about Eric and his sport. Take notes.
Then tell your partner four or more things about Cho and her sport.

You can say:

You can …
You need …
…

8c   UNIT 3, p. 64 PARTNER B

Which sport do you like better? Tell your partner about it.

You can say:

I like … better.
I think it's …
…

Chores

12a   UNIT 4, p. 85 PARTNER B, skill: reading p. 144

Ava's parents have got a lot of chores. Who does what and how often?
Copy the table. Then read about Ava's dad and write his chores in the table.

	mum	dad
always		*makes breakfast on Saturdays, …*
usually		
often		
sometimes		
never		

Ava's dad: There are five of us – and our dog, Ollie. That means we have a lot of work to do at home. But we share our chores. I always make breakfast on Saturdays and I always clean the kitchen. I always take out the rubbish, too. I often do the shopping and I often do the cooking on Fridays because Ava's mum works late. I usually make the beds and tidy and vacuum our bedroom. I sometimes empty the dishwasher but that is usually Ava's job. And I never tidy the children's rooms. That's their job!

12b UNIT 4, p. 85 PARTNER B

Answer your partner's questions about Ava's dad.

Then ask your partner about Ava's mum's chores and complete the table.

Draw an *X* when there is no answer.

You can answer:

He always / never / … makes / cleans / …
I don't know. / It's not in the text.

You can ask:

What does Ava's mum always / never / … do?

12c UNIT 4, P. 85 PARTNER B

Work with your partner. Look at your tables and check them. Is everything correct?

12d UNIT 4, p. 85 PARTNER B

Which of the jobs from the table would you choose? Tell your partner.

Shopping

7 UNIT 5, p. 105 PARTNER B, wordbank: shopping p. 159

You are in a clothes shop and would like to buy a T-shirt. Look at the boxes and do a role play. Your partner starts.

1 Partner A beginnt.		**7** Partner A reagiert.	

2 Begrüße den Verkäufer / die Verkäuferin und sage, dass du nach einem T-Shirt suchst.

8 Sage, dass es passt und du es kaufen möchtest. Frage nach dem Preis.

3 Partner A antwortet.

9 Partner A antwortet.

4 Du findest ein T-Shirt, hättest es aber lieber in Rot.

10 Bezahle mit £15.

5 Partner A reagiert.

11 Partner A reagiert.

6 Sage, dass du das T-Shirt in Größe M brauchst.

12 Bedanke und verabschiede dich.

All about pets  DIGITAL+

Introduction skill: projects p.149

People all over the world have got pets. Books and films are full of cute, funny and clever pets. So what about a project on pets? There are many questions you can ask, for example:

· What pets are there?
· Where are they from?
· What is special about them?
· What do they need?

Find answers to these and other interesting questions in a pets project!

Plan it

1 In class, collect ideas for topics. You can make notes in a word web. Here is an example:

2 Now collect ideas about what you could create. For example:

▶ care sheets for different pets
▶ photo stories or short video clips
▶ a role play about a scene in a pet shop
▶ ...

Care sheet for cats
• Give cats water and cat food.
• Don't give them sweets or chocolate!
• Don't give them milk!
• Clean ...

3 Now get together in small groups and make a detailed plan. Write down:

▶ what information you need
▶ how you can find information
▶ how you want to present your work
▶ what material you need for your project work (for example: computer, paper, glue, ...)
▶ who does what and when

Do it skill: searching the Internet p. 148

And ... action! Do research, interview people, collect pictures, write texts, ... and create an interesting care sheet, poster, photo story, video clip, role play, ...

Check it

Check everything. Are there any spelling or grammar mistakes? Are the pictures big enough? Is everything easy to understand? If you want to give a presentation, practise it before you give it.

Present it

Present your work. You can ask your classmates for feedback after the presentation.

Breakfast from all over the world  DIGITAL+

Introduction   skill: projects p. 149

Bread, rice, muesli, eggs, sausages, jam, fruit, vegetables, … ? People around the world eat lots of different things for breakfast.
Here is something to think about:

· What is your breakfast like?
· What do other children eat for breakfast?
· What are traditional breakfast dishes from different countries?

Find out about these and other interesting questions in a breakfast project!

Plan it

1 **In class, think about what your project could be about. You can collect ideas or questions in a list. Here is an example:**

► What do the children in our class eat for breakfast?
► What do children in other countries eat for breakfast?
► What are traditional breakfast dishes from different countries?
► How do you prepare different breakfast dishes?
► What makes a healthy breakfast?
► What would our class's dream breakfast look like?
► …

2 **Now collect ideas about what you could do to answer your questions and what you could create. For example, you could:**

▶ create a poster to show the results of a survey on what your classmates eat for breakfast.
▶ create a menu for a dream breakfast.
▶ make an international breakfast recipe book with photos and recipes.
▶ make a podcast on traditional breakfast dishes from different countries.
▶ ...

Tip

You can make a class product, for example a recipe book: every group creates one page and you put everything together in the end.

3 **Now get together in small groups and make a detailed plan. Write down:**

▶ what information you need
▶ how you can get the information (do research, do a survey and interview people, ...)
▶ how you want to present your work
▶ what material you need for your project work (for example: computer, paper, glue, ...)
▶ who does what and when

Tip

When you as a group have a plan about what to do and how to present your work, you can ask your classmates from other groups for feedback on your plan.

Do it   skill: searching the Internet p. 148

And ... action! Do research, do a survey, interview people, try recipes, collect pictures, write texts, ... and create an interesting poster, menu, recipe book, podcast, ...

Check it

Check everything. Are there any spelling or grammar mistakes? Are the pictures big enough? Is everything easy to understand? If you are planning to give a presentation, practise it before you present it.

Present it

Present your work. You can ask your classmates for feedback after the presentation.

1 WORKING WITH WORDS
Wortschatzarbeit

Wenn man eine Fremdsprache lernt, muss man häufig die Bedeutung von Wörtern nachschlagen, wenn man sie sich nicht erschließen kann. Natürlich muss man sich auch viele neue Wörter merken. Hier findest du einige Tipps zum Umgang mit Vokabular.

1. Neue Wörter ohne Wörterbuch verstehen
▶ Falls es in einem Text Wörter gibt, die du noch nicht kennst, probiere Folgendes:
▶ Kannst du die Bedeutung aus dem Textzusammenhang erschließen?
▶ Kennst du gleiche oder ähnliche Wörter im Deutschen oder in einer anderen Sprache?
▶ Sind dir einzelne Teile eines englischen Wortes schon bekannt? Was könnte zum Beispiel *unhappy* bedeuten? Denke an die Bedeutung von *happy* (=glücklich).

2. So arbeitest du mit einem Wörterbuch
▶ Unbekannte Wörter kannst du in einem Wörterbuch nachschlagen.
▶ Sieh gut hin: Die Wörter sind alphabetisch geordnet. Du musst nicht nur auf den ersten Buchstaben im Wort achten, sondern auch auf den zweiten oder sogar den dritten. Das Wort *back* steht zum Beispiel vor *banana*.
▶ Ein Wort hat manchmal mehrere Bedeutungen. Sieh dir also alle Einträge zu dem Wort an, damit du die Übersetzung findest, die am besten passt.
▶ Ab Seite 213 in diesem Buch findest du das *Dictionary*. Dort kannst du alle englischen Wörter und Redewendungen aus *Notting Hill Gate 5* nachschlagen.

3. So arbeitest du mit den *wordbanks*
▶ Wörter, Ausdrücke und Sätze stehen nach Wortfeldern sortiert in den *wordbanks* ab Seite 150.
▶ Wenn du über ein bestimmtes Thema sprechen oder schreiben möchtest, findest du hier Unterstützung.

4. So kannst du dir Wörter merken
▶ Lies dir die Lernwörter in der Wortliste immer wieder laut vor bis du sie dir eingeprägt hast.
▶ Sammle Wörter oder Wortkombinationen *(chunks)* in Listen oder *word webs*.
▶ Lege eigene *wordbanks* zu bestimmten Themen an. Du kannst deine *wordbanks* auch mit Bildern versehen.

▨ Tipp: Nutze Online-Wörterbücher

· Wörterbücher gibt es auch online oder als App. Du kannst ein Wort eingeben und bekommst Übersetzungsvorschläge.
· Hier kannst du dir oft auch anhören, wie ein Wort ausgesprochen wird.
· Kläre vorher, ob du ein Online-Wörterbuch oder eine App im Unterricht verwenden darfst.

2 LISTENING
Hören

Du musst nicht jedes einzelne Wort verstehen, wenn du dir etwas auf Englisch anhörst. Die folgenden Schritte helfen dir dabei, die wichtigen Informationen aus Hörtexten herauszuhören.

1. Vor dem Hören
▸ Überlege: Worum könnte es gehen? Was weißt du schon über das Thema?
▸ Gibt es Bilder? Was ist darauf zu sehen? Vielleicht kannst du vor dem Hören schon etwas über die Situation herausfinden.
▸ Gibt es eine Höraufgabe im Buch? Dann lies sie dir genau durch. Was sollst du herausfinden?

2. Während des Hörens
▸ Höre dir den Hörtext einmal ganz an und verschaffe dir einen Überblick: Wer spricht worüber? Vielleicht kannst du auch schon etwas heraushören, das du für die Bearbeitung der Aufgabe brauchst.
▸ Achte auch auf die Stimmen der Sprechenden und auf Hintergrundgeräusche. Sie können dir helfen zu verstehen, worum es geht.
▸ Schau dir noch einmal an, was du herausfinden sollst. Dann höre wieder zu und mache dir Notizen. Notiere nur Stichwörter, keine ganzen Sätze.
▸ Wenn du die Höraufgabe noch nicht lösen kannst, höre dir den Hörtext noch einmal an.

3. Nach dem Hören
▸ Konntest du alles heraushören, was du für die Höraufgabe herausfinden solltest?
▸ Falls ja, vergleiche deine Ergebnisse mit denen eines Partners oder einer Partnerin.
▸ Gibt es Stellen, an denen du gar nicht verstehst, worum es geht? Suche dir einen Partner oder eine Partnerin. Versucht, zusammen den Text zu verstehen.

🌿 Tipp: Nutze jede Gelegenheit, um Englisch zu hören

· Mit den Hörtexten zu Notting Hill Gate kannst du auch zu Hause dein Hörverstehen trainieren. Auf www.westermann.de/128200 findest du alle Hörtexte zum Textbook und zum Workbook.
· Wenn du englische Musik hörst, achte auf den Text. Was kannst du schon verstehen? Viele Liedtexte findest du im Internet und kannst sie beim Hören mitlesen.
· Sieh dir Filme, Serien oder Berichte zu Themen, die dich interessieren auf Englisch an. Auf DVDs oder bei Streaming-Diensten kannst du fast immer den englischen Ton und englische Untertitel einschalten.

3 TALKING WITH PEOPLE
Mit anderen sprechen

Wenn du dich auf Englisch unterhältst, ist es ganz normal, dass du nicht alles verstehst und dich nicht immer perfekt ausdrücken kannst. Mit der Zeit wirst du aber immer sicherer werden. Folgende Tipps können dir helfen, dich beim Sprechen zu verbessern.

1. Versuche, so viel wie möglich auf Englisch auszudrücken

▶ Wenn du über ein bestimmtes Thema sprechen willst, überlege dir vorher einige Ausdrücke, die du im Gespräch verwenden kannst. Die *wordbanks* ab Seite 150 können dir dabei helfen.

▶ Wenn du etwas nicht verstanden hast, bitte darum, dass es wiederholt wird:
„Can you say that again, please?" oder: *„Can you repeat that, please?"*

▶ Wenn dir ein Wort nicht einfällt, kannst du es umschreiben:
„Excuse me, I need a … erm … it's a school thing. I can write with it."

2. Rollenspiele

▶ Rollenspiele sind eine gute Methode, um dein Englisch zu trainieren.

▶ In der Gruppe könnt ihr das, was ihr sagen wollt, auf einzelne Kärtchen schreiben. Nummeriert sie und legt sie in der richtigen Reihenfolge hin.

▶ Mit der Methode *read – look up – speak* kannst du deine Rolle auswendig lernen: Du liest deinen Satz still, siehst dann auf und sprichst ihn.

▶ Versetze dich in die Person hinein, die du darstellst. Überlege, in welcher Stimmung die Person ist.

▶ Denke beim Sprechen an den passenden Gesichtsausdruck (Mimik) und die passende Bewegung (Gestik).

▶ Halte beim Sprechen Augenkontakt zu deinem Gegenüber.

▶ Im Englischen drückt man sich oft sehr höflich aus. Achte daher auf eine höfliche Ausdrucksweise und verwende an passenden Stellen *thank you, please* und *excuse me*.

▶ Wechselt auch mal die Rollen und übt mit anderen Partnern. So lernt ihr, spontan zu reagieren.

3. Sprich so oft Englisch, wie du kannst

▶ Höre dir die Hörtexte aus deinem Englischbuch an und lies die Texte laut mit. Versuche, die Aussprache der Sprecherinnen und Sprecher nachzuahmen.

▶ Singe englische Lieder mit.

▶ Unterhalte dich auf Englisch mit jemandem, der ebenfalls Englisch sprechen kann.

▨ Tipp: Nimm dich auf

· Lies einen Text aus dem Buch laut vor oder sprich Englisch und nimm dich auf. Dann kannst du dich selbst anhören und überprüfen, wie dein Englisch klingt.

· Auch Dialoge und Rollenspiele könnt ihr aufnehmen und so gemeinsam überprüfen, ob es noch etwas zu verbessern gibt.

4 WRITING
Schreiben

Wenn du einen Text schreiben willst, gehst du am besten
Schritt für Schritt vor.

1. Planen

▷ Überlege: Was für einen Text möchtest du schreiben – einen Dialog, eine Postkarte, eine
Geschichte? An wen richtet sich der Text?

▷ Überlege dir eine Reihenfolge. Was schreibst du zuerst, was folgt darauf, was steht am Ende?

▷ Sammle Ideen und Wörter zum Thema deines Textes in einem *word web* oder einer Liste.
Die *wordbanks* ab Seite 150 können dir dabei helfen.

▷ Sieh dir Texte im Buch an, die sich mit dem gleichen Thema beschäftigen und die gleiche Form
haben. Sie können als Muster für deinen Text dienen, wie z.B. *A weekend poem* auf Seite 57.

2. Schreiben

▷ Schreibe erst einmal kurze, einfache Sätze auf.

▷ Dann überarbeite deine Sätze.

▷ Beginne deine Sätze nicht immer mit dem gleichen Wort, damit dein Text abwechslungsreicher
wird. Zum Beispiel:
Football is great. Football is my favourite sport.
Football is great. It is my favourite sport.

▷ Verbinde Sätze mit *and, or, but, so* oder *because*. Zum Beispiel:
My football boots are red. My shirt is blue.
My football boots are red and my shirt is blue.

▷ Überlege dir eine passende Überschrift zu deinem Text.

3. Überarbeiten

▷ Sieh dir deinen Text noch einmal genau an. Wenn du möchtest, kannst du jemanden bitten, sich
deinen Text anzuschauen und dir Feedback zu geben.

▷ Bist du bei der Grammatik unsicher? Schau im Grammatik-Teil ab Seite 166 nach.

▷ Falls nötig, schreibe eine zweite, verbesserte Version deines Textes.

▨ Tipp: Benutze Textverarbeitungsprogramme

· Wenn du deinen Text mithilfe eines Textverarbeitungsprogramms am Computer schreibst,
kannst du zunächst Ideen und nützliche Wörter in einem Dokument sammeln und speichern.
Du kannst deine Ideensammlung und deinen Text dann jederzeit bearbeiten, ändern und
ergänzen.

5 READING
Lesen

Im Englischunterricht begegnen dir viele unterschiedliche Textsorten: Dialoge, Bildergeschichten, kurze Artikel, Gedichte, ...
Hier sind einige Tipps, die dir beim Verstehen der Texte helfen.

1. Vor dem Lesen

▸ Hat der Text eine Überschrift? Welche Hinweise gibt sie dir?

▸ Gibt es Bilder zum Text? Verraten sie dir vielleicht etwas über den Text?

▸ Überlege: Worum könnte es gehen? Weißt du schon etwas über das Thema?

▸ Wie lautet die Frage, die du beantworten sollst? Lies sie dir gründlich durch.

2. Während des Lesens

▸ Konzentriere dich auf die Leseaufgabe, die du beantworten sollst.

▸ Versuche, beim ersten Lesen grob zu verstehen, worum es geht. Du musst nicht jedes einzelne Wort verstehen.

▸ Versuche, Schlüsselwörter *(keywords)* im Text zu finden und notiere sie dir. In eigenen Büchern oder auf Kopien kannst du sie auch markieren.

▸ Um zu prüfen, ob du einen Text wirklich verstanden hast, lies ihn noch einmal und beantworte die folgenden Fragen, soweit es möglich ist:

Who?	**Where?**	**When?**	**What?**
Wer ist dabei?	Wo passiert es?	Wann passiert es?	Was passiert?

Schau dir zum Beispiel *Saturday family breakfast* auf Seite 52 an:

Who?	*Ava's family*
Where?	*in the kitchen*
When?	*9 o'clock on Saturday*
What?	*have breakfast*

3. Nach dem Lesen

▸ Vergleiche deine Ergebnisse mit denen einer Partnerin oder eines Partners. Was habt ihr herausgefunden? Haben sich eure Vermutungen, worum es gehen könnte, bestätigt?

Tipp: Suche dir englische Texte zu Themen, die dich interessieren

· Du kannst im Internet und in Büchereien nach interessanten Texten auf Englisch suchen.

· Am Ende jeder Unit in diesem Buch findest du ein Kapitel der Geschichte *Blaze and the Edinburgh dragons*.

· Auf den *Practise-reading*-Seiten im Workbook kannst du hilfreiche Lesestrategien ausprobieren.

6 MEDIATION
Sprachmittlung

Manchmal gibt es Situationen, in denen du jemandem helfen musst, der deine Sprache oder eine Fremdsprache nicht so gut kann wie du.

Hier erfährst du, wie das funktioniert:

---

1. Gib den Sinn wieder

Es kommt nicht darauf an, dass du alles Wort für Wort übersetzt. Wichtiger ist es, den Sinn wiederzugeben. Es muss nur klar werden, worum es geht.

> Do you play football? I just love playing football! I'm in a football team. I can run really fast.

> Er spielt auch gerne Fußball.

2. Bilde kurze Sätze

Bilde einfache, kurze Sätze. Unwichtige Einzelheiten kannst du weglassen.

> Was steht denn da?

> **Book club**
> Do you like books?
> Come to the book club!
> Where: in the library
> When: Mondays at lunchtime
> We read one new book every month.
> This month it's *Favourite School Stories*.

> Die Buch-AG trifft sich jeden Montag in der Mittagspause. Sie lesen jeden Monat ein anderes Buch.

Tipp: Habe keine Angst vor Fehlern!

- Wenn dir ein wichtiges Wort nicht einfällt, kannst du es umschreiben. Du weißt zum Beispiel nicht, was „Geschenk" auf Englisch heißt? Dann kannst du sagen: „*You give it to a friend. It's for a birthday.*"
- Versuche, dich an Redewendungen aus dem Englischunterricht zu erinnern – zum Beispiel daran, dass du mit „*What about …?*" Vorschläge machen kannst.

7 PRESENTATIONS
Präsentationen halten

Manchmal musst du vor der Klasse etwas präsentieren.
Folgende Tipps können dir dabei helfen:

1. Bevor du etwas präsentierst

▸ Überlege: Was möchtest du zu deinem Thema sagen? Wie viel Zeit hast du für deinen Vortrag?

▸ Sammle deine Ideen und schreibe sie auf, zum Beispiel in einem *word web* oder in einer Liste.

▸ Gliedere deinen Vortrag: Überlege, in welcher Reihenfolge du deine Ideen vorstellen und wie du anfangen möchtest.

▸ Du kannst auch ein Poster mit Bildern oder Fotos anfertigen. Wenn du Bilder oder Texte aus dem Internet oder aus einem Buch kopiert hast, vermerke immer, wo du sie gefunden hast.

▸ Notiere Stichpunkte zu dem, was du sagen möchtest, auf Karteikarten.

▸ Übe deinen Vortrag vor dem Spiegel, vor Freunden oder vor deiner Familie.

2. Während du präsentierst

▸ Sprich langsam und deutlich.

▸ Sieh deine Zuhörer an, wenn du sprichst.

▸ Versuche, frei zu sprechen. Du kannst die wichtigsten Punkte von deinen Notizen oder deinem Poster ablesen.

So sieht ein gelungenes Poster aus:
· ansprechende Überschrift
· interessante Informationen, aber nicht zu viel Text
· lesbare Schrift
· passende Bilder mit Bildunterschriften

Hello everyone. Today I'd like to tell you something about …

This picture shows …

In this picture you can see …

Thank you for listening. Have you got any questions?

🌿 Tipp: Überprüfe deine Aussprache

· Du kannst deinen Vortrag zur Probe aufnehmen, zum Beispiel mit dem Handy. Prüfe dann, ob du flüssig, verständlich und langsam genug gesprochen hast.

· Wenn du dir bei der Aussprache eines Wortes nicht sicher bist, kannst du dir das Wort in einem Online-Wörterbuch anhören.

Feedback geben und bekommen

Es ist hilfreich, von anderen Feedback zu bekommen – denn auch wenn man sein Bestes gegeben hat, gibt es oft noch etwas, das verbessert werden kann. Hier sind einige Hilfen und nützliche Formulierungen:

1. Feedback geben

▶ Fange immer mit einer Sache an, die dir gut gefallen hat.

▶ Dann kannst du Vorschläge machen, wie ein Text, eine Präsentation oder ein Rollenspiel noch besser werden kann.

I think your presentation is very interesting …

… but I can't read your poster. The writing is too small.

I really like the pictures in your presentation …

… but you always use "nice". Why don't you use words like … or … to make it more interesting?

You have got a lot of great ideas, for example …

… but I can't understand you. Can you talk a bit louder?

Your presentation is easy to understand …

… but your poster is a bit boring. Maybe you can add some pictures?

Your presentation was really good! Well done!

2. Feedback bekommen

▶ Wenn du Feedback bekommst, mache dir Notizen.

▶ Sieh dir die Verbesserungsvorschläge genau an und überlege, wie du sie umsetzen kannst.

▶ Merke dir die Punkte und versuche, sie beim nächsten Mal direkt zu berücksichtigen.

Tipp: Immer höflich bleiben!

· Besonders wenn du Feedback gibst, ist es wichtig, dass du freundlich und sachlich bleibst.

· Denke daran, dass das Feedback hilfreich sein soll. Wenn du etwas kritisierst, dann versuche, auch einen Verbesserungsvorschlag zu machen.

9 SEARCHING THE INTERNET
Im Internet recherchieren

Hier erfährst du, wie du im Internet zu einem Thema recherchieren kannst.

1. Benutze eine Suchmaschine

▸ Gute Suchbegriffe erleichtern dir die Suche im Internet. Versuche, möglichst genau zu formulieren, wonach du suchst – und zwar auf Englisch.

▸ Gib die Suchbegriffe in eine Suchmaschine ein.

▸ Es kann sein, dass die Suchmaschine eine riesige Anzahl an Treffern anzeigt. Oft genügt es, sich die ersten zehn bis 20 Suchergebnisse anzuschauen.

2. Suche auf englischsprachigen Seiten

▸ Suche am besten gleich auf englischsprachigen Seiten – dann steht dir der nötige Wortschatz gleich zur Verfügung. Bei vielen Suchmaschinen kannst du Englisch als Sprache wählen.

▸ Es gibt Webseiten, auf denen du Informationen in einfacherem Englisch finden kannst. Dein Lehrer oder deine Lehrerin kann dir helfen, sie zu finden.

3. Halte nützliche Informationen fest

▸ Überfliege erst einmal die Seiten, die dir interessant erscheinen. Dafür brauchst du nicht jedes Wort zu verstehen.

▸ Wenn du interessante Webseiten gefunden hast, kannst du dir Notizen zu den Inhalten machen.

▸ Denke daran, dir auch das Datum der Recherche aufzuschreiben und die Quelle zu sichern. Die Quelle ist die URL. Das ist die Adresse der Webseite, die du einfach aus der obersten Zeile in deinem Browser kopieren und speichern kannst. So weißt du später noch, wo du die Informationen gefunden hast.

▸ Wenn du Textausschnitte für deine eigenen Texte unverändert aus dem Internet übernimmst, musst du sie als Zitate kenntlich machen und die Quelle und das Datum, an dem du sie gefunden hast, angeben.

Tipp: Sei kritisch

· Informationen, die du im Internet findest, sind nicht immer richtig.

· Sei deshalb kritisch und überprüfe die Informationen noch einmal auf anderen Seiten oder in einem Lexikon.

· Einige Webseiten sind vertrauenswürdiger als andere. Suche möglichst auf Seiten, von denen du weißt, dass du dich auf die Informationen verlassen kannst. Deine Lehrkraft kann dir sicher Tipps geben.

10 PROJECTS
Projektarbeit

In einem Projekt geht es darum, etwas zu einem Thema herauszufinden und die Ergebnisse zu präsentieren. Die folgenden Schritte sind bei der Projektarbeit wichtig:

1. Vorbereiten

Überlegt mit der ganzen Klasse, was euch an einem bestimmten Thema interessiert und welche Fragen ihr beantworten möchtet. Macht euch außerdem Gedanken darüber, wie ihr eure Ergebnisse präsentieren könnt. Kommt dann in Gruppen zusammen und klärt, welche Gruppe was bearbeitet.

2. Planen

Plant eure Projektarbeit und macht euch Notizen zu folgenden Fragen:
- **Wie** wollt ihr eure Ergebnisse präsentieren?
- **Woher** bekommt ihr eure Informationen? (Internetrecherche, Bücherei, Interview, …)
- **Was** benötigt ihr? (Material, technische Ausstattung, …)
- **Wer** macht was bis wann?

Ihr könnt euch in der Klasse gegenseitig Feedback zu euren Plänen geben.

3. Das Projekt durchführen

Führt euer Projekt durch. Versucht, möglichst viele interessante Informationen zu eurem Thema zu finden. Haltet euch dabei an eure Planung und bereitet die Informationen so auf, dass ihr sie einem Publikum präsentieren könnt.

4. Überarbeiten

Wenn ihr eure Materialien erstellt habt, solltet ihr sie noch einmal überprüfen. Achtet darauf, dass alles verständlich, gut lesbar und interessant ist und schaut, ob ihr noch Fehler findet. Ihr könnt auch eure Lehrerin oder euren Lehrer um Rückmeldung bitten.

5. Präsentieren

Schließlich präsentiert ihr eure Ergebnisse. Überlegt euch vorher, wer was vorstellt und übt die Präsentation. Ihr könnt eure Präsentation vor der Klasse halten oder auch vor einem größeren Publikum, zum Beispiel am Tag der offenen Tür in eurer Schule.

Tipp: So findet ihr weitere Informationen

- Kennt ihr einen Experten oder eine Expertin für euer Projektthema? Vielleicht könnt ihr ihn oder sie befragen und das Interview aufnehmen.
- Gibt es Filme, in denen es um euer Projektthema geht? Vielleicht könnt ihr Ausschnitte daraus in eure Präsentation einbauen.

Animals

DIGITAL+ video 20

Pets

dog

guinea pig

hamster

Looking after a pet

You clean a hamster's cage.
You feed your fish.
You play with your cat.
You have to take the dog for walks.
Cats need water and cat food.

cat

rabbit

goldfish

budgie

Wild animals

tiger

elephant

lion

monkey

parrot

bear

crocodile

snake

bat

squirrel

bird

mouse

one mouse – two mice

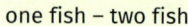
seagull

fish

one fish – two fish

Farm animals

horse

cow

pig

sheep

one sheep –
two sheep

chicken

About me

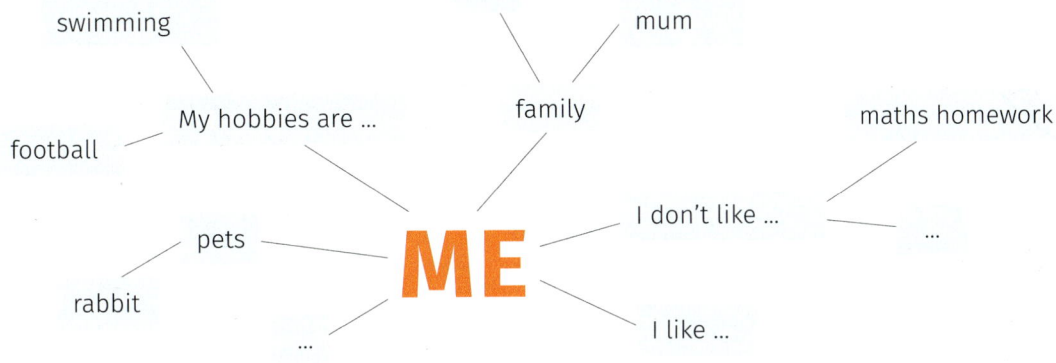

swimming

mum

...

My hobbies are ...

family

football

maths homework

pets

I don't like ...

ME

...

rabbit

...

I like ...

I don't like ...

This is me

My name is ...
I live in ... with ...
I'm from ...
I come from ...
My phone number is ...
I have got ... sisters and ... brothers.
I haven't got any brothers and sisters.
My brother is ... years old.
I haven't got a pet.
My hobby is playing computer games.
I listen to pop and rock music but I don't
like rap music.
My best friend is ...
I'm a ... fan.
I like dogs, skateboarding, ...
I love books, chocolate, ...
I hate spinach, homework, ...

In my room

I've got a lot of books in my room.
My favourite book is ...
This is my bed. It's my favourite place in
my room.
Here you can see the animal posters in my
room. My favourite animals are elephants.

Questions

What's your name?
Where are you from?
How old are you?
Are you from ..., too?
What's your favourite ...?
Can I have your phone number?
Have you got a pet?

Places

DIGITAL+ video 21

Places in my home town/area/neighbourhood

> house · garden · street ·
> underground station · school ·
> park · playground · zoo ·
> swimming pool · indoor skate park ·
> shopping centre · market · shop ·
> supermarket · flea market · sweet shop ·
> cinema · museum · restaurant · café ·
> fish and chip shop · river · lake ·
> sea · pier · beach · seaside ·
> tower · castle · mountain · farm

Places can be …

> beautiful · brilliant · cool · famous ·
> good · great · green ·
> nice · quiet · special · spooky

> big   ↔ small
> boring ↔ interesting
> new   ↔ old
> indoors ↔ outdoors

I live in a city. There are many houses and a lot of streets in my home town.

There is an underground station near my house.

On Thursdays there is a market in my neighbourhood. You can buy food from all over the world there. My favourite stall is a sweet stall.

There is a castle not far from my home town. It's a famous sight and lots of tourists go there.

I like it at the beach. It's a great place to relax and have fun.

We have got a big park. You can go skateboarding and ride your bike there. There is also a tree house where you can play.

Where …?

in

in front of

next to

behind

between

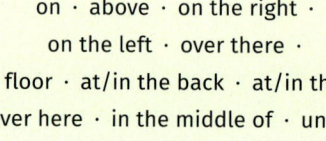

> on · above · on the right ·
> on the left · over there ·
> on the floor · at/in the back · at/in the front ·
> over here · in the middle of · under

Clothes

DIGITAL+ video 22

School uniform

tie

shirt

blazer

skirt

(a pair of) trousers

(a pair of) shoes

(a pair of) jeans

sweatshirt

T-shirt

sports clothes

cap

hat

scarf

glove(s)

jumper

jacket

shorts

socks

pyjamas

dress

costume

helmet

What colour is your …?

red · white · blue · green · purple · yellow · pink · black · orange · brown · grey

Body parts

DIGITAL+ video 23

ear   finger   eye head   hair

face

nose

mouth

tooth

cheek

shoulder

arm

back

stomach, tummy

hand

leg

knee

foot

toe

one tooth – two teeth
one foot – two feet

You can …

open your eyes · jump up high · clap your hands · stamp your feet · run · close your eyes

In the morning you …

take a shower · wash your feet · brush your teeth · clean your ears · comb your hair · style your hair

School

DIGITAL+ video 24

Let's pack your bag!

pencil sharpener

lunchbox

(a sheet of) paper

notepad

bottle

schoolbag

folder

exercise book

calculator

a pair of scissors

eraser

glue

pencil case

ruler

felt-tip

pencil

pen

coloured pencil

In the classroom

bin · board · bookshelf · chair · clock · desk · map · noticeboard · poster ·

School clubs

book club · cooking club · drama club · football team · school band · science club

Subjects on my timetable

art · English · French · geography · history · ICT (= Information and Communication Technology) · maths · music · PE (= Physical Education) · RE (= Religious Education) · science

People

classmate · form tutor · headteacher · student · teacher

School life

assembly · break · form time · homework · lesson · registration · school clubs · school uniform

Rooms and places

indoors: assembly hall · cafeteria · classroom · gym · library · music room · school kitchen · science lab
outdoors: sports ground

My favourite subjects are French and history.

I go to the book club on Mondays.

Time

What time is it?

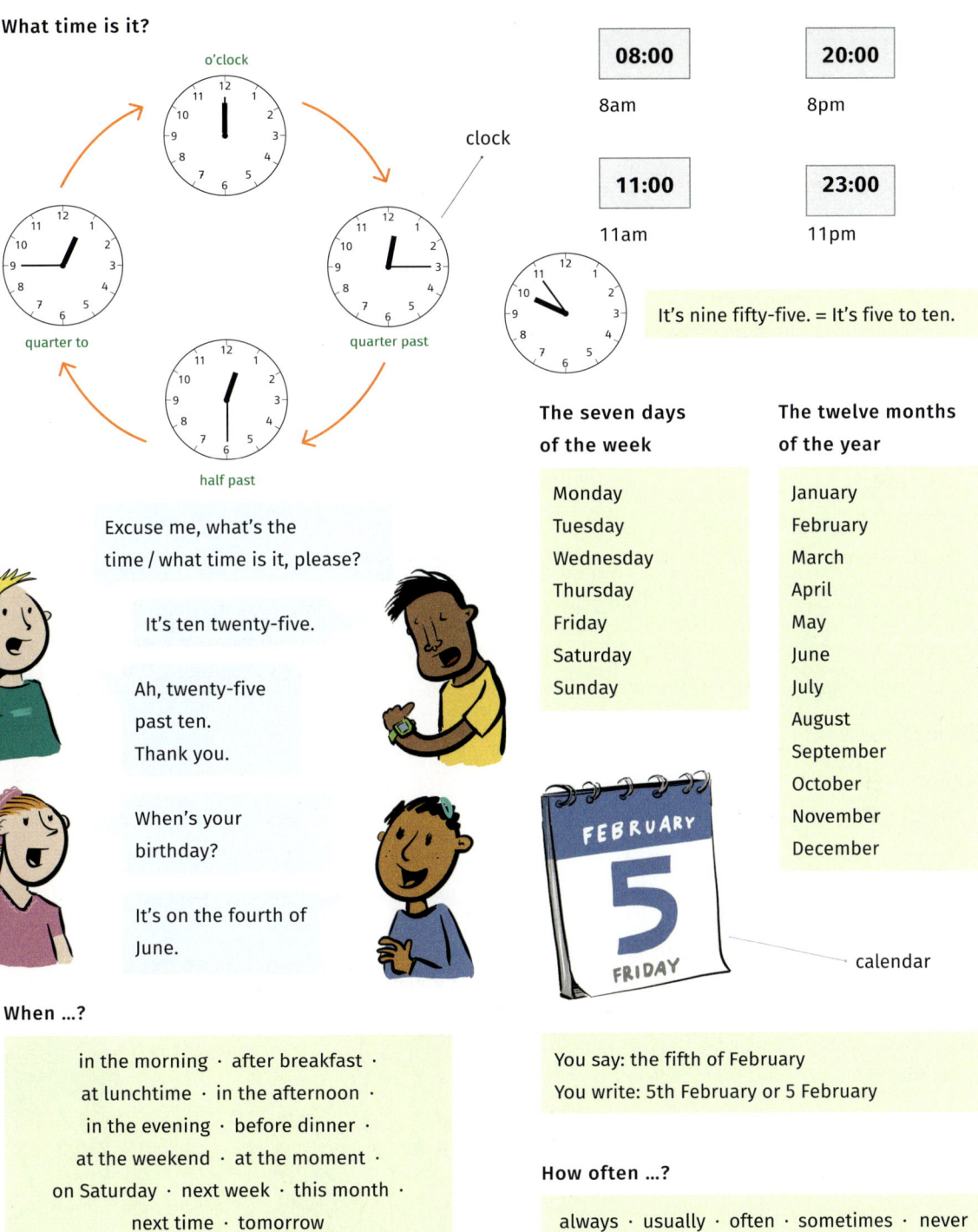

o'clock

clock

quarter past

half past

quarter to

| 08:00 | 20:00 |
| 8am | 8pm |

| 11:00 | 23:00 |
| 11am | 11pm |

It's nine fifty-five. = It's five to ten.

The seven days of the week

Monday
Tuesday
Wednesday
Thursday
Friday
Saturday
Sunday

The twelve months of the year

January
February
March
April
May
June
July
August
September
October
November
December

Excuse me, what's the time / what time is it, please?

It's ten twenty-five.

Ah, twenty-five past ten.
Thank you.

When's your birthday?

It's on the fourth of June.

FEBRUARY
5
FRIDAY

calendar

When …?

in the morning · after breakfast ·
at lunchtime · in the afternoon ·
in the evening · before dinner ·
at the weekend · at the moment ·
on Saturday · next week · this month ·
next time · tomorrow

in the mornings · in the afternoons ·
in the evenings · at the weekends · daily ·
every morning · on Saturdays · every month

You say: the fifth of February
You write: 5th February or 5 February

How often …?

always · usually · often · sometimes · never

In what order …?

first · then · in the end ·
before · after

Food

DIGITAL+ video 25

Things to eat and drink

Breakfast
cereal · muesli · porridge ·
milk · cheese · yoghurt ·
bread · rolls · toast · pancake ·
butter · chocolate spread · jam ·
eggs · bacon · ham ·
baked beans · (vegetarian) sausages

Lunch/Dinner
main courses: spaghetti · hamburger ·
pizza · fish and chips · steak ·
chilli con carne · vegetarian chilli
sides: chips · rice · salad

Dessert
vanilla ice cream · apple pie · cake

Snacks/Sweets
cheese and onion crisps ·
salt and vinegar crisps · sandwiches ·
biscuits · cupcakes · chocolate

Drinks
(orange) juice · water · lemonade ·
coffee · tea

Setting the table

sugar · pepper · salt · cup · glass · plate · teaspoon · fork · (table-) spoon · knife

You can buy …

a bag of crisps · a bottle of lemonade ·
a box of cornflakes · some water ·
a packet of biscuits

You can …

bake a cake · cook spaghetti ·
make breakfast · get a takeaway for lunch ·
have dinner with your family

Fruit

apple · banana · cherry · lemon

mango · melon · orange · strawberry

Vegetables

broccoli · carrot · cucumber ·
spinach · tomato

You can have a meal …

at the breakfast table · at a café ·
at a fish and chip shop · in the kitchen ·
in the school cafeteria · at a restaurant

My favourite food is
vegetarian chilli.
Yummy! I always have
vegetarian sausages for
breakfast on Saturdays.

I don't eat sausages.
But I like spaghetti
– and chocolate ice
cream.

I'm really hungry
now. Let's go and
get some pizza.

Free time

DIGITAL+ video 26

Weekend plans

> sleep in · have a big family breakfast ·
> stay up late · stay in bed · relax

Things to do in your free time

> play computer games (online or offline) ·
> read books · listen to music · do sports ·
> meet friends · play board games · watch TV ·
> go skateboarding · cook · do karaoke ·
> go to the cinema · be creative · do a contest ·
> play an instrument · do arts and crafts ·
> make music · do experiments ·
> watch a film · go on a treasure hunt

Sports

> swim · dance · climb · ice-skate · ski
> **play:** football · (ice) hockey · table tennis ·
> matches at the weekend
> **do:** yoga · karate · gymnastics · athletics
> **ride:** a bike · a horse

> It's a game for two or four players.
> There are 15 players in each team.
> Keep the ball inside the lines!
> Hit the ball over the net!
> Kick, throw or catch the ball!
> Try to get the ball behind the goal line!
> You score points for every goal.
> The fastest team wins.

Places

> swimming pool · racetrack · gym · ice rink ·
> tennis court · rugby field · climbing wall ·
> football ground · mini golf course

> I go swimming at the swimming pool.
> I've got dancing lessons at the gym.
> They play football on the football ground.
> The hockey team practises on the hockey field.

We can go there …

> by train · by bus · by car · by bike ·
> by boat · by underground · on foot

A day out

Let's go on a day trip to Brighton at the weekend. There's so much to do. Look at this map!

Excellent plan. I'd love to go to the beach.

Let's go to Brighton Palace Pier. It's open daily from 10am to 10pm.

What about the Upside Down House? It's only £5.00. You can even buy the tickets online and we could walk there from the pier.

Good idea. And we could have fish and chips at the seaside for lunch.

At home

DIGITAL+ video 27

My bedroom

In my room, there is:
a computer · a bed ·
a table · a picture on the wall
In my room, there are:
toys · books · clothes ·
board games · posters ·
computer games · bookshelves

This is where I do my homework.
I keep my comics on the shelf.

Rooms in a house

bathroom · bedroom · kitchen · living room

Furniture and other things

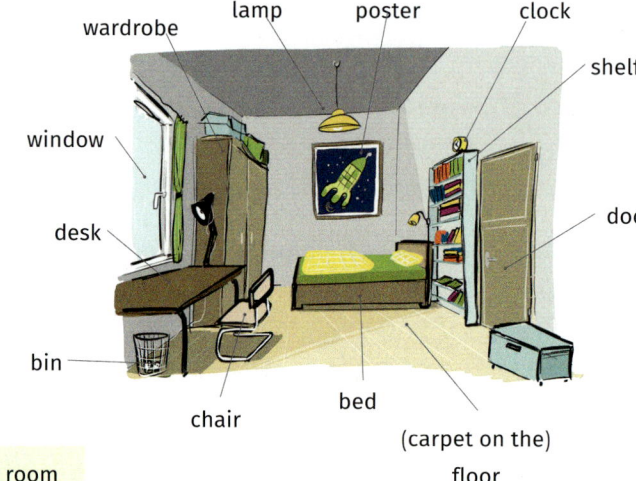

wardrobe lamp poster clock
window
shelf
desk
door
bin
chair bed
(carpet on the)
floor

My home

I live in a small house on a very big street.
The house isn't big but I like it.

There are five rooms: a kitchen, a bathroom,
a living room and two bedrooms – one for
my parents and one for me.

In the bathroom there's a shower, a toilet
and a washing machine.
In the kitchen we've got a fridge, a freezer
and a dishwasher.

We haven't got a garden but we've got a balcony
with lots of flowers. It's a good place to relax.

Chores

**There are a lot of jobs to
do around the house.
You have to …**

do the cooking ·
tidy up · clean the bathroom ·
make your bed · clean up after dinner ·
take out the rubbish · vacuum the floor ·
set the table for breakfast · do the shopping ·
load the dishwasher · empty the dishwasher ·
take the dog for a walk · tidy the living room

Our room is
a mess!

Our room is so
messy because you
never help.
I always have to do
everything on my
own.

We really have to
tidy up and vacuum
our bedroom!

Let's share the
chores! It's nice
when everything is
clean and tidy.

Shopping

DIGITAL+ video 25

Could I have a bag, please?

Excuse me. Where are the sandwiches, please?

Let's get some ice cream.

Can you get three bottles of lemonade, please?

shopkeeper

till

Let's pay then. The till is over there.

Let's buy a melon. They only cost £2.90 each.

customer

How much money have we got?

British money

£6.50 = six pounds fifty

75p = seventy-five p *or* seventy-five pence

100 pence = 1 pound (£)

You can go shopping at …

a shop · the supermarket · a corner shop ·
a shopping centre · a sweet shop ·
a market with lots of stalls · a souvenir shop ·
a second-hand clothes shop · a flea market

The shopkeeper says:

Hello.
Can I help you?
It's over there. Next to the …
What size do you need?
Here you are.
That's 6 pounds 50, please.
Here's your change.
Thank you and goodbye.
Have a nice day.

The customer says:

Excuse me, I'm looking for …
Could I have …, please?
Have you got …?
I need size M.
It fits. I'll take it.
How much is it?
I'd like this one, please.
Thank you, bye.

Family

A family tree

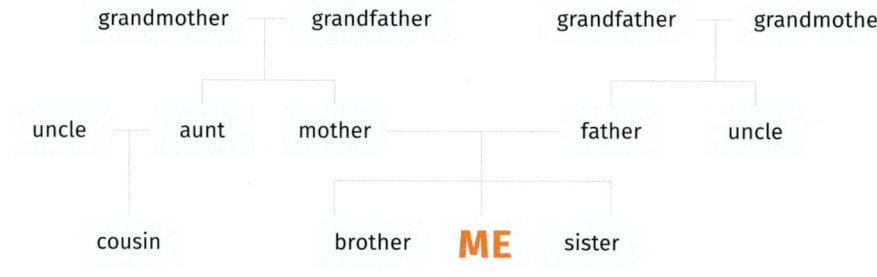

grandmother — grandfather   grandfather — grandmother

uncle — aunt   mother   father   uncle

cousin   brother   **ME**   sister

Girls and women

mother
mum
stepmother
daughter
sister
grandmother
grandma
granddaughter
aunt
cousin
wife
partner
stepsister
half sister

Boys and men

father
dad
stepfather
son
brother
grandfather
grandpa
grandson
uncle
cousin
husband
partner
stepbrother
half brother

Families can be …

 … a single mum and two children.

 … two dads, three children and a dog.

 … a mum, a dad and a child.

 …

Brothers and sisters can be …

 … two brothers, one half sister and a stepbrother.

 …

My brothers are twins.

My parents are divorced. My mum has got a new husband and my dad has got a new wife.

My little sister is six years old.

I have got two grandfathers and two grandmothers. They are my grandparents.

My uncle's wife is my aunt. They have got three children. Their children are my cousins.

I've got three cousins: Tom, Ben and Anna.

Party time

Happy birthday!

birthday cake

presents

balloons

invitation

candles

music

decorations

sing

dance

Party planning

list of ideas · to-do list · playlist ·
guest list · shopping list

Party activities

sing · play games · take funny pictures ·
open the presents · go on a treasure hunt ·
wear funny costumes · dance ·
dress up · do karaoke ·
have a barbecue · eat cake · drink lemonade

To-do list

write invitations
bake a cake
make biscuits
put up decorations
go shopping
  - buy candles and balloons
  - get food and drinks
make pizza

Dear Ava,
I would like to invite you
to my birthday party.
WHEN: 10th October 3pm
WHERE: Wonderlab, Science Museum
WHAT TO BRING: Just yourself
WHAT TO EXPECT: Exciting experiments,
a live show and a lot of fun!

Please tell me if you can come.
George

George's parties are the
best. We always have so
much fun!

Classroom phrases

Wenn man ankommt oder geht

Good morning.	Guten Morgen.
What's for homework?	Was haben wir als Hausaufgabe auf?
See you tomorrow.	Bis morgen.
Bye.	Tschüs.

Wenn es ein Problem gibt

Sorry I'm late.	Tut mir leid, dass ich zu spät bin.
Sorry, I haven't got my exercise book with me.	Tut mir leid, ich habe mein Heft nicht dabei.
Sorry, I haven't got my homework with me.	Tut mir leid, ich habe meine Hausaufgaben nicht dabei.
What's the matter?	Was ist los?
I'm fine.	Mir geht's gut.
I feel sick.	Mir ist schlecht.
I've got a headache.	Ich habe Kopfschmerzen.
Can I open the window, please?	Kann ich bitte das Fenster öffnen?
Can I go to the toilet, please?	Kann ich bitte zur Toilette gehen?

Wenn man Hilfe braucht

Can you help me, please?	Können Sie / Kannst du mir bitte helfen?
I've got a question.	Ich habe eine Frage.
I don't understand this.	Ich verstehe das hier nicht.
How do I do this exercise?	Wie mache ich diese Aufgabe?
What's … in English / German?	Was heißt … auf Englisch / Deutsch?
What does … mean?	Was bedeutet …?
Is that correct?	Ist das richtig?
Can you write that on the board, please?	Können Sie das bitte an die Tafel schreiben?
Can you spell that, please?	Können Sie das bitte buchstabieren?
Can you say that again, please?	Können Sie / Kannst du das bitte noch einmal sagen?
Can we listen to the audio track again, please?	Können wir den Audiotrack bitte noch einmal hören?
Sorry, I don't know.	Tut mir leid, das weiß ich nicht.
What page, please?	Auf welcher Seite bitte?

Wenn man zusammen arbeitet oder spielt

Whose turn is it?	Wer ist dran?
Do you want to work with me?	Möchtest du mit mir arbeiten?
Let's check …	Lass uns … überprüfen.
Let's compare …	Lass uns … vergleichen.

Wenn man mit dem Computer arbeitet

What's your email address?	Wie ist deine E-Mail-Adresse?
You can click on this link.	Du kannst auf diesen Link klicken.
Can I print that out?	Kann ich das ausdrucken?
Can I download it?	Kann ich es herunterladen?
I saved it.	Ich habe es gespeichert.

Was die Lehrerin oder der Lehrer sagt

Open your books at page …	Öffnet eure Bücher auf Seite …
Turn to page …	Blättert zu Seite …
Look at line …	Seht euch Zeile … an.
Look at the next paragraph.	Seht euch den nächsten Absatz an.
Read the text on page …	Lies / Lest den Text auf Seite …
Work in pairs / in groups of four.	Arbeitet zu zweit / zu viert.
Sit in a circle.	Bildet einen Sitzkreis.
Listen to track number …	Hör dir / Hört euch Track Nummer … an.
Write about …	Schreibe / Schreibt über …
Talk about …	Sprich / Sprecht über …
Ask questions about …	Stelle / Stellt Fragen zu …
Answer the question, please.	Beantworte / Beantwortet bitte die Frage.
Match the sentences.	Ordne / Ordnet die Sätze zu.
Who wants to read out the text?	Wer möchte den Text vorlesen?
Write down the answers.	Schreibt die Antworten auf.
Act out the dialogue.	Spiel / Spielt den Dialog vor.
Change roles.	Tauscht die Rollen.
Make your own dialogue.	Entwirf / Entwerft selbst ein Gespräch.
Take a card.	Nimm / Nehmt eine Karte.
Come to the board, please.	Komm / Kommt bitte zur Tafel.
Do this exercise at home, please.	Macht diese Aufgabe bitte zu Hause.
Be quiet, please.	Sei / Seid bitte ruhig.
Sit down, please.	Setz dich bitte. / Setzt euch bitte.
Please speak up.	Sprich / Sprecht bitte lauter.
You can do better.	Das kannst du besser.
Try again.	Versuch es noch einmal.
That's it.	Das ist es. / Richtig!
Well done.	Gut gemacht.

Deutscher Begriff	Englischer Begriff	Beispiele	Grammatik-Kapitel
Apostroph	apostrophe /əˈpɒstrəfi/	Harry's sister, Ava's dog	14
Artikel (Begleiter)	article /ˈɑːtɪkl/		6
bestimmt	definite /ˈdefnət/	the	6a
unbestimmt	indefinite /ɪnˈdefnət/	a, an	6b
Aussagesatz	statement /ˈsteɪtment/	I love spaghetti.	10
bejaht	positive /ˈpɒzətɪv/	Tarek likes hockey.	1a, 2a, 8a, 11a, 16a, 18a
verneint	negative /ˈnegətɪv/	Ava doesn't like carrots.	1b, 2b, 8b, 11b, 16b, 18b
Befehlsform (Imperativ)	imperative /ɪmˈperətɪv/	Open your books, please. Don't forget your pencil.	5
einfache Gegenwart (Präsens)	simple present /ˌsɪmpl ˈpreznt/	Harry lives in Notting Hill.	8, 9
einfache Vergangenheit (Präteritum)	simple past /ˌsɪmpl ˈpɑːst/	It was a sunny day.	18
Entscheidungsfrage (Ja/Nein-Frage)	yes/no-question /jes ˈnəʊ ˌkwestʃn/	Are you from Notting Hill?	3a, 4a, 9a, 12a, 17a
Fragewort	question word /ˈkwestʃn wɜːd/	who, what, when, where, why	3b, 4b, 9b, 12b, 13, 17b
Frage mit Fragewort	wh-question /ˌdʌbljuː ˈeɪtʃ ˌkwestʃn/	What's your name?	3b, 4b, 9b, 12b, 13, 17b
Grundform des Verbs (Infinitiv)	infinitive /ɪnˈfɪnətɪv/	be, go, like	1a, 2a, 5, 8, 11, 16
Häufigkeitsadverb	adverb of frequency /ˌædvɜːb əv ˈfriːkwənsi/	always, sometimes, never	15
Konsonant (Mitlaut)	consonant /ˈkɒnsənənt/		7a, 8a, 16a
stimmlos	voiceless /ˈvɔɪsləs/	k, p, t	7a
stimmhaft	voiced /vɔɪst/	g, b, d	7a
Kurzantwort	short answer /ˈʃɔːtˌɑːnsə/	Are you eleven? Yes, I am.	3a, 4a, 9a, 12a, 17a, 18c
Kurzform	short form /ˈʃɔːt fɔːm/	'm, 's, isn't, aren't	1, 2, 3, 4, 5, 8, 16, 17, 18
Langform	long form /ˈlɒŋ fɔːm/	am, is, is not, are not	1, 2, 8, 11, 16, 18

Deutscher Begriff	Englischer Begriff	Beispiele	Grammatik-Kapitel
Nomen (Substantiv, Hauptwort)	noun /naʊn/	school, book, dog	7, 14
Objekt (Satzergänzung)	object /ˈɒbdʒɪkt/	Harry loves <u>music.</u>	10, 13, 15
Objektpronomen	object pronoun /ˌɒbdʒɪkt ˈprəʊnaʊn/	me, you, him, her, it, us, you, them	10
Personalpronomen	personal pronoun /ˌpɜːsnl ˈprəʊnaʊn/	I, you, he, she, it, we, you, they	10
Plural (Mehrzahl) regelmäßig unregelmäßig	plural /ˈplʊərəl/ regular /ˈregjʊlə/ irregular /ɪˈregjʊlə/	schools, books children, teeth	7, 14 7a, 14a 7b, 14a
Possessivbegleiter (besitzanzeigender Begleiter)	possessive determiner /pəˌzesɪv dɪˈtɜːmɪnə/	my, your, his, her, its, our, your, their	14b
s-Form (des Verbs)	s-form /ˈes fɔːm/	likes, goes, does	8a
s-Genitiv	s-genitive /ˈes ˌdʒenətɪv/	Ava<u>'s</u> dog	14
Singular (Einzahl)	singular /ˈsɪŋgjʊlə/	one house, one apple	7, 14
Subjekt (Satzgegenstand)	subject /ˈsʌbdʒekt/	<u>Harry</u> loves music.	9b, 10, 13, 15
Verb (Tätigkeitswort)	verb /vɜːb/	play, like, be	1, 2, 3, 4, 5, 8, 9, 10, 11, 13, 15, 16, 18
Vergangenheitsform	past form /ˈpɑːst fɔːm/	was, were	18
Verlaufsform der Gegenwart	present progressive /ˌpreznt prəʊˈgresɪv/	We <u>are having</u> a party.	16, 17
Verneinung verneint, negativ	negation /nɪˈgeɪʃn/ negative /ˈnegətɪv/	I <u>don't like</u> carrots.	8b, 16b, 18b
Vokal (Selbstlaut)	vowel /ˈvaʊəl/	a, e, i , o, u	6, 7a, 16a

1 THE VERB BE: STATEMENTS
Das Verb *be*: Aussagen

> Hi, I'm Ava, I'm eleven.
> Our house is in Notting Hill.
> It isn't big but it's nice.
> Noah and Joshua are my
> brothers. They're twelve and
> six years old.

Du brauchst die Formen von *be* zum Beispiel dann, wenn du über dich selbst, über andere oder über Dinge sprechen möchtest.

a) Bejahte Aussagesätze mit *be*

Zur Grundform *be* gehören die Formen *am, are* und *is*. Diese Formen gibt es als Kurzformen *(short forms)* und Langformen *(long forms)*. Die Kurzformen verwendest du meistens beim Sprechen und in persönlichen Briefen und E-Mails, in Textnachrichten oder Chats. Die Langformen verwendet man eher beim förmlichen Schreiben.

DIGITAL+ video 28

	Langform	Kurzform		
Singular	I am	I'm		Ich bin …
	You are	You're		Du bist … / Sie sind …
	He/She/It is	He's/She's/It's		Er/Sie/Es ist …
Plural	We are	We're	eleven.	Wir sind …
	You are	You're		Ihr seid … / Sie sind …
	They are	They're		Sie sind …

b) Verneinte Aussagesätze mit *be*

Die Formen von *be* kannst du verneinen, indem du *not* einfügst.
Auch hier gibt es Kurz- und Langformen.

	Langform	Kurzform		
Singular	I am not	I'm not		Ich bin nicht …
	You are not	You aren't		Du bist nicht … / Sie sind nicht …
	He/She/It is not	He/She/It isn't		Er/Sie/Es ist nicht …
Plural	We are not	We aren't	eleven.	Wir sind nicht …
	You are not	You aren't		Ihr seid nicht … / Sie sind nicht …
	They are not	They aren't		Sie sind nicht …

2 THE VERB HAVE GOT: STATEMENTS
Das Verb *have got*: Aussagen

Hi, I'm Harry. I've got a sister, Lily. She has got a lot of things. In our room we've got two rabbits. They have got a cage. I've got a red guitar.

Have got heißt auf Deutsch „haben". Man kann damit ausdrücken, dass jemand etwas hat oder besitzt.

a) Bejahte Aussagesätze mit *have got*

Zu der Grundform von *have got* gibt es zwei Formen: *have got* und *has got*. In der Tabelle kannst du sehen, wann man welche Form benutzt. Auch hier gibt es Kurzformen *(short forms)* und Langformen *(long forms)*.

DIGITAL+ video 29

	Langform	Kurzform		
Singular	I have got	I've got		*Ich habe …*
	You have got	You've got		*Du hast … / Sie haben …*
	He/She/It has got	He's/She's/It's got		*Er/Sie/Es hat …*
Plural	We have got	We've got	a dog.	*Wir haben …*
	You have got	You've got		*Ihr habt … / Sie haben …*
	They have got	They've got		*Sie haben …*

Is und *has* haben die gleiche Kurzform:
She's my sister. = She is my sister.
She's got a lot of books. = She has got a lot of books.

b) Verneinte Aussagesätze mit *have got*

Wenn man sagen möchte, dass man etwas nicht hat, stellt man das Wort *not* zwischen *have* und *got* bzw. zwischen *has* und *got*. Meistens verwendet man die Kurzformen *haven't* und *hasn't*.

	Langform	Kurzform		
Singular	I have not got	I haven't got		*Ich habe keinen …*
	You have not got	You haven't got		*Du hast keinen … / Sie haben keinen …*
	He/She/It has not got	He/She/It hasn't got		*Er/Sie/Es hat keinen …*
Plural	We have not got	We haven't got	a dog.	*Wir haben keinen …*
	You have not got	You haven't got		*Ihr habt keinen … / Sie haben keinen …*
	They have not got	They haven't got		*Sie haben keinen …*

3 THE VERB BE: QUESTIONS
Das Verb *be*: Fragen

Entscheidungsfragen sind Fragen, die man mit „Ja" oder „Nein" beantworten kann.
Im Englischen antwortet man darauf meistens mit Kurzantworten.

a) Entscheidungsfragen und Kurzantworten mit *be*

Wenn du eine Entscheidungsfrage mit einer Form von *be* (*am, are* oder *is*) stellen möchtest, stellst du diese an den Satzanfang.
***Is** Ava from Notting Hill?*

DIGITAL+ video 28

In der Kurzantwort wird dann die passende Form von *be* verwendet.
Nur mit „*Yes.*" oder „*No.*" zu antworten, klingt etwas unhöflich.
***Is** Ava from Notting Hill? – Yes, she **is**.*

	Entscheidungsfrage	Kurzantwort	Kurzantwort
Singular	Am I in your team?	Yes, you are.	No, you aren't.
	Are you eleven?	Yes, I am.	No, I'm not.
	Is he/she/it twelve?	Yes, he/she/it is.	No, he/she/it isn't.
Plural	Are we too loud?	Yes, you are.	No, you aren't.
	Are you hungry?	Yes, we are.	No, we aren't.
	Are they from London?	Yes, they are.	No, they aren't.

b) Fragen mit Fragewort und *be*

What, where und *who* sind Fragewörter. Wenn du eine Frage mit einem Fragewort stellen willst, stellst du das Fragewort an den Satzanfang.
***What is** your name? – My name is Ava.*
***Where is** your friend from? – He is from Brighton.*
***Who is** that? – That is my little brother.*

Auch bei den Fragen gilt, dass man Kurzformen vor allem in gesprochener Sprache (oder in persönlichen Briefen, SMS, E-Mails oder Chats) verwendet.
***What's** your name?*
***Where's** your friend from?*
***Who's** that?*

4 THE VERB HAVE GOT: QUESTIONS
Das Verb *have got*: Fragen

> Have you got a pet?

> No, I haven't.

Auch bei Entscheidungsfragen mit *have got* antwortet man meistens mit Kurzantworten.

a) Entscheidungsfragen und Kurzantworten mit *have got*

Wenn du eine Entscheidungsfrage mit *have got* bzw. *has got* stellen möchtest, stellst du *have* bzw. *has* an den Satzanfang.
Has *Harry* ***got*** *a sister?*

DIGITAL+ video 29

In der Kurzantwort wird dann *have* bzw. *has* wiederholt.
Has *Harry* ***got*** *a sister? – Yes, he* ***has***.

	Entscheidungsfrage	Kurzantwort	Kurzantwort
Singular	Have I got my phone?	Yes, you have.	No, you haven't.
	Have you got a dog?	Yes, I have.	No, I haven't.
	Has he/she/it got a brother?	Yes, he/she/it has.	No, he/she/it hasn't.
Plural	Have we got homework?	Yes, you have.	No, you haven't.
	Have you got a garden?	Yes, we have.	No, we haven't.
	Have they got a big house?	Yes, they have.	No, they haven't.

b) Fragen mit Fragewort und *have got*

Wenn du eine Frage mit einem Fragewort stellen willst, stellst du das Fragewort an den Satzanfang. Danach folgt dann *have* oder *has*:
What have *you* ***got***? – *I have got a rabbit.*
What have *the children* ***got***? – *They have got skateboards.*
Who has got *a dog?* – *Ava has got a dog.*

Auch hier verwendet man Kurzformen meistens beim Sprechen, in persönlichen Briefen, SMS, E-Mails oder Chats.
Who's got *a dog?*

5 THE IMPERATIVE
Die Befehlsform

Tarek, pack your bag, please.
And don't forget your pencils …

Mit Befehlsformen kannst du jemanden um etwas bitten oder jemanden auffordern, etwas zu tun.

a) Befehlsform

Im Englischen hat die Befehlsform (Imperativ) die gleiche Form wie die Grundform des Verbs.

Look!
Pack your schoolbag, please.
Be on time, please.
Listen to the teacher, please.

Die Befehlsform hat nur eine Form. Es spielt also keine Rolle, ob du eine oder mehrere Personen ansprichst oder ob du die Person mit du oder Sie anredest.

Help me, please.   Bitte **hilf** mir. / Bitte **helft** mir. / Bitte **helfen** Sie mir.

Wenn du die Befehlsform verwendest und kein *please* hinzufügst, kann das im Englischen sehr unfreundlich klingen. Höflicher ist es, wenn du *please* verwendest.

b) Verneinte Befehlsform

Wenn du sagen willst, dass jemand etwas nicht tun soll, benutzt du die verneinte Befehlsform. Hierfür stellst du *don't* vor das Verb. *Don't* ist die Kurzform von *do not*.

Don't worry!
Don't forget your pencil, please.
Don't be nervous.
Don't play football here, please.

6 THE ARTICLE
Der Artikel

I've got a guitar. The guitar is my favourite thing.

Auch im Englischen gibt es bestimmte und unbestimmte Artikel. Du brauchst sie zum Beispiel, wenn du über Dinge sprechen möchtest.

a) Der bestimmte Artikel *the*

Anders als im Deutschen gibt es im Englischen nur eine Form des bestimmten Artikels: *the*.

the desk	*der* Schreibtisch
the school	*die* Schule
the book	*das* Buch
the chairs	*die* Stühle

Achtung bei der Aussprache von *the*: Wenn das nachfolgende Wort mit einem Vokallaut beginnt, wird *the* nicht /ðə/ ausgesprochen, sondern /ðiː/.

the /ðə/	**the** /ðiː/
the book	**the** exercise book

Hier zählt nur die Aussprache des folgenden Wortes. Das Wort *uniform* zum Beispiel wird /ˈjunifoːm/ ausgesprochen, *the* wird daher bei *the uniform* /ðə/ ausgesprochen.

b) Der unbestimmte Artikel *a / an*

„Ein" und „eine" sind die unbestimmten Artikel im Deutschen. Im Englischen heißt der unbestimmte Artikel *a* oder *an*.
Ob du *a* oder *an* verwendest, hängt von der Aussprache des folgenden Wortes ab: Beginnt dieses mit einem Vokallaut, benutzt du *an*.

a /ə/	**an** /ən/
a book	**an** exercise book

Auch hier zählt nur die Aussprache. Es heißt daher *a uniform,* da das Wort /ˈjunifoːm/ ausgesprochen wird.

7 THE PLURAL FORMS OF NOUNS
Die Pluralformen der Nomen

Have you got your folders and exercise books? And put your bottles and lunchboxes in your bags, please.

Wenn du über mehrere Dinge sprechen willst, verwendest du die Pluralformen der Nomen.

a) Regelmäßige Pluralformen

Die meisten englischen Nomen haben im Plural die Endung *-s.*
Achte auf die unterschiedliche Aussprache:

Singular	Plural
a book	two book**s** /-s/
one pen	four pen**s** /-z/

Nach stimmlosen (harten) Konsonanten klingt das *-s* wie das Zischen einer Schlange /-s/.
Nach stimmhaften (weichen) Konsonanten oder Vokalen klingt es wie das Summen einer Biene /-z/.

Nomen, die auf *-s, -ss, -sh, -ch* oder *-x* enden, erhalten im Plural ein *-es:*

Singular	Plural
a box	two box**es** /-ɪz/
one sandwich	three sandwich**es** /-ɪz/

Bei Nomen, die auf *-y* enden, gilt: Steht ein Konsonant (Mitlaut) vor dem *-y,*
so wird das *-y* im Plural zu *-ies:*

Singular	Plural
a story	two stor**ies** /-iz/
my hobby	my hobb**ies** /-iz/

Beachte auch die Schreibung und die Aussprache bei den Pluralformen der folgenden Wörter:
bookshel**f** /ˈbʊkˌʃelf/ → bookshel**ves** /ˈbʊkˌʃelvz/
li**fe** /laɪf/ → li**ves** /laɪvz/

b) Unregelmäßige Pluralformen

Manche Nomen haben unregelmäßige Pluralformen. Am besten lernst du diese immer zusammen mit der Singularform. Sie stehen in der Wortliste ab Seite 187 in Klammern hinter dem Nomen: *foot (pl feet)*

Singular	Plural
one foot	two f**ee**t
one child	lots of child**ren**

8 THE SIMPLE PRESENT: STATEMENTS
Die einfache Gegenwart: Aussagen

> I read in the library every Monday.
> I love books!

Das *simple present* verwendest du,
- wenn jemand etwas regelmäßig tut oder wenn etwas regelmäßig stattfindet,
- wenn etwas über längere Zeit oder allgemein gültig ist.

a) Bejahte Aussagesätze im *simple present*

Das *simple present* hat meistens die gleiche Form wie die Grundform des Verbs. Nur in der 3. Person Singular *(he, she, it)* hängst du ein *-s* an.

DIGITAL+ video 30

Singular	I	play		Ich spiele …
	You	play		Du spielst … / Sie spielen …
	He/She/It	play**s**	football.	Er/Sie/Es spielt …
Plural	We	play		Wir spielen …
	You	play		Ihr spielt … / Sie spielen …
	They	play		Sie spielen …

Vorsicht: Es gibt bei der s-Form in der 3. Person Singular einige Besonderheiten bei der Rechtschreibung:
– Endet das Verb mit *-ss, -sh, -ch oder -x,* hängst du in der 3. Person Singular ein *-es* an: *Lily sometimes watch**es** videos on her phone.*
– Auch bei *do* und *go* fügst du in der 3. Person Singular *-es* an. Beachte die Aussprache: *do**es*** wird /dʌz/ ausgesprochen, *go**es*** wird /gəʊz/ ausgesprochen.
– Bei Verben, die auf *y* enden (zum Beispiel *worry*), gilt Folgendes: Steht ein Konsonant vor dem *y,* so wird das *y* in der 3. Person Singular zu *ies: Tarek worr**ies** about his first day at the new school.*

b) Verneinte Aussagesätze im *simple present*

Für die Verneinung fügst du *don't (= do not)* bzw. bei der 3. Person Singular *doesn't (= does not)* ein.

	Langform	Kurzform		
Singular	I do not	I don't		Ich spiele nicht …
	You do not	You don't		Du spielst nicht … / Sie spielen nicht …
	He/She/It does not	He/She/It doesn't		Er/Sie/Es spielt nicht …
Plural	We do not	We don't	play football.	Wir spielen nicht …
	You do not	You don't		Ihr spielt nicht … / Sie spielen nicht …
	They do not	They don't		Sie spielen nicht …

9 THE SIMPLE PRESENT: QUESTIONS
Die einfache Gegenwart: Fragen

> Do you like your new school, Lily?
>
> Yes, I do. – What do you think about your new school uniform?

Auf Entscheidungsfragen antwortest du meistens mit einer Kurzantwort. Fragen mit Fragewort beginnen zum Beispiel mit *what*, *where* oder *when*.

a) Entscheidungsfragen und Kurzantworten im *simple present*

Wie man Entscheidungsfragen mit den Verben *be* und *have got* bildet, hast du schon bei Grammatik-Thema 3 (Seite 168) und 4 (Seite 169) gesehen.

DIGITAL+ video 30

Wenn du Entscheidungsfragen mit anderen Verben im *simple present* stellen möchtest, stellst du *do* oder *does* an den Satzanfang. Bei der 3. Person Singular hat das Hauptverb dann kein *-s*. Das *-s* steckt schon in *does*. In den Kurzantworten wird *do* oder *does* aufgegriffen.

	Entscheidungsfrage	Kurzantwort	Kurzantwort
Singular	Do I worry too much?	Yes, you do.	No, you don't.
	Do you live in Notting Hill?	Yes, I do.	No, I don't.
	Does he/she/it like carrots?	Yes, he/she/it does.	No, he/she/it doesn't.
Plural	Do we need our books?	Yes, you do.	No, you don't.
	Do you like dogs?	Yes, we do.	No, we don't.
	Do they go to Holland Park School?	Yes, they do.	No, they don't.

b) Fragen mit Fragewort im *simple present*

Bei Fragen mit Fragewort steht das Fragewort am Satzanfang. Es steht vor *do* oder *does*.

__What do__ you __think__ about your new school? – I like it.
__Where do__ you __play__ football? – We play on the sports ground.
__When does__ school __start__? – School starts at 9 o'clock.

Bei Fragen mit *who* braucht man kein zusätzliches *do* oder *does*, wenn *who* nach dem Subjekt fragt:

__Who__ lives in Notting Hill? – __Ava__ lives in Notting Hill.
__Who__ likes rock music? – __Harry__ likes rock music.

10 WORD ORDER IN STATEMENTS
Die Wortstellung im Aussagesatz

> I like eggs for breakfast.
> Noah eats vegetarian sausages.
> Joshua likes cereal.
> We love breakfast!

Aussagesätze werden im Englischen nach einem bestimmten Muster gebildet.

Subjekt, Verb und Objekt stehen in englischen Aussagesätzen immer in dieser Reihenfolge:

Subjekt – Verb – Objekt (S – V – O).

Im Anschluss können noch weitere Ergänzungen folgen.

Subjekt	Verb	Objekt	Ergänzung
Noah	eats	vegetarian sausages.	
Ava	likes	eggs and bacon	for breakfast.
Ava's dad	drinks	tea	in the morning.
Ava and Noah	meet	their friends	at the weekend.
Tarek	plays	hockey	on Saturdays.

Anstatt ein Nomen mehrmals zu verwenden, kannst du es durch ein Personalpronomen ersetzen, wenn klar ist, worauf es sich bezieht.
Ava *meets* ***Harry*** *at the weekend.*
She *meets* ***him*** *at the skate park.*

Die Personalpronomen *I, you, he, she, it, we* und *they* kennst du bereits, sie stehen an der Subjektposition im Satz. Man nennt sie daher auch Subjektpronomen. Wenn die Personalpronomen in der Objektposition stehen, verwendest du Objektpronomen.

Subjektpronomen	Objektpronomen
I	me
you	you
he	him
she	her
it	it
we	us
you	you
they	them

11 CAN: STATEMENTS
Can: Aussagen

I can dance, but I can't play an instrument.

Wenn du sagen möchtest, was jemand tun oder nicht tun kann, benutzt du *can* bzw. *can't*.
Mit *can* bzw. *can't* kann man auch ausdrücken, dass etwas erlaubt oder nicht erlaubt ist.

a) Bejahte Aussagesätze mit *can*

Can steht mit der Grundform des Verbs (Infinitiv) und bleibt in allen Personen gleich.

DIGITAL+ video 31

Singular	I			*Ich kann …*
	You			*Du kannst / Sie können …*
	He/She/It	can	swim.	*Er/Sie/Es kann …*
Plural	We			*Wir können …*
	You			*Ihr könnt / Sie können …*
	They			*Sie können …*

b) Verneinte Aussagesätze mit *can*

Wenn du ausdrücken willst, dass jemand etwas nicht tun kann, verwendest du *can't*.
Die Langform von *can't* lautet *cannot*. Die Langform *cannot* wird allerdings eher selten verwendet.

Singular	I			*Ich kann nicht …*
	You			*Du kannst / Sie können nicht …*
	He/She/It	can't	swim.	*Er/Sie/Es kann nicht …*
Plural	We			*Wir können nicht …*
	You			*Ihr könnt / Sie können nicht …*
	They			*Sie können nicht …*

Mit *can* bzw. *can't* kann man auch ausdrücken, dass etwas erlaubt oder nicht erlaubt ist:

*Mum says I **can** go to the park later.*
*You **can't** swim here.*

12 CAN: QUESTIONS
Can: Fragen

Wenn du fragen möchtest, was jemand tun oder nicht tun kann, benutzt du *can* bzw. *can't*.
Mit *can* bzw. *can't* kannst du auch danach fragen, was erlaubt oder nicht erlaubt ist.

Can we **go** to the park and play football, Uncle Sami?

Yes, we **can**. Let's go!

a) Entscheidungsfragen und Kurzantworten mit *can*

Auf Entscheidungsfragen antwortet man meistens nicht mit einem ganzen Satz, sondern mit einer Kurzantwort. Nur mit „*Yes.*" oder „*No.*" zu antworten ist etwas unhöflich.

DIGITAL+ video 31

	Entscheidungsfrage	Kurzantwort	Kurzantwort
Singular	Can I help you?	Yes, you can.	No, you can't.
	Can you play the piano?	Yes, I can.	No, I can't.
	Can he/she/it swim?	Yes, he/she/it can.	No, he/she/it can't.
Plural	Can we play football here?	Yes, you can.	No, you can't.
	Can you sing?	Yes, we can.	No, we can't.
	Can they speak English?	Yes, they can.	No, they can't.

b) Fragen mit Fragewort und *can*

Bei Fragen mit Fragewort stellst du das Fragewort an den Satzanfang, noch vor *can*.

*Where can you **play** basketball? – You can play basketball in a sports hall.*
*When can I **go** to the park? – You can go there in the afternoon.*

13 QUESTIONS WITH QUESTION WORDS (REVISION)
Fragen mit Fragewort *(revision)*

What, where, when und *who* sind Fragewörter. Wenn du eine Frage mit einem Fragewort stellen möchtest, stellst du das Fragewort an den Satzanfang.

What can we do?

Where can we go?

Du hast schon gelernt, wie du mit verschiedenen Verben Fragen mit Fragewort bildest. Eine Übersicht zur Wortstellung findest du hier.

a) Fragen mit *do/does*

Fragewort	do/does	Subjekt	Verb	Objekt/Ergänzung
What	do	I	need?	
What	does	Tarek	think?	
Where	do	the children	play	the game?

Bei Fragen mit *who* braucht man kein zusätzliches *do* oder *does*, wenn *who* nach dem Subjekt fragt:
Who lives *in Notting Hill?*
Ava lives *in Notting Hill.*

b) Fragen mit *can*

Fragewort	can	Subjekt	Verb	Objekt/Ergänzung
What	can	I	do?	
When	can	the children	start	the game?
Where	can	we	play?	

c) Fragen mit *have got*

Fragewort	have/has	Subjekt	got	Objekt/Ergänzung
What	have	I	got?	
What	has	Lily	got	in her schoolbag?
What	have	the children	got?	

d) Fragen mit *be*

Fragewort	Form von *be*	Subjekt	Objekt/Ergänzung
Where	am	I?	
When	is	your birthday?	
Where	are	the children	in the afternoon?

14 POSSESSIVES
Besitzverhältnisse ausdrücken

It's my turn to clean Double and Trouble's cage. Their cage is really dirty. Next week it's Lily's turn again!

Wenn du sagen möchtest, wem etwas gehört oder zu wem etwas gehört, kannst du dies mithilfe des s-Genitivs ausdrücken oder Possessivbegleiter verwenden.

a) Der s-Genitiv

Im Singular hängst du bei Nomen einen Apostroph und ein s an ('s):

Tarek's room is tidy.
The girl's room is big.
Thomas's house is small.

Bei mehreren Namen hängt man 's nur an den letzten Namen an.
This is Harry and Lily's room.

Achte auf die unterschiedliche Schreibung im Englischen und im Deutschen:
Ava's room – Avas Zimmer

Bei regelmäßigen Pluralformen fügst du nur einen Apostroph an das Plural-s an:
The girls' room is very big.

Bei unregelmäßigen Pluralformen, die nicht auf -s enden, bildest du den s-Genitiv mit 's:
The children's room is very big.

Der s-Genitiv wird meistens dann verwendet, wenn etwas (zu) einer Person oder einem Tier gehört. Wenn es um eine Sache geht, zu der etwas gehört, verwendet man meistens eine Konstruktion mit *of*:
The name of the school is Holland Park School.

b) Possessivbegleiter

Possessivbegleiter sind Wörter, die man statt eines Nomens mit s-Genitiv (zum Beispiel *Ava's*) verwenden kann, wenn klar ist, worauf sie sich beziehen:

Ava lives in a house in Notting Hill.
Her room is small.
(statt: **Ava's** room is small.)

Singular	My		Mein …
	Your		Dein/Ihr …
	His/Her/Its	house is big.	Sein/Ihr/Sein …
Plural	Our		Unser …
	Your		Euer/Ihr …
	Their		Ihr …

15
ADVERBS OF FREQUENCY
Häufigkeitsadverbien

I *usually* take Ollie for a walk.
We *often* go to the park and
play. We *sometimes* go
skateboarding together, too.
It's *never* boring with Ollie
and we *always* have lots of fun
together!

Die Wörter *always, usually, often,
sometimes* und *never* nennt man
Häufigkeitsadverbien. Mit ihnen
kannst du ausdrücken, wie häufig
etwas geschieht.

Anders als im Deutschen stehen Häufigkeitsadverbien im Englischen
fast immer <u>vor</u> dem Verb.

Subjekt	Häufigkeitsadverb	Verb	Objekt	Ergänzung
I	always	tidy	the living room	on Saturdays.
My parents	usually	do	the cooking.	
Ava	often	takes	Ollie	for a walk.
Tarek's dad	sometimes	cleans	the bathroom.	
You	never	help!		

Bei Sätzen mit *be* stehen dagegen Häufigkeitsadverbien nach *am, are* oder *is.*

Subjekt	Form von *be*	Häufigkeitsadverb	Ergänzung
I	am	always	hungry.
He	is	usually	at home on Sunday mornings.
We	are	often	in the park at the weekend.
I	am	sometimes	late.
It	is	never	boring at the swimming pool.

16 PRESENT PROGRESSIVE: STATEMENTS
Die Verlaufsform der Gegenwart: Aussagen

I'm doing my homework and Ollie is having fun in the garden.
That's not fair!

Das *present progressive* verwendest du, wenn du sagen möchtest, was jemand gerade tut oder was gerade passiert. Du benutzt es auch, wenn du beschreibst, was auf Bildern passiert.

a) Bejahte Aussagesätze im *present progressive*

So bildest du das *present progressive*:

Form von be (am, is, are) + Grundform des Verbs + **Endung -ing**.

DIGITAL+ video 32

	Langform	Kurzform		
Singular	I am	I'm		Ich esse gerade.
	You are	You're		Du isst/Sie essen gerade.
	He/She/It is	He's/She's/It's	eating.	Er/Sie/Es isst gerade.
Plural	We are	We're		Wir essen gerade.
	You are	You're		Ihr esst/Sie essen gerade.
	They are	They're		Sie essen gerade.

Endet das Verb auf ein stummes *-e*, dann fällt das *-e* in der Verlaufsform weg.

writ**e** → writ**ing**   *Lily is writ**ing** a birthday card.*
danc**e** → danc**ing**   *Harry is danc**ing**.*

Endet das Verb auf einem kurzen betonten Vokal + Konsonant, wird der Konsonant verdoppelt.

put → pu**tt**ing   *Tarek is pu**tt**ing food on the table.*
run → ru**nn**ing   *Ava is ru**nn**ing.*

b) Verneinte Aussagesätze im *present progressive*

Für die Verneinung fügst du ein *not* hinter der Form von *be* ein.
Hier wird dann oft die Kurzform verwendet:

*I **am not** making pizza.*   *I**'m not** making pizza.*
*Harry **is not** dancing.*   *Harry **isn't** dancing.*
*They **are not** watching TV.*   *They **aren't** watching TV.*

17 PRESENT PROGRESSIVE: QUESTIONS
Die Verlaufsform der Gegenwart: Fragen

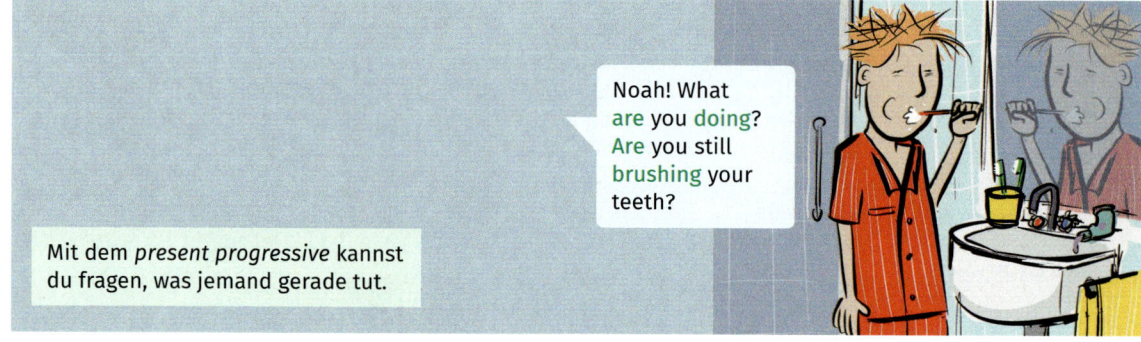

Noah! What **are** you **doing**? **Are** you still **brushing** your teeth?

Mit dem *present progressive* kannst du fragen, was jemand gerade tut.

a) Entscheidungsfragen und Kurzantworten im *present progressive*

Entscheidungsfragen im *present progressive* bildest du, indem du die Form von *be* (also *am, is* oder *are*) an den Satzanfang stellst.
In den Kurzantworten wird die Form von *be* aufgegriffen.
In verneinten Kurzantworten verwendet man meistens die Kurzformen.

DIGITAL+ video 32

	Entscheidungsfrage	Kurzantwort	Kurzantwort
Singular	Am I talking too fast?	Yes, you are.	No, you aren't.
	Are you doing your homework?	Yes, I am.	No, I'm not.
	Is he/she/it playing?	Yes, he/she/it is.	No, he/she/it isn't.
Plural	Are we talking too much?	Yes, you are.	No, you aren't.
	Are you working?	Yes, we are.	No, we aren't.
	Are they dancing?	Yes, they are.	No, they aren't.

b) Fragen mit Fragewort im *present progressive*

Bei Fragen mit Fragewort steht das Fragewort am Satzanfang:

What are *you* ***doing***? – Was machst du (gerade)?
Where are *you* ***going***? – Wohin gehst du (gerade)?

18 THE SIMPLE PAST OF BE
Die einfache Vergangenheit von *be*

We were at the beach last weekend. It was great! How was your weekend?

Das *simple* past verwendest du, wenn du über etwas sprechen willst, das in der Vergangenheit liegt und abgeschlossen ist, zum Beispiel wenn du berichtest, was du erlebt hast.

a) Bejahte Aussagesätze mit *was* und *were*

Das Verb *be* hat die zwei Vergangenheitsformen *was* und *were*:
I/he/she/it **was** – *you/we/they* **were**.

DIGITAL+ video 33

Singular	I	was		Ich war …
	You	were		Du warst … / Sie waren …
	He/She/It	was	in Brighton last year.	Er/Sie/Es war …
Plural	We	were		Wir waren …
	You	were		Ihr wart … / Sie waren …
	They	were		Sie waren …

b) Verneinte Aussagesätze mit *was* und *were*

Für die Verneinung fügst du nach *was* bzw. *were* ein *not* ein.
Auch hier gibt es Kurz- und Langformen.

	Langform	Kurzform		
Singular	I was not	I wasn't		Ich war nicht …
	You were not	You weren't		Du warst nicht … / Sie waren nicht …
	He/She/It was not	He/She/It wasn't	in Brighton last year.	Er/Sie/Es war nicht …
Plural	We were not	We weren't		Wir waren nicht …
	You were not	You weren't		Ihr wart nicht … / Sie waren nicht …
	They were not	They weren't		Sie waren nicht …

c) Fragen mit *was* und *were*

Die Fragen und Kurzantworten in der Vergangenheit werden analog zur Gegenwart gebildet:

***Was** Noah in Brighton last year? – Yes, he **was**. / No, he **wasn't**.*
***Were** the children in Brighton last year? – Yes, they **were**. / No, they **weren't**.*
***How was** the trip? – It **was** great.*
***Where were** the children? – They **were** in Brighton.*

Nach Vokabeln suchen

Alphabetische Wortliste *(Dictionary)*: Du suchst nach der Bedeutung eines einzelnen englischen Wortes, das im Textbook vorgekommen ist? Dann nutze die alphabetische Wortliste ab Seite 213. Hier findest du auch die Wörter aus der *Story*, aus den Projekten, aus den *Wordbanks* und von den *Get together-* und *Challenge*-Seiten. Einige englische Wörter, die im Englischen und im Deutschen gleich sind, findest du auf Seite 186.

Wortlisten nach Kapiteln *(Vocabulary)*: Du möchtest die Vokabeln zu einem ganzen Abschnitt im Buch lernen? Dann nutze die chronologische Wortliste ab Seite 187. Nach Kapiteln und Seitenzahlen sortiert findest du hier alle Wörter, die neu im Buch vorkommen.

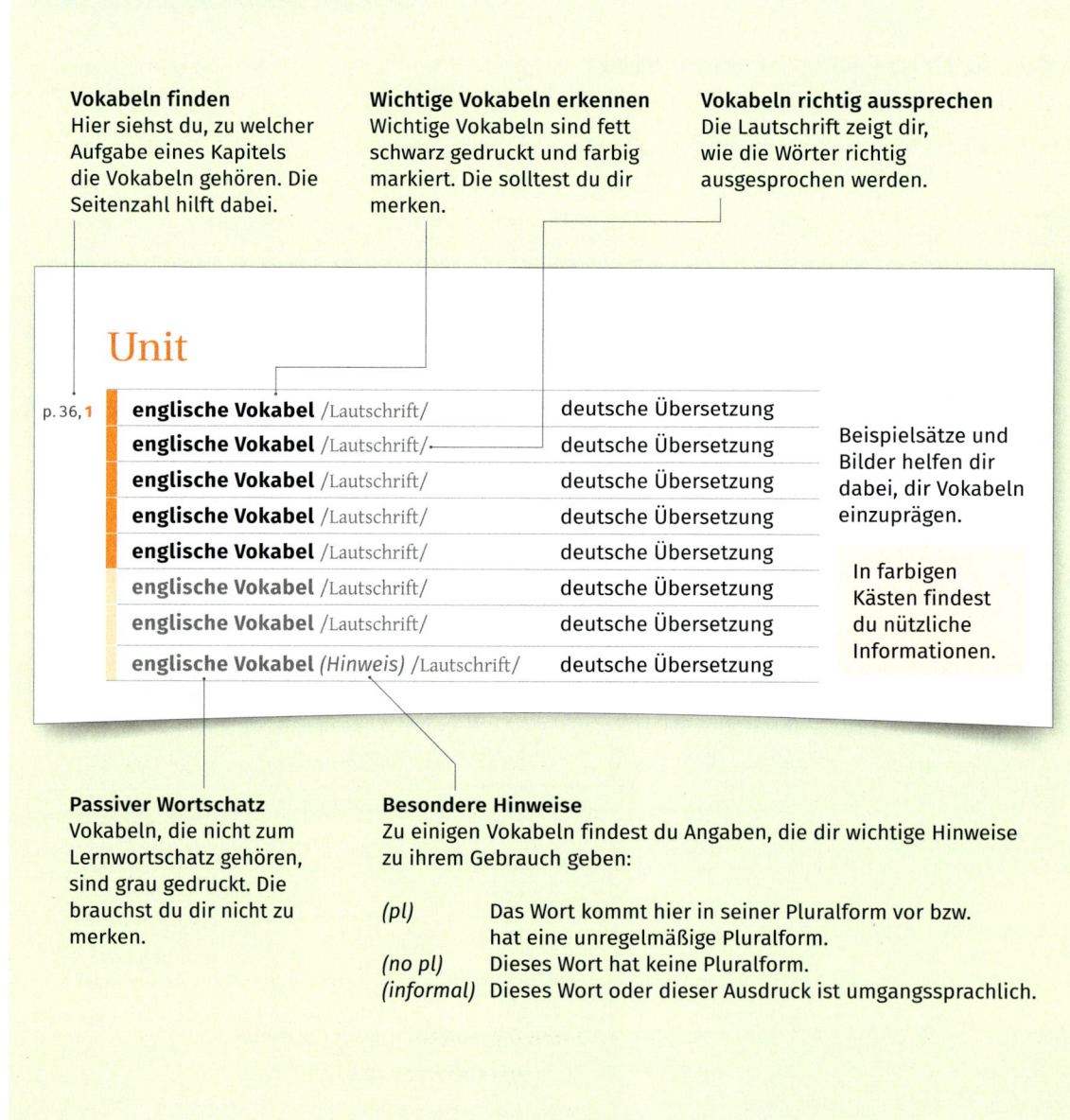

Vokabeln finden
Hier siehst du, zu welcher Aufgabe eines Kapitels die Vokabeln gehören. Die Seitenzahl hilft dabei.

Wichtige Vokabeln erkennen
Wichtige Vokabeln sind fett schwarz gedruckt und farbig markiert. Die solltest du dir merken.

Vokabeln richtig aussprechen
Die Lautschrift zeigt dir, wie die Wörter richtig ausgesprochen werden.

Unit

p. 36, **1**	**englische Vokabel** /Lautschrift/	deutsche Übersetzung
	englische Vokabel /Lautschrift/	deutsche Übersetzung
	englische Vokabel /Lautschrift/	deutsche Übersetzung
	englische Vokabel /Lautschrift/	deutsche Übersetzung
	englische Vokabel /Lautschrift/	deutsche Übersetzung
	englische Vokabel /Lautschrift/	deutsche Übersetzung
	englische Vokabel /Lautschrift/	deutsche Übersetzung
	englische Vokabel *(Hinweis)* /Lautschrift/	deutsche Übersetzung

Beispielsätze und Bilder helfen dir dabei, dir Vokabeln einzuprägen.

In farbigen Kästen findest du nützliche Informationen.

Passiver Wortschatz
Vokabeln, die nicht zum Lernwortschatz gehören, sind grau gedruckt. Die brauchst du dir nicht zu merken.

Besondere Hinweise
Zu einigen Vokabeln findest du Angaben, die dir wichtige Hinweise zu ihrem Gebrauch geben:

(pl) Das Wort kommt hier in seiner Pluralform vor bzw. hat eine unregelmäßige Pluralform.
(no pl) Dieses Wort hat keine Pluralform.
(informal) Dieses Wort oder dieser Ausdruck ist umgangssprachlich.

Die richtige Aussprache

Im Englischen spricht man Wörter oft anders aus als man sie schreibt.
Die Aussprache der Wörter wird mithilfe der Lautschrift in jedem Wörterbuch angegeben.
Man kann so auch neue Wörter richtig aussprechen, ohne sie vorher gehört zu haben.
Die Lautschrift ist eine Schrift, deren Symbole jeden Laut genau bezeichnen.
Hier ist eine Liste mit den Symbolen dieser Lautschrift zusammen mit Beispielwörtern.

The English alphabet

a	/eɪ/
b	/biː/
c	/siː/
d	/diː/
e	/iː/
f	/ef/
g	/dʒiː/
h	/eɪtʃ/
i	/aɪ/
j	/dʒeɪ/
k	/keɪ/
l	/el/
m	/em/
n	/en/
o	/əʊ/
p	/piː/
q	/kjuː/
r	/ɑː/
s	/es/
t	/tiː/
u	/juː/
v	/viː/
w	/ˈdʌbljuː/
x	/eks/
y	/waɪ/
z	/zed/

English sounds

Vokale

/ɑː/	**arm**
/ʌ/	**but**
/e/	**desk**
/ə/	**a, an**
/ɜː/	**girl, bird**
/æ/	**apple**
/ɪ/	**in, it**
/i/	**happy**
/iː/	**easy, eat**
/ɒ/	**orange, sorry**
/ɔː/	**all, call**
/ʊ/	**look**
/u/	**January**
/uː/	**boot**

Doppellaute

/aɪ/	**eye, by, buy**
/aʊ/	**our**
/eə/	**air, there**
/eɪ/	**take, they**
/ɪə/	**here**
/ɔɪ/	**boy**
/əʊ/	**go, old**
/ʊə/	**tour**

Konsonanten

/b/	**bag, club**
/d/	**duck, card**
/f/	**fish, laugh**
/g/	**get, dog**
/h/	**hot**
/j/	**you**
/k/	**can, duck**
/l/	**lot, small**
/m/	**more, mum**
/n/	**now, sun**
/ŋ/	**song, long**
/p/	**present, top**
/r/	**red, around**
/s/	**sister, class** *(stimmlos)*
/z/	**nose, dogs** *(stimmhaft)*
/t/	**time, cat**
/ʒ/	**television**
/dʒ/	**sausage**
/ʃ/	**fresh**
/tʃ/	**child, cheese**
/ð/	**these, mother** *(stimmhaft)*
/θ/	**bathroom, think** *(stimmlos)*
/v/	**very, have**
/w/	**what, word**

Betonungszeichen für die folgende Silbe

/ˈ/	**Hauptbetonung**
/ˌ/	**Nebenbetonung**

Bekannte Wörter

Viele Wörter sind im Englischen und im Deutschen so gut wie gleich. Manche unterscheiden sich nur durch die Groß- bzw. Kleinschreibung. Viele dieser Wörter, die in deinem Buch vorkommen, findest du hier. Bei denen, die anders ausgesprochen werden als im Deutschen, ist die Lautschrift farbig hervorgehoben.

ABC /ˌeɪbiːˈsiː/
alphabet /ˈælfəˌbet/
app /æp/
arm /ɑːm/
astronaut /ˈæstrəˌnɔːt/
audio /ˈɔːdiəʊ/
baby /ˈbeɪbi/
ball /bɔːl/
band /bænd/
blazer /ˈbleɪzə/
burger /ˈbɜːgə/
bus /bʌs/
butter /ˈbʌtə/
café /ˈkæfeɪ/
cafeteria /ˌkæfəˈtɪəriə/
chat /tʃæt/
clip /klɪp/
collage /ˈkɒlɑːʒ/
comic /ˈkɒmɪk/
computer /kəmˈpjuːtə/
cool /kuːl/
cornflakes /ˈkɔːnfleɪks/
crunch /krʌntʃ/
cupcake /ˈkʌpˌkeɪk/
digital /ˈdɪdʒɪtl/
domino /ˈdɒmɪnəʊ/
explosion /ɪkˈspləʊʒn/
fan /fæn/
fatbike /ˈfætbaɪk/
film /fɪlm/
finger /ˈfɪŋgə/
flyer /ˈflaɪə/
form /fɔːm/
glitter /ˈglɪtə/
gold(en) /gəʊld, ˈgəʊldn/
hamburger /ˈhæmˌbɜːgə/

hamster /ˈhæmstə/
hand /hænd/
handball /ˈhænbɔːl/
hey /heɪ/
hi /haɪ/
hip hop /ˈhɪp hɒp/
hobby /ˈhɒbi/
hockey /ˈhɒki/
hotel /həʊˈtel/
inline skater /ˌɪnlaɪn ˈskeɪtə/
instrument /ˈɪnstrʊmənt/
international /ˌɪntəˈnæʃnəl/
Internet /ˈɪntəˌnet/
jeans /dʒiːnz/
karaoke /ˌkæriˈəʊki/
karate /kəˈrɑːti/
lacrosse /ləˈkrɒs/
live /laɪv/
mango /ˈmæŋgəʊ/
material /məˈtɪəriəl/
million /ˈmɪljən/
mini /ˈmɪni/
minute /ˈmɪnɪt/
moment /ˈməʊmənt/
monster /ˈmɒnstə/
museum /mjuːˈziːəm/
name /neɪm/
national /ˈnæʃnəl/
nest /nest/
offline /ˌɒfˈlaɪn/
OK (= okay) /ˌəʊˈkeɪ/
online /ˈɒnlaɪn/
paddle boarding /ˈpædl ˌbɔːdɪŋ/
parade /pəˈreɪd/

park /pɑːk/
partner /ˈpɑːtnə/
party /ˈpɑːti/
person /ˈpɜːsn/
pier /pɪə/
pilot /ˈpaɪlət/
pink /pɪŋk/
pizza /ˈpiːtsə/
plan /plæn/
planet /ˈplænɪt/
playlist /ˈpleɪˌlɪst/
plural /ˈplʊərəl/
podcast /ˈpɒdˌkɑːst/
pool /puːl/
pop /pɒp/
popcorn /ˈpɒpkɔːn/
poster /ˈpəʊstə/
problem /ˈprɒbləm/
quiz /kwɪz/
rap /ræp/
rest /rest/
restaurant /ˈrestrɒnt/
rock /rɒk/
rugby /ˈrʌgbi/
sandwich /ˈsænwɪdʒ/
selfie /ˈselfi/
sensor /ˈsensə/
shorts /ʃɔːts/
show /ʃəʊ/
sightseeing /ˈsaɪtˌsiːɪŋ/
simulation /ˌsɪmjʊˈleɪʃn/
situation /ˌsɪtʃuˈeɪʃn/
skate park /ˈskeɪt pɑːk/
skateboard /ˈskeɪtbɔːd/
skateboarder, skater /ˈskeɪtbɔːdə, ˈskeɪtə/
slide show /ˈslaɪd ʃəʊ/

smartphone /ˈsmɑːtˌfəʊn/
smoothie /ˈsmuːði/
snack /snæk/
souvenir /ˌsuːvəˈnɪə/
spaghetti /spəˈgeti/
standard /ˈstændəd/
star /stɑː/
steak /steɪk/
sweatshirt /ˈswetˌʃɜːt/
T-shirt /ˈtiː ʃɜːt/
tablet /ˈtæblət/
talent /ˈtælənt/
team /tiːm/
teenager /ˈtiːnˌeɪdʒə/
tennis /ˈtenɪs/
test /test/
text /tekst/
ticket /ˈtɪkɪt/
tiger /ˈtaɪgə/
toast /təʊst/
tour /tʊə/
tourist /ˈtʊərɪst/
tutor /ˈtjuːtə/
uniform /ˈjuːnɪfɔːm/
verb /vɜːb/
video /ˈvɪdiəʊ/
video clip /ˈvɪdiəʊ klɪp/
video track /ˈvɪdiəʊ træk/
warm /wɔːm/
website /ˈwebˌsaɪt/
wild /waɪld/
yoga /ˈjəʊgə/
yoghurt /ˈjɒgət/
zoo /zuː/

Welcome

p. 6	**welcome (to)** /ˈwelkəm tʊ/	willkommen (in)
p. 7, **1**	**in** /ɪn/	in; auf
	the /ðə/	der/die/das
	street /striːt/	(die) Straße
	what /wɒt/	was; welche(r, s)
	can /kæn/	können
	you /juː/	du, dich, dir, man, ihr, euch, Sie, Ihnen
	(to) see /siː/	sehen
	(to) think about /ˈθɪŋk_əˌbaʊt/	denken an, nachdenken über
	colour /ˈkʌlə/	(die) Farbe
	food /fuːd/	(das) Essen
	animal /ˈænɪml/	(das) Tier
	people /ˈpiːpl/	(die) Leute, (die) Menschen
	(to) say /seɪ/	sagen
	I /aɪ/	ich
	a, an /ə/eɪ, ən/	ein(e)
	house /haʊs/	(das) Haus
p. 7, **2**	**ice cream** /ˈaɪs ˌkriːm/	(das) Eis
	(to) listen (to) /ˈlɪsn/	zuhören, anhören
	lots of /ˈlɒts_əv/	viel(e)
	but /bʌt/	aber
	which /wɪtʃ/	welche(r, s); was
	(he/she/it) is /ˌhiː/ʃiː/ɪtˈˌɪz/	(er/sie/es) ist
	the best /ðə ˈbest/	der/die/das beste
	let's (= let us) /lets, ˈlet_əs/	lass(t) uns …
	(to) let /let/	lassen
	us /ʌs/	uns
	for /fɔː/	für
	if /ɪf/	wenn; falls
	(to) like /laɪk/	mögen
	lemon /ˈlemən/	(die) Zitrone
	(to) touch /tʌtʃ/	berühren
	your /jɔː/	dein(e), euer / eure, Ihr(e)
	nose /nəʊz/	(die) Nase
	banana /bəˈnɑːnə/	(die) Banane
	toe /təʊ/	(der) Zeh
	chocolate /ˈtʃɒklət/	(die) Schokolade
	(to) close /kləʊz/	zumachen, schließen
	one /wʌn/	ein(e); eins
	eye /aɪ/	(das) Auge
	(to) jump /dʒʌmp/	springen
	up /ʌp/	nach oben, hinauf, oben

in a house
  in einem Haus
in the street
  auf der Straße

What **can you see**?
Was **kannst du /
kann man / können
Sie / könnt ihr sehen**?

I **can see you**.
Ich **kann dich /
Sie / euch sehen**.

A tiger is an **animal**.

I can see **a** skateboard.
I can see **an** animal.

Colours		Farben
green	/griːn/	grün
blue	/bluː/	blau
yellow	/ˈjeləʊ/	gelb
red	/red/	rot
orange	/ˈɒrɪndʒ/	orange
grey	/greɪ/	grau
brown	/braʊn/	braun
purple	/ˈpɜːpl/	violett, lila
black	/blæk/	schwarz
white	/waɪt/	weiß

lemon

to **touch your nose**

toes

to **close** one **eye**

	high /haɪ/	hoch
	and /ænd/	und
	sweet /swiːt/	süß
	then /ðen/	dann
	foot (*pl* **feet**) /fʊt, fiːt/	(der) Fuß
	(to) **sing** /sɪŋ/	singen
	(to) **do** /duː/	tun, machen
	move /muːv/	(die) Bewegung
	chant /tʃɑːnt/	(der) Sprechgesang
	flavour /ˈfleɪvə/	(die) Geschmacksrichtung
	(to) **get ready** /ˌget ˈredi/	sich fertig machen
	vanilla /vəˈnɪlə/	(die) Vanille
	yummy *(informal)* /ˈjʌmi/	lecker
	(to) **clap one's hands** /ˌklæp wʌnz ˈhændz/	in die Hände klatschen
	(to) **stamp one's foot** /ˌstæmp wʌnz ˈfʊt/	mit dem Fuß aufstampfen
p. 7, **3**	(to) **point (at/to)** /pɔɪnt/	deuten (auf), zeigen (auf)
	ice cream van /ˈaɪs kriːm ˌvæn/	(der) Eiswagen
p. 8, **4**	**new** /njuː/	neu
	friend /frend/	(der/die) Freund/in
	(to) **read along** /ˌriːd əˈlɒŋ/	mitlesen
	(to) **find out** /ˌfaɪnd ˈaʊt/	herausfinden
	about /əˈbaʊt/	über; an
	child (*pl* **children**) /tʃaɪld, ˈtʃɪldrən/	(das) Kind
	so /səʊ/	also
	where /weə/	wo; wohin
	(to) **go** /gəʊ/	gehen; fahren
	skateboarding /ˈskeɪtbɔːdɪŋ/	(das) Skateboardfahren
	there's (= **there is**) /ðeəz, ðeər ˈɪz/	dort ist; es gibt
	it /ɪt/	es
	really /ˈrɪəli/	wirklich
	are /ɑː/	bist, sind, seid
	from /frɒm/	von; aus
	I'm (= **I am**) /aɪm, ˈaɪ æm/	ich bin, ich heiße
	we /wiː/	wir
	(to) **live** /lɪv/	leben, wohnen
	now /naʊ/	jetzt
	my /maɪ/	mein(e)
	that /ðæt/	das; der / die / das (dort)
	little /ˈlɪtl/	klein
	brother /ˈbrʌðə/	(der) Bruder
	he /hiː/	er
	(to) **have got** /ˌhæv ˈgɒt/	haben

Numbers		Zahlen
one	/wʌn/	eins
two	/tuː/	zwei
three	/θriː/	drei
four	/fɔː/	vier
five	/faɪv/	fünf
six	/sɪks/	sechs
seven	/ˈsevn/	sieben
eight	/eɪt/	acht
nine	/naɪn/	neun
ten	/ten/	zehn
eleven	/ɪˈlevn/	elf
twelve	/twelv/	zwölf

Bei Telefonnummern sagt man für **0 oh**, sonst sagt man auch **zero**.

two **children** – one **child**

what's = what is
that's = that is
he's = he is
she's = she is
it's = it is
there's = there is

Where are you from?
Woher bist du? /
Woher seid ihr? /
Woher sind Sie?

That's my brother.
Das ist mein Bruder.

What's your name?
Wie heißt du?
Wie heißen Sie?
My name is …
Ich heiße …

	twin /twɪn/	(der) Zwilling; Zwillings-	I've got a **sister**. We're **twins**.
	sister /ˈsɪstə/	(die) Schwester	
	how /haʊ/	wie	
	old /əʊld/	alt	old ↔ new
	too /tuː/	auch	
	her /hɜː/	ihr/ihre; sie	**How old are you?** Wie alt bist du? / Wie alt seid ihr?
	she /ʃiː/	sie	
	great /greɪt/	groß; großartig	
	tomorrow /təˈmɒrəʊ/	morgen	What's your **sister's name?** Wie heißt deine Schwester?
	(to) **have** /hæv/	haben	**She** is eleven. Sie ist elf.
	phone number /ˈfəʊn ˌnʌmbə/	(die) Telefonnummer	**Her** name is Ava. Ihr Name ist Ava.
	(to) **text** /tekst/	eine Textnachricht schreiben	I can see **her**. Ich kann **sie** sehen.
	bye /baɪ/	tschüs(s)	
	indoor skate park /ˌɪndɔː ˈskeɪt pɑːk/	Hallenskatepark	
	sure (informal) /ʃɔː/	na klar, natürlich	
	see you tomorrow /ˌsiː jə təˈmɒrəʊ/	bis morgen	
p.9, **4**	**who** /huː/	wer	
	or /ɔː/	oder	
	number /ˈnʌmbə/	(die) Zahl; (die) Nummer; (die) Anzahl	
	(to) **want (to)** /wɒnt/	wollen	
	they /ðeɪ/	sie	
p.9, **5**	(to) **look (at)** /ˈlʊk‿ət/	(an)sehen, (an)schauen	
	picture /ˈpɪktʃə/	(das) Bild	
	this /ðɪs/	diese(r, s)	**This** is Tarek and that is his dad.
	Nice to meet you. /ˌnaɪs tə ˈmiːt jə/	Schön, dich / euch / Sie zu treffen.	

I	/aɪ/	ich
you	/juː/	du / Sie
he	/hiː/	er
she	/ʃiː/	sie
it	/ɪt/	es
we	/wiː/	wir
you	/juː/	ihr / Sie
they	/ðeɪ/	sie

	yes /jes/	ja	
	(to) **get together** /ˌget təˈgeðə/	zusammenkommen	
	group /gruːp/	(die) Gruppe	
	of /əv/	von; aus	
	(to) **act out** /ˌækt‿ˈaʊt/	nachspielen, vorspielen	
	scene /siːn/	(die) Szene	
	Come on! (informal) /ˌkʌm‿ˈɒn/	Komm(t) schon!	
	groups of five /ˌgruːps‿əv‿ˈfaɪv/	(die) Fünfergruppen	
p.10, **6**	(to) **talk (to)** /tɔːk/	sprechen (mit), reden (mit)	
	classmate /ˈklɑːsˌmeɪt/	(der/die) Klassenkamerad/in, (der/die) Mitschüler/in	Your **classmate** is a child in your class.
	hello /həˈləʊ/	hallo	
	(to) **ask questions** /ˌɑːsk ˈkwestʃnz/	Fragen stellen	
	(to) **ask** /ɑːsk/	fragen, bitten	to **ask** ↔ to **answer**
	(to) **answer** /ˈɑːnsə/	(be)antworten	
p.10, **7**	(to) **think** /θɪŋk/	denken, glauben	
	(to) **write** /raɪt/	schreiben	to **write**
	(to) **choose** /tʃuːz/	wählen; sich entscheiden	
	task /tɑːsk/	(die) Aufgabe	

menu /ˈmenju:/	(die) Speisekarte; (das) Menü
(to) **think of** /ˈθɪŋk_əv/	denken an, sich ausdenken
special /ˈspeʃl/	besondere(r, s); besonders
more /mɔ:/	mehr; weitere
on /ɒn/	auf, an, in
page /peɪdʒ/	(die) Seite
dialogue /ˈdaɪə.lɒg/	(das) Gespräch, (der) Dialog
verse /vɜ:s/	(die) Strophe, (der) Vers

You can see a girl **on** the phone **on** page 6. Man kann **auf** Seite 6 ein Mädchen **am** Telefon sehen.

Unit 1 | Part A   Me and my things

p. 11	**place** /pleɪs/	(der) Ort, (der) Platz
	city /ˈsɪti/	(die) Stadt, (die) Innenstadt
	station /ˈsteɪʃn/	(die) U-Bahn-Station, (der) Bahnhof
	shop /ʃɒp/	(das) Geschäft, (der) Laden
	part /pɑ:t/	(der/das) Teil
	me, to me /mi:, tə ˈmi:/	mir, mich, ich
	thing /θɪŋ/	(das) Ding, (der) Gegenstand
	neighbourhood /ˈneɪbə.hʊd/	(das) Viertel, (die) Nachbarschaft
p. 12, **1**	(to) **meet** /mi:t/	treffen; sich treffen
	(to) **collect** /kəˈlekt/	sammeln
	word /wɜ:d/	(das) Wort
	there are /ðeər_ˈɑ:/	dort sind; es gibt
	(to) **talk about** /ˈtɔ:k_ə.baʊt/	sprechen über
	here /hɪə/	hier; hierher
	room /ru:m/	(der) Platz, (der) Raum, (das) Zimmer
	with /wɪð/	mit; bei
	family /ˈfæmli/	(die) Familie
	mum /mʌm/	(die) Mama, (die) Mutti
	dad /dæd/	(der) Papa, (der) Vati
	our /aʊə/	unser(e)
	not /nɒt/	nicht
	big /bɪg/	groß
	small /smɔ:l/	klein
	garden /ˈgɑ:dn/	(der) Garten
	playing /ˈpleɪɪŋ/	(das) Spielen
	game /geɪm/	(das) Spiel
	these (*pl of* **this**) /ði:z/	diese; das
	dog /dɒg/	(der) Hund
	year /jɪə/	(das) Jahr
	a lot (of) /ə ˈlɒt/	viel(e), jede Menge
	trick /trɪk/	(der) Trick, (das) Kunststück
	even /ˈi:vn/	selbst, sogar
	favourite /ˈfeɪvrət/	(der) Liebling; Lieblings-
	toy /tɔɪ/	(das) Spielzeug

London is a **city**.

Can you text **me**? Kannst du **mir** eine SMS schreiben? Can you see **me**? Kannst du **mich** sehen? That's **me**! Das bin **ich**!

A **dialogue** is when you **talk about** something with someone.

There are **rooms** in a house.

I haven't got a **big garden** – my **garden** isn't **big**. I've got a **small garden** – my **garden** is **small**.

Ollie is a **dog**.

a lot of = **lots of**

I like spaghetti. Ava like**s** spaghetti. Ollie like**s** spaghetti, too.

	always /ˈɔːlweɪz/	immer	
	hungry /ˈhʌŋgri/	hungrig	
	carrot /ˈkærət/	(die) Möhre, (die) Karotte	A **carrot** is a vegetable.
	his /hɪz/	sein; seine(r, s)	
	(to) **love** /lʌv/	lieben, sehr mögen	
	(to) **hate** /heɪt/	hassen; nicht ausstehen können	to **hate** ↔ to **love**
p. 13, **1**	**again** /əˈgen/	wieder, noch einmal	
	true /truː/	wahr	
	false /fɔːls/	falsch	**false** ↔ **true**
	(to) **correct** /kəˈrekt/	korrigieren	Ava**'s** dog Avas Hund
	statement /ˈsteɪtmənt/	(die) Äußerung, (die) Aussage	Ava**'s** brothers / hobbies
	(to) **write down** /ˌraɪt ˈdaʊn/	aufschreiben	Avas Brüder / Hobbys
	them /ðem/	sie, ihnen	
	(to) **work** /wɜːk/	arbeiten	Can you see the people?
	(to) **check** /tʃek/	überprüfen, kontrollieren	Yes, I can see **them**.
p. 13, **2**	**level** /ˈlevl/	(die) Stufe, (das / der) Level	Kannst du die Leute sehen? Ja, ich kann **sie**
	(to) **complete** /kəmˈpliːt/	vervollständigen	sehen.
	sentence /ˈsentəns/	(der) Satz	I can talk to **them**.
	What about ...? /ˌwɒt̬ ə̯baʊt ˈ.../	Was ist mit ...? / Wie wäre es mit ...?	Ich kann mit **ihnen** sprechen.
p. 14, **Grammar**	**long** /lɒŋ/	lang	
	short /ʃɔːt/	kurz	**long** ↔ **short**
	(to) **be** /biː/	sein	Ava and Joshua **are**
	grammar /ˈgræmə/	(die) Grammatik	from London. They**'re**
	help /help/	(die) Hilfe	from Notting Hill.
p. 14, **3**	(to) **find** /faɪnd/	finden	
	matching /ˈmætʃɪŋ/	zusammenpassend	Harry**'s** room and Lily**'s** room =
p. 14, **4**	**phone** /fəʊn/	(das) Telefon	Harry and Lily**'s** room
p. 15, **6**	**rabbit** /ˈræbɪt/	(das) Kaninchen	
	bed /bed/	(das) Bett	
	book /bʊk/	(das) Buch	**book**
	funny /ˈfʌni/	lustig, komisch	
	never /ˈnevə/	nie, niemals	
	(to) **love doing something** /lʌv ˈduːɪŋ ˌsʌmθɪŋ/	etwas sehr gern tun	
	(to) **play** /pleɪ/	spielen	
	so /səʊ/	deshalb, daher	
	very /ˈveri/	sehr	
	cage /keɪdʒ/	(der) Käfig	
	football /ˈfʊtˌbɔːl/	(der) Fußball	
	also /ˈɔːlsəʊ/	auch	
	music /ˈmjuːzɪk/	(die) Musik	He **loves** mak**ing music**.
	guitar /gɪˈtɑː/	(die) Gitarre	He can **play** the **guitar**.
	every /ˈevri/	jede(r, s)	
	evening /ˈiːvnɪŋ/	(der) Abend	

	loud /laʊd/	laut
	sock /sɒk/	(die) Socke
	board game /ˈbɔːd ɡeɪm/	(das) Brettspiel
	(to) take turns /ˌteɪk ˈtɜːnz/	sich abwechseln
p. 16, **7**	**sport** /spɔːt/	(der) Sport, (die) Sportart
	some /sʌm/	einige, ein paar; etwas
	(he/she) is talking about /ˌhiː/ˌʃiː_ɪz ˈtɔːkɪŋ_əˌbaʊt/	(er/sie) spricht gerade über
p. 16, **8**	(to) **make** /meɪk/	machen
	word web /ˈwɜːd web/	(das) Wortnetz
	him /hɪm/	ihm, ihn
	class /klɑːs/	(die) Klasse, (die) Unterrichtsstunde
	pet /pet/	(das) Haustier
	list /lɪst/	(die) Liste
	to /tʊ/	(um) zu
	alphabetical /ˌælfəˈbetɪkl/	alphabetisch
p. 17, **9**	(to) **know** /nəʊ/	wissen, kennen
	(to) **use** /juːz/	benutzen
	box /bɒks/	(der) Kasten, (die) Kiste
p. 17, **10**	**poem** /ˈpəʊɪm/	(das) Gedicht
	all /ɔːl/	alle, alles
	homework /ˈhəʊmwɜːk/	(die) Hausaufgaben
	way /weɪ/	(der) Weg, (die) Art
	chocolate cake /ˈtʃɒklət keɪk/	(der) Schokoladenkuchen
	puppy /ˈpʌpi/	(der) junge Hund, (der) Welpe
	riding a bike /ˌraɪdɪŋ_ə ˈbaɪk/	(das) Fahrradfahren
	spinach /ˈspɪnɪdʒ/	(der) Spinat
	stinky /ˈstɪŋki/	stinkend
	smell /smel/	(der) Geruch
	(to) **yell** /jel/	laut schreien, brüllen
	shopping /ˈʃɒpɪŋ/	(das) Einkaufen
	ten-mile hike /ˌten maɪl ˈhaɪk/	*(die) Wanderung von zehn Meilen*
	rhyming pair /ˈraɪmɪŋ peə/	(das) Reimpaar
	(to) **read out** /ˌriːd_ˈaʊt/	(laut) vorlesen
p. 17, **11**	(to) **watch** /wɒtʃ/	beobachten, ansehen
	(to) **tell** /tel/	erzählen
	German /ˈdʒɜːmən/	Deutsch; deutsch
	That's me. /ˌðæts ˈmiː /	Das bin ich.
p. 18, **13**	**information** *(no pl)* /ˌɪnfəˈmeɪʃn/	(die) Informationen
	(to) **unscramble** /ʌnˈskræmbl/	ordnen, in die richtige Reihenfolge bringen
p. 18, **14**	**cat** /kæt/	(die) Katze
	odd one out /ˌɒd wʌn_ˈaʊt/	*(das) Wort, das nicht zu den anderen passt*
p. 19, **15**	**yourself** /jɔːˈself/	dir, dich; sich

me	/miː/	mich
you	/juː/	dich / Sie
him	/hɪm/	ihn
her	/hɜː/	sie
it	/ɪt/	es
us	/ʌs/	uns
you	/juː/	euch / Sie
them	/ðem/	sie

I give **him** a book.
Ich gebe **ihm** ein Buch.
I see **him**. Ich sehe **ihn**.

one **box**   three **boxes**

There are four **puppies** in the picture.

shopping

to **watch** = to look at

You can find lots of **information** in school books.

cat

before /bɪˈfɔː/	bevor	
(to) **start** /stɑːt/	anfangen, beginnen	to **start** ↔ to stop
step /step/	(die) Stufe, (der) Schritt	
would /wʊd/	würde(st, n, t)	
(to) **make notes** /ˌmeɪk ˈnəʊts/	sich Notizen machen	
no /nəʊ/	kein(e)	
(to) **show** /ʃəʊ/	zeigen	
something /ˈsʌmθɪŋ/	etwas	
(to) **take a picture** /ˌteɪk ə ˈpɪktʃə/	ein Foto machen	
(to) **draw** /drɔː/	zeichnen	
note /nəʊt/	(die) Nachricht, (die) Notiz	

He **is taking a picture**.

Unit 1 | Part B My neighbourhood

p. 20, **1**

photo /ˈfəʊtəʊ/	(das) Foto	
(to) **read** /riːd/	lesen	
(to) **travel** /ˈtrævl/	reisen; fahren	If you live in Germany, you have to **travel** to go to England.
to /tʊ/	in, nach, zu, an	
fast /fɑːst/	schnell	
easy /ˈiːzi/	leicht, einfach	
at /æt/	an, in, bei, um	
best /best/	beste(r, s)	
market /ˈmɑːkɪt/	(der) Markt	 **market**
many /ˈmeni/	viele	
(to) **buy** /baɪ/	kaufen	
clothes *(pl)* /kləʊðz/	(die) Kleider, (die) Kleidung	
from all over the world /frəm ˌɔːl ˌəʊvə ðə ˈwɜːld/	aus der ganzen Welt	
cinema /ˈsɪnəmə/	(das) Kino	 **cinema**
kid /kɪd/	(das) Kind	
club /klʌb/	(die) AG, (der) Klub	
creative /kriˈeɪtɪv/	kreativ	
(to) **try** /traɪ/	(aus)probieren, versuchen	
(to) **decorate** /ˈdekəreɪt/	schmücken, dekorieren	
biscuit /ˈbɪskɪt/	(der) Keks	
(to) **take** /teɪk/	nehmen, bringen	
personal /ˈpɜːsnəl/	persönlich	
home /həʊm/	nach Hause	They are going **home**.
(he/she) is looking at /ˌhiːˈʃiː ɪz ˈlʊkɪŋ ət/	(er/sie) sieht sich gerade … an	
web page /ˈweb peɪdʒ/	(die) Webseite, (die) Internetseite	
on /ɒn/	*hier:* mit	
underground /ˈʌndəˌɡraʊnd/	(die) U-Bahn	 **underground**
stall /stɔːl/	(der) Stand	
second-hand /ˌsekənd ˈhænd/	gebraucht	

	(to) **be fun** /ˌbiː ˈfʌn/	Spaß machen	
p. 21, **1**	**dancing** /ˈdɑːnsɪŋ/	(das) Tanzen	
	August /ˈɔːɡəst/	(der) August	**August** is a month.
	over /ˈəʊvə/	über, hinüber; vorbei	
	(to) **come** /kʌm/	kommen	
	maybe /ˈmeɪbi/	vielleicht	
	costume /ˈkɒstjuːm/	(das) Kostüm	
	(to) **take somebody on a tour** /ˌteɪk ˌsʌmbədi ˌɒn ə ˈtʊə/	mit jemandem einen Rundgang / eine Tour machen	
p. 21, **2**	(to) **walk** /wɔːk/	gehen	
	(to) **stop** /stɒp/	stehen bleiben, anhalten	
	shopping centre /ˈʃɒpɪŋ ˌsentə/	(das) Einkaufszentrum	
	playground /ˈpleɪˌɡraʊnd/	(der) Spielplatz	You can go shopping at a **shopping centre**.
	swimming pool /ˈswɪmɪŋ puːl/	(das) Schwimmbad	
	school /skuːl/	(die) Schule	
	good /ɡʊd/	gut	Are there good schools in your neighbourhood? Yes, there are.
	interesting /ˈɪntrəstɪŋ/	interessant	
	no /nəʊ/	nein	
p. 22, **Grammar**	**question** /ˈkwestʃn/	(die) Frage	**Short answers**
p. 22, **3**	**answer** /ˈɑːnsə/	(die) Antwort	
	(to) **match (with / to)** /mætʃ/	zuordnen	
p. 22, **5**	**correct** /kəˈrekt/	richtig, korrekt	
	famous /ˈfeɪməs/	berühmt	
p. 23, **6**	**ready** /ˈredi/	fertig, bereit	
	can't (= cannot) /kɑːnt, ˈkænɒt/	nicht können	
	(to) **wait** /weɪt/	(er)warten	
	brilliant /ˈbrɪljənt/	genial, klasse	
	over there /ˌəʊvə ˈðeə/	dort (drüben)	
	it's (= it is) /ɪts, ˈɪt ɪz/	hier: es kostet	
	only /ˈəʊnli/	nur, bloß; erst	The T-shirt is **only** five pounds. Das T-Shirt kostet **nur** fünf Pfund. Basketball is my **only** hobby. Basketball ist mein **einziges** Hobby.
	pound (= £) /paʊnd/	(das) Pfund (britische Währung)	
	(you) guys (pl, informal) /ɡaɪz/	Leute (umgangssprachl. Anrede)	
	I can't wait! /aɪ ˌkɑːnt ˈweɪt/	Ich kann es nicht erwarten!	
	fish and chip shop /ˌfɪʃ ən ˈtʃɪp ʃɒp/	(der) Fischimbiss	
	fish and chips /ˌfɪʃ ən ˈtʃɪps/	Fisch mit Pommes	
p. 23, **7**	**only** /ˈəʊnli/	einzige(r, s)	
	everyone /ˈevriwʌn/	alle; jeder	
	lesson /ˈlesn/	(die) Stunde, (der) Unterricht	
	event /ɪˈvent/	(das) Ereignis, (die) Veranstaltung	A party is an **event**.
	road /rəʊd/	(die) Straße	
	when /wen/	wann	
	open /ˈəʊpən/	offen, geöffnet	
	daily /ˈdeɪli/	täglich	**daily** = every day
	to /tʊ/	bis	

Short answers

Yes, there is.	No, there isn't.
Yes, there are.	No, there aren't.
Yes, we have.	No, we haven't.
Yes, it is.	No, it isn't.

much /mʌtʃ/	viel	
per /pɜ:/	pro	
session /ˈseʃn/	(die) Stunde, (die) Session	
skater's paradise /ˌskeɪtəz ˈpærədaɪs/	*(das) Paradies für Skater*	
paradise /ˈpærədaɪs/	(das) Paradies	
indoor /ˌɪnˈdɔ:/	Hallen-	
BMX biker /ˌbi:emˈeks ˌbaɪkə/	(der/die) BMX-Fahrer/in	
beginner /bɪˈɡɪnə/	(der/die) Anfänger/in	
professional /prəˈfeʃnəl/	(der) Profi	

p. 24, 8

there /ðeə/	dort, dahin	**there** ↔ here
nice /naɪs/	schön; nett	
quiet /ˈkwaɪət/	leise; ruhig	**quiet** ↔ loud
after /ˈɑːftə/	nach	
(to) relax /rɪˈlæks/	entspannen	
beautiful /ˈbju:təfl/	schön	
nature /ˈneɪtʃə/	(die) Natur	
walk /wɔ:k/	(der) Spaziergang	
I don't like ... /ˌaɪ ˈdəʊnt laɪk/	Ich mag ... nicht.	
bad /bæd/	schlecht; schlimm	**bad** ↔ good
boring /ˈbɔːrɪŋ/	langweilig	**boring** ↔ interesting
(to) (be) called /ˌbi: ˈkɔ:ld/	heißen, genannt werden	
o'clock /əˈklɒk/	Uhr *(bei Nennung einer Uhrzeit)*	
weather /ˈweðə/	(das) Wetter	
too /tu:/	zu	
(to) come back /ˌkʌm ˈbæk/	zurückkommen	
another /əˈnʌðə/	noch ein/e; ein anderer/ein anderes/ eine andere	
day /deɪ/	(der) Tag	
(to) get /ɡet/	bekommen, holen, kaufen	
idea /aɪˈdɪə/	(die) Idee	
Japanese /ˌdʒæpəˈni:z/	japanisch	
bat /bæt/	(die) Fledermaus	
ugh *(informal)* /ʌɡ/	i, igitt	
the Science Museum /ðə ˈsaɪəns mju:ˌzi:əm/	(das) Naturwissenschaftsmuseum	
lab (= laboratory) /læb, ləˈbɒrətri/	(das) Labor	
next time /ˈnekst ˌtaɪm/	nächstes Mal	
indoors /ˌɪnˈdɔ:z/	drinnen, im Haus	
in the end /ɪn ði ˈend/	am Ende, schließlich	

The weather is **too** warm today. Heute ist das Wetter **zu** warm.
I like chocolate and I like cake, **too**. Ich mag Schokolade und ich mag **auch** Kuchen.

bat

p. 25, 9

missing /ˈmɪsɪŋ/	fehlend	**missing** = not there
letter /ˈletə/	(der) Buchstabe	
search /sɜ:tʃ/	(die) Suche	
acrostic /əˈkrɒstɪk/	(das) Akrostichon, (der) Leistenvers	
riddle /ˈrɪdl/	(das) Rätsel	

p. 25, **10**	**different** /ˈdɪfrənt/	anders; andere(r, s); verschiedene(r, s)	
p. 26, **11**	**(to) fill in** /ˌfɪlˈˈɪn/	eintragen, ausfüllen	
	gap /gæp/	(die) Lücke	
	(to) cost /kɒst/	kosten	
p. 26, **12**	**(to) describe** /dɪˈskraɪb/	beschreiben	
p. 26, **13**	**(to) repeat** /riˈpiːt/	wiederholen	to **repeat** = to say or do again
p. 27, **14**	**area** /ˈeərɪə/	(das) Gebiet, (die) Region	
	fact file /ˈfækt faɪl/	(der) Steckbrief	There is information in a **fact file**.
	(to) add /æd/	hinzufügen	
	How much is it? /ˌhaʊ mʌtʃˈˈɪzˈɪt/	Wie viel kostet es?	
	painting /ˈpeɪntɪŋ/	(das) Bild, (das) Gemälde	
	(to) display /dɪˈspleɪ/	aushängen; zeigen	to **display** = to show
	classroom /ˈklɑːsˌruːm/	(das) Klassenzimmer	
	(to) put /pʊt/	setzen, stellen, legen	
	together /təˈgeðə/	zusammen	
	someone /ˈsʌmwʌn/	jemand, irgendwer	
	who /huː/	der/die/das	
	(to) speak /spiːk/	sprechen, reden	People in England, Scotland and Wales **speak English**.
	English /ˈɪŋglɪʃ/	(das) Englisch; englisch	
	castle /ˈkɑːsl/	(die) Burg, (das) Schloss	
	brochure /ˈbrəʊʃə/	(die) Broschüre	

Unit 2 | Part A Back to school

p. 31	**the same** /ðə ˈseɪm/	der/die/das Gleiche; derselbe/dieselbe/dasselbe	**Don't worry!** Mach dir keine Sorgen! / Macht euch keine Sorgen!
	back /bæk/	zurück	
	life (pl **lives**) /laɪf, laɪvz/	(das) Leben	**Don't forget …!** Vergiss … nicht! / Vergesst … nicht!
p. 32, **1**	**(to) worry** /ˈwʌri/	sich Sorgen machen	
	next /nekst/	nächste(r, s)	
	quarter /ˈkwɔːtə/	(das) Viertel	**quarter past** = 15 minutes **past**
	past /pɑːst/	nach	
	(to) pack /pæk/	packen	
	schoolbag /ˈskuːlˌbæg/	(die) Schultasche	
	nervous /ˈnɜːvəs/	nervös	You are often **nervous** when you do something for the **first** time.
	first /fɜːst/	erste(r, s)	
	well /wel/	nun	
	a bit /ə ˈbɪt/	ein bisschen	**a bit** ↔ a lot
	pm (= post meridiem) /ˌpiːˈem, ˌpəʊst məˈrɪdiəm/	nachmittags, abends *(nur hinter Uhrzeit zwischen 12 Uhr mittags und Mitternacht)*	
	folder /ˈfəʊldə/	(die) Mappe, (der) Ordner	
	exercise book /ˈeksəsaɪz ˌbʊk/	(das) Heft	
	pencil case /ˈpensl ˌkeɪs/	(das) Federmäppchen	**pencil case**
	pen /pen/	(der) Stift	
	pencil /ˈpensl/	(der) Bleistift	

	eraser /ɪˈreɪzə/	(der) Radiergummi	eraser	
	(to) forget /fəˈget/	vergessen		
	ruler /ˈruːlə/	(das) Lineal	ruler	
	calculator /ˈkælkjʊˌleɪtə/	(der) Taschenrechner		
	please /pliːz/	bitte		
	glue /gluː/	(der) Klebstoff		
	(a pair of) scissors /ˈsɪzəz/	(die) Schere	(a pair of) scissors	
	notepad /ˈnəʊtˌpæd/	(der) Notizblock		
	pencil sharpener /ˈpensl ˌʃɑːpnə/	(der) Bleistiftspitzer		
	felt-tip /ˈfeltˌtɪp/	(der) Filzstift		
	thanks /θæŋks/	danke	for help als Hilfe, zur Hilfe	
	help /help/	(die) Hilfe		
	time /taɪm/	(die) Zeit		
	checklist /ˈtʃeklɪst/	(die) Checkliste		
p. 33, 2	dream /driːm/	(der) Traum		
	(to) be about /ˌbiː‿əˈbaʊt/	gehen um, handeln von		
p. 33, 3	assembly /əˈsembli/	(die) (Schüler)versammlung		
	Good morning! /ˌgʊd ˈmɔːnɪŋ/	Guten Morgen!		
	boy /bɔɪ/	(der) Junge		
	girl /gɜːl/	(das) Mädchen	He's a boy. She's a girl.	
	Mr /ˈmɪstə/	Herr (Anrede)		
	today /təˈdeɪ/	heute		
	exciting /ɪkˈsaɪtɪŋ/	aufregend	exciting ↔ boring	
	morning /ˈmɔːnɪŋ/	(der) Morgen		
	important /ɪmˈpɔːtnt/	wichtig	If you are never late, you are always on time.	
	on time /ˌɒn ˈtaɪm/	pünktlich		
	registration /ˌredʒɪˈstreɪʃn/	(die) Überprüfung der Anwesenheit		
	lunch /lʌntʃ/	(das) Mittagessen		
	half /hɑːf/	halb		
	activity /ækˈtɪvəti/	(die) Aktivität		
	afternoon /ˌɑːftəˈnuːn/	(der) Nachmittag		
	noticeboard /ˈnəʊtɪsˌbɔːd/	(das) Schwarze Brett	You can find information on a noticeboard.	
	(to) hope /həʊp/	hoffen	in the morning /ˌɪn ðə ˈmɔːnɪŋ/ am Morgen	
	any /ˈeni/	(irgend)ein(e)		
	office /ˈɒfɪs/	(das) Büro		
	headteacher /ˌhedˈtiːtʃə/	(der/die) Schulleiter/in, (der/die) Rektor/in	in the afternoon /ˌɪn ðiˌɑːftəˈnuːn/ am Nachmittag	
	to /tʊ/	hier: vor	in the evening /ˌɪn ðiˌˈiːvnɪŋ/ am Abend	
p. 33, 4	wordbank /ˈwɜːdbæŋk/	(die) Wortsammlung		
	own /əʊn/	eigene(r, s)		
	teacher /ˈtiːtʃə/	(der/die) Lehrer/in		
p. 34, 5	(to) open /ˈəʊpən/	öffnen, aufmachen	to open ↔ to close	
p. 34, 6	command /kəˈmɑːnd/	(der) Befehl		
	action /ˈækʃn/	(die) Handlung		

	(to) **mime** /maɪm/	mimen, pantomimisch darstellen
p. 34, **7**	**clock** /klɒk/	(die) Uhr
	to /tʊ/	*hier:* vor
p. 35, **8**	(to) **happen** /ˈhæpən/	geschehen, passieren
p. 35, **9**	**timetable** /ˈtaɪmteɪbl/	(der) Stundenplan
	subject /ˈsʌbdʒɪkt/	(das) Schulfach
	(to) **name** /neɪm/	(be)nennen
	am (= ante meridiem) /ˌeɪˈem, ˌænti məˈrɪdiəm/	morgens, vormittags *(nur hinter Uhrzeit zwischen Mitternacht und 12 Uhr mittags)*
	form /fɔːm/	(die) Klasse
	maths *(informal)* /mæθ/	Mathe *(Schulfach)*
	French /frentʃ/	(das) Französisch
	ICT (= Information and Communication Technology) /ˌaɪˌsiːˈtiː, ɪnfəˈmeɪʃn̩ ən kəˌmjuːnɪˈkeɪʃn̩ tekˌnɒlədʒi/	Informatik *(Schulfach)*
	break /breɪk/	(die) Pause
	science /ˈsaɪəns/	(die) Naturwissenschaft
	art /ɑːt/	(die) Kunst
	geography /dʒiˈɒɡrəfi/	(die) Erdkunde
	history /ˈhɪstri/	(die) Geschichte
	PE (= Physical Education) /ˌpiːˈiː, ˌfɪzɪkl̩ edjʊˈkeɪʃn̩/	Sport *(Schulfach)*
	RE (= Religious Education) /ˌɑːrˈiː, reˌlɪdʒəs edjʊˈkeɪʃn̩/	Religion *(Schulfach)*
	form time /ˈfɔːm taɪm/	*(die) Klassenlehrerstunde*
	school day /ˈskuːl ˌdeɪ/	(der) Schultag
p. 36, **10**	**bottle** /ˈbɒtl/	(die) Flasche
	sorry /ˈsɒri/	es tut mir leid, Entschuldigung
	late /leɪt/	(zu) spät
	(to) **sit down** /ˌsɪtˈdaʊn/	sich hinsetzen
	cold /kəʊld/	kalt
	Excuse me! /ɪkˈskjuːz ˌmi/	Entschuldigung!
	toilet /ˈtɔɪlət/	(die) Toilette
	window /ˈwɪndəʊ/	(das) Fenster
	double /ˈdʌbl/	doppelt, Doppel-
	(to) **borrow** /ˈbɒrəʊ/	(aus)leihen
	Here you are! /ˌhɪə juˈɑː/	Hier, bitte!
	(to) **spell** /spel/	buchstabieren
	board /bɔːtl/	(die) Tafel, (das) Brett
	chair /tʃeə/	(der) Stuhl
	desk /desk/	(der) Schreibtisch
	bin /bɪn/	(der) Abfalleimer
	map /mæp/	(die) Karte
	bookshelf (*pl* **bookshelves**) /ˈbʊkʃelf, ˈbʊkʃelvz/	(das) Bücherregal

What's the time, please?
Wie spät ist es, bitte?
What time is it?
Wie spät ist es?

Monday /ˈmʌndeɪ/
(der) Montag
Tuesday /ˈtjuːzdeɪ/
(der) Dienstag
Wednesday /ˈwenzdeɪ/
(der) Mittwoch
Thursday /ˈθɜːzdeɪ/
(der) Donnerstag
Friday /ˈfraɪdeɪ/
(der) Freitag
Saturday /ˈsætədeɪ/
(der) Samstag
Sunday /ˈsʌndeɪ/
(der) Sonntag

Science and **art** are school **subjects**.

Man sagt **Excuse me!**, wenn man jemanden anspricht, um ihn oder sie nach dem Weg zu fragen oder wenn man an jemandem vorbei möchte.
Sorry! sagt man, wenn man sich für etwas entschuldigen möchte, z. B., wenn man zu spät kommt.

When you **spell** "spell", you say "s-p-e-**double** l".

bin

	lunchbox /ˈlʌntʃbɒks/	(die) Frühstücksdose	
p. 37, **11**	(to) **label** /ˈleɪbl/	beschriften	
p. 37, **12**	(to) **record** /riˈkɔːd/	aufnehmen	
	game of dominoes /ˌɡeɪm‿əv ˈdɒmɪnəʊz/	(das) Dominospiel	
p. 37, **13**	**song** /sɒŋ/	(das) Lied	They are singing a **song**.
	(to) **sing along** /ˌsɪŋ‿əˈlɒŋ/	mitsingen	**everybody** = all the
	everybody /ˈevriˌbɒdi/	alle; jeder	people
	as /əz/	als; wie; während	
	before /bɪˈfɔː/	zuvor, vorher	
	(to) **sing out** /ˌsɪŋ‿ˈaʊt/	laut singen	
	chorus /ˈkɔːrəs/	(der) Refrain	
	so far /ˈsəʊ fɑː/	bisher	
	once more /ˌwʌns ˈmɔː/	noch einmal	
	we've done /ˌwiːv ˈdʌn/	wir haben getan	
p. 38, **14**	**noun** /naʊn/	(das) Hauptwort, (das) Substantiv, (das) Nomen	"Song" is a **noun**, "to sing" is a verb.
	article /ˈɑːtɪkl/	(der) Artikel	
	apple /ˈæpl/	(der) Apfel	
	orange /ˈɒrɪndʒ/	(die) Orange, (die) Apfelsine	**orange**
p. 38, **15**	**phrase** /freɪz/	(der) Satz, (der) Ausdruck	
p. 38, **16**	**spelling** /ˈspelɪŋ/	(das) Buchstabieren, (die) Rechtschreibung	
p. 39, **17**	**challenge** /ˈtʃæləndʒ/	(die) Herausforderung	
	card /kɑːd/	(die) Karte	
	player /ˈpleɪə/	(der/die) Spieler/in	
	(to) **place** /pleɪs/	platzieren, stellen	

Unit 2 | Part B   School life

p. 40, **1**	**library** /ˈlaɪbrəri/	(die) Bücherei	**(on) Mondays** /ˈmʌndeɪz/ montags
	month /mʌnθ/	(der) Monat	**(on) Tuesdays** /ˈtjuːzdeɪz/ dienstags
	story /ˈstɔːri/	(die) Geschichte, (die) Erzählung	**(on) Wednesdays** /ˈwenzdeɪz/ mittwochs
	Mrs /ˈmɪsɪz/	Frau *(Anrede)*	**(on) Thursdays** /ˈθɜːzdeɪz/ donnerstags
	cooking /ˈkʊkɪŋ/	(das) Kochen; Koch-	**(on) Fridays** /ˈfraɪdeɪz/ freitags
	(to) **join** /dʒɔɪn/	mitmachen (bei)	**(on) Saturdays** /ˈsætədeɪz/ samstags
	student /ˈstjuːdnt/	(der/die) Schüler/in	**(on) Sundays** /ˈsʌndeɪz/ sonntags
	kitchen /ˈkɪtʃən/	(die) Küche	
	(to) **need** /niːd/	brauchen	
	(to) **practise** /ˈpræktɪs/	üben; trainieren	If you want to be good at something, you have to **practise** a lot.
	gym (= gymnasium) /dʒɪm, dʒɪmˈneɪziəm/	(die) Turnhalle	
	match /mætʃ/	(das) Spiel	You can do **experiments** at the science club.
	experiment /ɪkˈsperɪmənt/	(das) Experiment, (der) Versuch	
	(to) **bring** /brɪŋ/	mitbringen	
	chips *(pl)* /tʃɪps/	(die) Pommes frites	

	rice /raɪs/	(der) Reis
	What's on? *(informal)* /ˌwɒts‿'ɒn/	Was ist los?
	lunchtime /'lʌntʃtaɪm/	(die) Mittagszeit, (die) Mittagspause
	drama /'drɑːmə/	Theater-, Schauspiel-
	assembly hall /ə'sembli ˌhɔːl/	(die) Aula
	main (course) /'meɪn kɔːs/	(das) Hauptgericht
	chilli con carne /ˌtʃɪli kɒn 'kɑːni/	*Chili con Carne*
	vegetarian chilli /ˌvedʒə'teəriən ˌtʃɪli/	*vegetarisches Chili*
	side (dish) /'saɪd‿dɪʃ/	(die) Beilage
	dessert /dɪ'zɜːt/	(der) Nachtisch
	apple pie /'æpl ˌpaɪ/	(der) gedeckte Apfelkuchen
p. 41, **1**	**week** /wiːk/	(die) Woche
p. 41, **2**	**I don't know.** /ˌaɪ ˌdəʊnt 'nəʊ/	Ich weiß es nicht.
	(to) sound /saʊnd/	klingen, sich anhören
	sometimes /'sʌmtaɪmz/	manchmal
	enough /ɪ'nʌf/	genug
	before /bɪ'fɔː/	vor
	first /fɜːst/	zuerst
p. 41, **3**	**top** /tɒp/	beste(r, s)
p. 43, **7**	**uncle** /'ʌŋkl/	(der) Onkel
	(to) like best /ˌlaɪk 'best/	am liebsten mögen
	else /els/	anders, sonst
	useful /'juːsfl/	nützlich
	(to) cook /kʊk/	kochen
	(to) teach /tiːtʃ/	unterrichten
	term /tɜːm/	(das) Trimester
	when /wen/	wenn; als
	(to) rain /reɪn/	regnen
	sports ground /'spɔːts graʊnd/	(der) Sportplatz
	right now /ˌraɪt 'naʊ/	jetzt, sofort, gleich
p. 44, **8**	**How are you?** /ˌhaʊ‿'ɑː jʊ/	Wie geht es dir / euch / Ihnen?
	I'm good, thanks. /aɪm 'gʊd ˌθæŋks/	Es geht mir gut, danke.
	a lot /ə 'lɒt/	viel, sehr; oft
	(to) miss /mɪs/	vermissen, verpassen
	without /wɪð'aʊt/	ohne
	still /stɪl/	(immer) noch
	(to) look /lʊk/	aussehen
	(to) wear /weə/	tragen *(Kleidung)*
	skirt /skɜːt/	(der) Rock
	(a pair of) trousers /ə ˌpeər‿əv 'traʊzəz/	(die) Hosen
	shirt /ʃɜːt/	(das) Hemd
	tie /taɪ/	(die) Krawatte
	their /ðeə/	ihr(e)

to **play the guitar**	Gitarre spielen
to **play the piano**	Klavier spielen
to **play football**	Fußball spielen
to **play hockey**	Hockey spielen

There are seven days in a **week**.

before ↔ after

Your **uncle** is your mum or dad's brother.

How are you? **I'm good, thanks.**

Short answers

Yes, I do.	No, I don't.
Yes, he / she does.	No, he / she doesn't.
Yes, they do.	No, they don't.

They are wearing **ties**.

	(to) **say hello to somebody** /ˌseɪ həˈləʊ tə ˌsʌmbədi/	jemanden (be)grüßen	
p. 45, **10**	(to) **design** /dɪˈzaɪn/	entwerfen	
	(to) **create** /kriˈeɪt/	erschaffen, erzeugen	
p. 45, **11**	(to) **understand** /ˌʌndəˈstænd/	verstehen	**everything** = all the things
	everything /ˈevriθɪŋ/	alles	
	exchange student /ɪksˈtʃeɪndʒ ˌstjuːdnt/	(der/die) Austauschschüler/in	
p. 46, **13**	(to) **copy** /ˈkɒpi/	abschreiben	
	into /ˈɪntuː/	in	
	(to) **eat** /iːt/	essen	to **eat**
p. 46, **14**	(to) **present (to)** /priˈzent/	präsentieren, vorstellen	
	outside /ˌaʊtˈsaɪd/	außen; (nach) draußen	
	start /stɑːt/	(der) Anfang, (der) Beginn	
	each /iːtʃ/	jede(r, s)	
	sports hall /ˈspɔːts hɔːl/	(die) Sporthalle	
p. 47, **15**	(to) **prepare** /priˈpeə/	vorbereiten	**What can you see?** Was kannst du sehen?
	presentation /ˌpreznˈteɪʃn/	(die) Präsentation, (der) Vortrag	**What do you like?** Was magst du?
	for example /fərˌɪgˈzɑːmpl/	zum Beispiel	**What don't you like?** Was magst du nicht?
	(to) **decide** /dɪˈsaɪd/	entscheiden; sich entscheiden	
	could /kʊd/	könnte(st, n, t)	
	topic /ˈtɒpɪk/	(das) Thema	
	(to) **interview** /ˈɪntəˌvjuː/	interviewen, befragen	
	work /wɜːk/	(die) Arbeit, (das) Werk	
	outdoors /ˌaʊtˈdɔːz/	draußen, im Freien	

Unit 3 | Part A At the weekend

			at the weekend **am** Wochenende **on** Monday, Tuesday, … **am** Montag, Dienstag, …
p. 51	**free time** /friːˈtaɪm/	(die) Freizeit	
	weekend /ˌwiːkˈend/	(das) Wochenende	
p. 52, **1**	**breakfast** /ˈbrekfəst/	(das) Frühstück	
	egg /eg/	(das) Ei	**for breakfast** zum Frühstück
	tomato /təˈmɑːtəʊ/	(die) Tomate	**for lunch** zum Mittagessen
	juice /dʒuːs/	(der) Saft	**for dinner** zum Abendessen
	coffee /ˈkɒfi/	(der) Kaffee	
	tea /tiː/	(der) Tee	**orange juice** Orangensaft
	milk /mɪlk/	(die) Milch	**tomato juice** Tomatensaft
	(to) **set the table** /ˌset ðə ˈteɪbl/	den Tisch decken	
	plate /pleɪt/	(der) Teller	
	cup /kʌp/	(die) Tasse	
	knife /naɪf/	(das) Messer	
	fork /fɔːk/	(die) Gabel	
	spoon /spuːn/	(der) Löffel	
	table /ˈteɪbl/	(der) Tisch	
	fruit /fruːt/	(die) Frucht, (das) Obst	A banana is a **fruit**.
	(to) **help** /help/	helfen	

	(to) **clean (up)** /kliːn, ˌkliːnˈʌp/	sauber machen
	(to) **pass** /pɑːs/	geben, herüberreichen
	(to) **drink** /drɪŋk/	trinken
	bacon /ˈbeɪkən/	(der) Schinkenspeck
	sausage /ˈsɒsɪdʒ/	(die) Wurst, (das) Würstchen
	vegetarian /ˌvedʒəˈteəriən/	vegetarisch
	baked beans (pl) /ˌbeɪkt ˈbiːnz/	*(die) Bohnen in Tomatensauce*
	cereal /ˈsɪəriəl/	(die) Frühstücksflocken
	jam /dʒæm/	(die) Marmelade
	chocolate spread /ˈtʃɒklət spred/	(der) Schokoladenaufstrich
p. 53, 3	**perfect** /ˈpɜːfɪkt/	perfekt
p. 54, 4	(to) **watch TV** /ˌwɒtʃ tiː ˈviː/	Fernsehen gucken
p. 54, 5	**shelf** /ʃelf/	(das) Regal
p. 54, 6	(to) **hear** /hɪə/	hören
p. 55, 7	(to) **hurry (up)** /ˌhʌriˈʌp/	sich beeilen
	body /ˈbɒdi/	(der) Körper
	bathroom /ˈbɑːθˌruːm/	(das) Badezimmer
	(to) leave /liːv/	weggehen
	just /dʒʌst/	nur, bloß
	second /ˈsekənd/	(die) Sekunde
	(to) **need to** /ˈniːd tʊ/	müssen
	ear /ɪə/	(das) Ohr
	(to) **wash** /wɒʃ/	waschen; sich waschen
	later /ˈleɪtə/	später
	(to) **take** /teɪk/	benötigen, brauchen
	(to) **brush one's teeth** /ˌbrʌʃ wʌnz ˈtiːθ/	sich die Zähne putzen
	hair /heə/	(das) Haar, (die) Haare
	body part /ˈbɒdi pɑːt/	(das) Körperteil
	(to) **take a shower** /ˌteɪk ə ˈʃaʊə/	duschen
	(to) **style one's hair** /ˌstaɪl wʌnz ˈheə/	sich frisieren
	smelly feet (pl) /ˌsmeli ˈfiːt/	Stinkefüße
	perfection /pəˈfekʃn/	(die) Perfektion
	(to) **comb** /kəʊm/	kämmen
	(to) **go out** /ˌgəʊˈaʊt/	*hier:* Gassi gehen; hinausgehen
	(to) **make up** /ˌmeɪkˈʌp/	erfinden, sich ausdenken
p. 56, 8	**each other** /ˌiːtʃˈʌðə/	einander
	(to) **plan** /plæn/	planen
	swimming /ˈswɪmɪŋ/	(das) Schwimmen
	(to) **pick up** /ˌpɪkˈʌp/	aufheben, abholen
	(to) **have** /hæv/	essen; trinken
	planner /ˈplænə/	(der) Kalender, (der) Planer
	granny (informal) /ˈgræni/	(die) Oma, (die) Omi
	(to) **sleep in** /ˌsliːpˈɪn/	ausschlafen

to **drink**

The boy **is watching TV**.

"**Just**" can mean "only".

He **is brushing** his **teeth**.

If I see you and you see me, we see **each other**.

granny

sunshine

	Indian /ˈɪndiən/	indisch	
	takeaway /ˈteɪkəˌweɪ/	(das) Essen zum Mitnehmen	
p.56, **9**	**message** /ˈmesɪdʒ/	(die) Nachricht, (die) Botschaft	
p.57, **11**	**sunshine** /ˈsʌnʃaɪn/	(der) Sonnenschein	
	(to) **be right** /ˌbiː ˈraɪt/	recht haben	
	pretty /ˈprɪti/	ziemlich	
	idea /aɪˈdɪə/	(die) Vorstellung	
	meal /miːl/	(die) Mahlzeit, (das) Essen	
	(to) **stay** /steɪ/	bleiben, wohnen	
	all /ɔːl/	ganz, völlig	
	dinner /ˈdɪnə/	(das) Abendessen	
	right /raɪt/	richtig	
	(to) **take notes (on)** /ˌteɪk ˈnəʊts/	sich Notizen machen (zu)	
	watermelon /ˈwɔːtəˌmelən/	(die) Wassermelone	
	(to) **stay up late** /ˌsteɪ ˌʌp ˈleɪt/	lange aufbleiben	
	flea market /ˈfliː ˌmɑːkɪt/	(der) Flohmarkt	
	pancake /ˈpænˌkeɪk/	(der) Pfannkuchen	
	on /ɒn/	*hier:* über	
p.58, **13**	(to) **imagine** /ɪˈmædʒɪn/	sich etwas vorstellen	
p.58, **14**	(to) **sort** /sɔːt/	sortieren	
	scrambled /ˈskræmbld/	durcheinander gebracht	
	(to) **scramble** /ˈskræmbl/	durcheinander bringen	
p.59, **15**	**version** /ˈvɜːʃn/	(die) Version, (die) Fassung	
	feedback /ˈfiːdbæk/	(das) Feedback, (die) Rückmeldung	
	final /ˈfaɪnl/	letzte(r, s); endgültig	

Breakfast is the **meal** you eat in the morning and **dinner** is the **meal** you eat in the evening.

watermelon

Unit 3 | Part B Sports and hobbies

p.60, **2**	(to) **dance** /dɑːns/	tanzen	
p.61, **3**	(to) **ride a bike** /ˌraɪd ə ˈbaɪk/	Fahrrad fahren	
	(to) **do gymnastics** /ˌduː dʒɪmˈnæstɪks/	turnen	
	table tennis /ˈteɪbl ˌtenɪs/	(das) Tischtennis	
	(to) **climb** /klaɪm/	auf etwas (hinauf)steigen, klettern	
	(to) **do athletics** /ˌduː æθˈletɪks/	Leichtathletik machen	
	(to) **ride a horse** /ˌraɪd ə ˈhɔːs/	reiten	
	piano /piˈænəʊ/	(das) Klavier	
	(to) **ice-skate** /ˈaɪsˌskeɪt/	Schlittschuh laufen	
	(to) **guess** /ges/	(er)raten	
	(to) **do arts and crafts** /ˌduː ˌɑːts ən ˈkrɑːfts/	basteln	
p.62, **Grammar**	**guessing game** /ˈgesɪŋ ˌgeɪm/	(das) Ratespiel	
	(to) **swim** /swɪm/	schwimmen	
p.62, **5**	(to) **ride** /raɪd/	fahren; reiten	
	example /ɪgˈzɑːmpl/	(das) Beispiel	
p.63, **7**	**racetrack** /ˈreɪsˌtræk/	(die) Rennbahn	

They **are riding** their **bikes**.

You have to be fit to **do athletics**.

Can you …?
Yes, I can. /jes ˌaɪ ˈkæn/ Ja.
No, I can't. /ˌnəʊ ˌaɪ ˈkɑːnt/ Nein.

	ice rink /ˈaɪs rɪŋk/	(die) Schlittschuhbahn
	tennis court /ˈtenɪs kɔːt/	(der) Tennisplatz
	football ground /ˈfʊtˌbɔːl graʊnd/	(der) Fußballplatz
	climbing wall /ˈklaɪmɪŋ wɔːl/	(die) Kletterwand
	mini golf course /ˈmɪni gɒlf ˌkɔːs/	(die) Minigolfanlage
p. 64, **9**	**unusual** /ʌnˈjuːʒuəl/	ungewöhnlich
	sportsperson /ˈspɔːtsˌpɜːsn/	(der/die) Sportler/in
p. 65, **10**	**alone** /əˈləʊn/	allein
	other /ˈʌðə/	andere(r, s)
	kind /kaɪnd/	(die) Art, (die) Sorte
	court /kɔːt/	(der) Platz
	net /net/	(das) Netz
	middle /ˈmɪdl/	(die) Mitte
	(to) **hit** /hɪt/	schlagen
	(to) **keep** /kiːp/	halten, behalten, aufbewahren
	inside /ˈɪnˌsaɪd/	innerhalb
	line /laɪn/	(die) Linie; (die) Zeile
	point /pɔɪnt/	(der) Punkt
	out /aʊt/	heraus, hinaus; aus
	field /fiːld/	(das) Feld
	goal /gəʊl/	(das) Tor
	like /laɪk/	wie
	round /raʊnd/	rund
	behind /bɪˈhaɪnd/	hinter
	(to) **kick** /kɪk/	treten
	(to) **throw** /θrəʊ/	werfen
	(to) **catch** /kætʃ/	fangen
	(to) **include** /ɪnˈkluːd/	beinhalten; einbeziehen
	fact /fækt/	(die) Tatsache, (der) Fakt
	(to) **have to** /ˈhæv tə/	müssen
	(to) **get into** /ˌget ˈɪntʊ/	sich auseinandersetzen mit
	console /ˈkɒnsəʊl/	(die) Konsole
	racket /ˈrækɪt/	(der) Schläger
	(to) **tackle** /ˈtækl/	angreifen
	(to) **score** /skɔː/	einen Punkt machen
	goal line /ˈgəʊl ˌlaɪn/	(die) Ziellinie
	at least /ət ˈliːst/	mindestens, wenigstens
	number /ˈnʌmbə/	(die) Anzahl
p. 66, **12**	**opposite** /ˈɒpəzɪt/	(das) Gegenteil
p. 67, **13**	**if** /ɪf/	ob
	on one's own /ˌɒn ˌwʌnz ˈəʊn/	allein
	rule /ruːl/	(die) Regel
	(to) **explain** /ɪkˈspleɪn/	erklären
	equipment /ɪˈkwɪpmənt/	(die) Ausrüstung, (die) Ausstattung

Golf is an **unusual** sport for a child.

There is always a **net** in the **middle** of a tennis **court**.

There are two **goals** on a football **field**.

You have to **kick** a ball to play football.

tennis **racket**

on one's own = not with other people

(to) **give a presentation** /ˌgɪv_ə ˌpreznˈteɪʃn/	eine Präsentation halten	

Unit 4 | Part A At home with friends

Cleaning is a **chore**.

p. 71	**at home** /ˌæt ˈhəʊm/	zu Hause	
	chore /tʃɔː/	(die) lästige Aufgabe, (die) Hausarbeit	
p. 72, **1**	(to) **share** /ʃeə/	teilen	
	(to) **paint** /peɪnt/	(an)malen	
	extra /ˈekstrə/	zusätzlich	
	sure /ʃɔː/	sicher	
	why /waɪ/	warum	
	drink /drɪŋk/	(das) Trinken, (das) Getränk	Orange juice is a **drink**.
	excellent /ˈeksələnt/	ausgezeichnet	**excellent** = very good
	(to) **escape** /ɪˈskeɪp/	fliehen, entkommen	
	contest /ˈkɒntest/	(der) Wettbewerb	
	modelling /ˈmɒdlɪŋ/	(das) Modeln	
	(to) **check out** *(informal)* /ˌtʃek_ˈaʊt/	sich ansehen; ausprobieren	
	corner shop /ˈkɔːnə ʃɒp/	(der) Laden an der Ecke, (der) Tante-Emma-Laden	
p. 73, **1**	(to) **list** /lɪst/	auflisten	to **list** = to make a list
p. 73, **2**	(to) **give** /gɪv/	geben	
	bag /bæg/	(die) Tasche, (die) Tüte	
	money /ˈmʌni/	(das) Geld	
	lemonade /ˌleməˈneɪd/	(die) Limonade	
p. 73, **3**	**rainy** /ˈreɪni/	regnerisch	
	often /ˈɒfn/	oft, häufig	
p. 74, **5**	**at / in the front** /ˌæt / ˌɪn ðə ˈfrʌnt/	vorne	**at / in the front**
p. 75, **6**	**cake** /keɪk/	(der) Kuchen	
	packet /ˈpækɪt/	(die) Packung	
	at / in the back /ˌæt / ˌɪn ðə ˈbæk/	hinten	
	water /ˈwɔːtə/	(das) Wasser	**Water** is a **drink**.
	Of course! /əv ˈkɔːs/	Natürlich!	
	salt /sɔːlt/	(das) Salz	
	What ... would you like? /ˌwɒt ... wəd jə ˈlaɪk/	Was für ein / eine ... hättest du / hättet ihr / hätten Sie gern?	
	cheese /tʃiːz/	(der) Käse	
	between /bɪˈtwiːn/	zwischen	**between**
	next to /ˈnekst_tə/	neben	
	above /əˈbʌv/	über	
	in front of /ˌɪn ˈfrʌnt_əv/	vor	
	thanks a lot /ˌθæŋks_ə ˈlɒt/	vielen Dank	
	(to) **pay** /peɪ/	(be)zahlen	
	reading /ˈriːdɪŋ/	(das) Lesen	**Reading** is her hobby.
	shopping /ˈʃɒpɪŋ/	(das) Einkaufen; Einkaufs-	

	I spy with my little eye. /aɪ ˌspaɪ wɪð ˌmaɪ ˌlɪtl̩ ˈaɪ/	*Ich sehe was, was du nicht siehst.*
	box /bɒks/	*hier:* (die) Packung
	crisps *(pl)* /krɪsps/	(die) Chips
	vinegar /ˈvɪnɪɡə/	(der) Essig
	onion /ˈʌnjən/	(die) Zwiebel
	freezer /ˈfriːzə/	(der) Gefrierschrank
	fridge /frɪdʒ/	(der) Kühlschrank
	melon /ˈmelən/	(die) Melone
	role play /ˈrəʊl pleɪ/	(das) Rollenspiel
p.76, **7**	(to) **remember** /rɪˈmembə/	sich erinnern an
	bedroom /ˈbedruːm/	(das) Schlafzimmer
	floor /flɔː/	(der) Fußboden
	on the right /ˌɒn ðə ˈraɪt/	rechts, auf der rechten Seite
	whose /huːz/	wessen
	under /ˈʌndə/	unter
	everywhere /ˈevriweə/	überall
	on the left /ˌɒn ðə ˈleft/	links, auf der linken Seite
	thank you /ˈθæŋk ju/	danke
	heavy /ˈhevi/	schwer
	tidy /ˈtaɪdi/	ordentlich, aufgeräumt
	(to) **be a mess** /ˌbi‿ə ˈmes/	unordentlich sein
	cap /kæp/	(die) Mütze
	messy /ˈmesi/	unordentlich
	stuff *(informal)* /stʌf/	(das) Zeug
	(to) **be rubbish** /ˌbiː ˈrʌbɪʃ/	Quatsch sein
	the messy one /ðə ˈmesi wʌn/	der/die/das Unordentliche
	all over the place /ˌɔːl‿ˌəʊvə ðə ˈpleɪs/	überall
	erm *(informal)* /ɜːm/	ähm
	lamp /læmp/	(die) Lampe
	design /dɪˈzaɪn/	(der) Entwurf, (das) Design
	cute /kjuːt/	süß, niedlich
	done /dʌn/	fertig, erledigt
p.77, **8**	**furniture** /ˈfɜːnɪtʃə/	(das) Möbel(stück)
	snake /sneɪk/	(die) Schlange
p.77, **9**	**sweet** /swiːt/	(die) Süßigkeit
p.77, **10**	(to) **focus on** /ˈfəʊkəs‿ɒn/	sich konzentrieren auf
p.78, **11**	**member** /ˈmembə/	(das) Mitglied
	(to) **do research** /ˌduː rɪˈsɜːtʃ/	recherchieren
	job /dʒɒb/	(die) Aufgabe
p.78, **12**	**language** /ˈlæŋɡwɪdʒ/	(die) Sprache
	goodbye /ˌɡʊdˈbaɪ/	auf Wiedersehen
	its /ɪts/	sein(e), ihr(e) *(sächlich)*
p.79, **13**	(to) **search** /sɜːtʃ/	suchen

freezer
fridge

The cat is **under** the chair.

The **bedroom** is very **tidy**.

lamp

furniture: a bed, a sofa, ...

This is a dog with **its** puppies.

(to) **search the Internet** /ˌsɜːtʃ ði ˈɪntənet/	im Internet suchen	to **search the Internet** = to use a computer to look for information
term /tɜːm/	(der) Begriff	
introduction /ˌɪntrəˈdʌkʃn/	(die) Einleitung	
(to) **introduce** /ˌɪntrəˈdjuːs/	einführen; vorstellen	
main /meɪn/	Haupt-	
detail /ˈdiːteɪl/	(das) Detail, (die) Einzelheit	
end /end/	(das) Ende, (der) Schluss	**end** ↔ start
(to) **edit** /ˈedɪt/	bearbeiten	
necessary /ˈnesəsri/	notwendig, erforderlich	**necessary** = what you need
fun /fʌn/	lustig, witzig	
(to) **say goodbye (to somebody)** /ˌseɪ ɡʊdˈbaɪ tə ˌsʌmbədi/	sich von jemandem verabschieden	
(to) **script** /skrɪpt/	das Drehbuch zu etwas schreiben	

Unit 4 | Part B Chores

text (message) /ˈtekst ˌmesɪdʒ/	(die) Textnachricht	
place /pleɪs/	*hier:* (das) Haus, (das) Zuhause	
home /həʊm/	zu Hause, daheim	
that /ðæt/	dass	
(to) **do the shopping** /ˌduː ðə ˈʃɒpɪŋ/	einkaufen	
(to) **do the cooking** /ˌduː ðə ˈkʊkɪŋ/	kochen	
hour /ˈaʊə/	(die) Stunde	
fine /faɪn/	in Ordnung, gut	
parents *(pl)* /ˈpeərənts/	(die) Eltern	
(to) **take a dog for a walk** /ˌteɪk ə ˌdɒɡ fər ə ˈwɔːk/	mit einem Hund Gassi gehen	
this evening /ðɪs ˈiːvnɪŋ/	heute Abend	
love /lʌv/	viele Grüße, alles Liebe *(in Briefen)*	
Fri (= Friday) /ˈfraɪdeɪ/	(der) Freitag	
(to) **work late** /ˌwɜːk ˈleɪt/	länger arbeiten	
for another half hour /fər əˌnʌðə hɑːf ˈaʊə/	noch eine halbe Stunde	
(to) **make sure** /ˌmeɪk ˈʃɔː/	darauf achten, dass	
already /ɔːlˈredi/	schon, bereits	
(to) **be one's turn** /ˌbiː wʌnz ˈtɜːn/	an der Reihe sein	
(to) **vacuum** /ˈvækjuəm/	staubsaugen	
usually /ˈjuːʒuəli/	gewöhnlich, normalerweise	
(to) **empty** /ˈempti/	ausleeren; ausräumen	
dishwasher /ˈdɪʃˌwɒʃə/	(die) Spülmaschine	
(to) **tidy (up)** /ˈtaɪdi, ˌtaɪdiˈʌp/	aufräumen	
living room /ˈlɪvɪŋ ˌruːm/	(das) Wohnzimmer	
anything /ˈeniˌθɪŋ/	irgendetwas	
because /bɪˈkɒz/	weil, da	
(to) **take out** /ˌteɪk ˈaʊt/	hinausbringen	

p. 80, 1
p. 80, 2

He **is doing the cooking**.

one **hour** = sixty minutes

it's my turn
  ich bin an der Reihe
it's your turn
  du bist an der Reihe
it's his / her turn
  er / sie ist an der Reihe
it's our turn
it's your turn
it's their turn

The boy **is tidying up**.

	rubbish /ˈrʌbɪʃ/	(der) Müll
	(to) **load** /ləʊd/	laden
	time /taɪm/	(das) Mal
	fun /fʌn/	(der) Spaß
	like that /ˌlaɪk ˈðæt/	so
	cleaning /ˈkliːnɪŋ/	*hier:* beim Reinigen
p. 82, **7**	**fish** (*pl* **fish** *or* **fishes**) /fɪʃ, fɪʃ, fɪʃɪz/	(der) Fisch
p. 83, **8**	**solution** /səˈluːʃn/	(die) Lösung
	dirty /ˈdɜːti/	dreckig, schmutzig
	switch on /ˌswɪtʃ ˈɒn/	einschalten
	clean /kliːn/	sauber
	near /nɪə/	nahe, in der Nähe von
	ad (= advertisement) /æd, ədˈvɜːtɪsmənt/	(die) Anzeige
	robot /ˈrəʊbɒt/	(der) Roboter
	washing machine /ˈwɒʃɪŋ məˌʃiːn/	(die) Waschmaschine
	to belong /bɪˈlɒŋ/	hingehören
p. 83, **9**	**competition** /ˌkɒmpəˈtɪʃn/	(der) Wettbewerb
p. 84, **10**	(to) **begin** /bɪˈgɪn/	anfangen, beginnen
	(to) **look after** /ˌlʊk ˈɑːftə/	sich kümmern um; aufpassen auf
	hole /həʊl/	(das) Loch
	(to) **look for** /ˈlʊk fə/	suchen nach
	away /əˈweɪ/	weg
	treat /triːt/	(die) Leckerei
	(to) **dig** /dɪg/	graben
	squirrel /ˈskwɪrəl/	(das) Eichhörnchen
	excuse /ɪkˈskjuːs/	(die) Entschuldigung
p. 85, **10**	**busy** /ˈbɪzi/	beschäftigt
p. 85, **11**	**terrible** /ˈterəbl/	schrecklich
p. 86, **13**	**mother** /ˈmʌðə/	(die) Mutter
p. 87, **15**	**typical** /ˈtɪpɪkl/	typisch
	recording /rɪˈkɔːdɪŋ/	(die) Aufnahme

this time diesmal, dieses Mal
next time nächstes Mal

1 **fish**   3 **fish** (or **fishes**)

clean ↔ **dirty**

robot

to **begin** = to start

When you go to school, get a lot of homework and have a lot of hobbies, you are very **busy**.

Unit 5 | Part A   Happy birthday!

p. 91	**Happy birthday (to you)!** /ˌhæpi ˈbɜːθdeɪ tʊ juː/	Herzlichen Glückwunsch zum Geburtstag!
	happy /ˈhæpi/	glücklich
	birthday /ˈbɜːθdeɪ/	(der) Geburtstag
	like this /ˌlaɪk ˈðɪs/	so
	day out /ˌdeɪ ˈaʊt/	*(der) Ausflugstag*
p. 92, **2**	(to) **have a barbecue** /ˌhæv ə ˈbɑːbɪˌkjuː/	grillen, eine Grillparty machen
p. 92, **3**	(to) **send** /send/	schicken
	Poland /ˈpəʊlənd/	Polen

	invitation /ˌɪnvɪˈteɪʃn/	(die) Einladung
	(to) **bake** /beɪk/	backen
	balloon /bəˈluːn/	(der) Luftballon
	candle /ˈkændl/	(die) Kerze
	guest /gest/	(der) Gast
	(to) **arrive** /əˈraɪv/	ankommen
	present /ˈpreznt/	(das) Geschenk
	grandma (informal) /ˈɡrænˌmɑː/	(die) Oma
	keyword /ˈkiːˌwɜːd/	(das) Schlüsselwort, (das) Stichwort
	mess /mes/	(die) Unordnung
	set up /ˌsetˈʌp/	aufbauen
	grandpa (informal) /ˈɡrænˌpɑː/	(der) Opa
	delicious /dɪˈlɪʃəs/	köstlich, lecker
p. 94, 5	(to) **sleep** /sliːp/	schlafen
p. 94, 6	**present progressive** /ˌpreznt prəʊˈɡresɪv/	(die) Verlaufsform der Gegenwart
p. 95, 7	**calendar** /ˈkælɪndə/	(der) Kalender
	(to) **hear** /hɪə/	hören
	(to) **rap along** /ˌræpəˈlɒŋ/	mitrappen
	(to) **stand up** /ˌstændˈʌp/	aufstehen
	twenty-first /ˌtwentiˈfɜːst/	einundzwanzigste(r, s)
p. 95, 8	**grandmother** /ˈɡrænˌmʌðə/	(die) Großmutter
	husband /ˈhʌzbənd/	(der) Ehemann
	cousin /ˈkʌzn/	(der/die) Cousin/e
	wife /waɪf/	(die) Ehefrau
	woman (pl **women**) /ˈwʊmən, ˈwɪmɪn/	(die) Frau
	daughter /ˈdɔːtə/	(die) Tochter
	aunt /ɑːnt/	(die) Tante
	man (pl **men**) /mæn, men/	(der) Mann
	father /ˈfɑːðə/	(der) Vater
	son /sʌn/	(der) Sohn
	grandfather /ˈɡrænˌfɑːðə/	(der) Großvater
	family tree /ˌfæmli ˈtriː/	(der) Familienstammbaum
	divorced /dɪˈvɔːst/	geschieden
	granddaughter /ˈɡrænˌdɔːtə/	(die) Enkelin
	grandson /ˈɡrænˌsʌn/	(der) Enkel
p. 96, 9	(to) **build** /bɪld/	bauen
	world /wɜːld/	(die) Welt
	face /feɪs/	(das) Gesicht
	sun /sʌn/	(die) Sonne
	moon /muːn/	(der) Mond
	star /stɑː/	(der) Stern
	light /laɪt/	(das) Licht
	sleepover /ˈsliːpˌəʊvə/	(die) Übernachtung

balloons

presents

January /ˈdʒænjuəri/	(der) Januar
February /ˈfebruəri/	(der) Februar
March /mɑːtʃ/	(der) März
April /ˈeɪprəl/	(der) April
May /meɪ/	(der) Mai
June /dʒuːn/	(der) Juni
July /dʒʊˈlaɪ/	(der) Juli
August /ˈɔːɡəst/	(der) August
September /sepˈtembə/	(der) September
October /ɒkˈtəʊbə/	(der) Oktober
November /nəʊˈvembə/	(der) November
December /dɪˈsembə/	(der) Dezember

at the moment /ˌæt ðə ˈməʊmənt/ im Moment

There's a lot of **light** when the **sun** is shining.

(to) **have** /hæv/	*hier:* machen	
mattress /ˈmætrəs/	(die) Matratze	
sleeping mat /ˈsliːpɪŋ mæt/	(die) Schlafmatte	
pillow /ˈpɪləʊ/	(das) Kissen	
sleeping bag /ˈsliːpɪŋ bæg/	(der) Schlafsack	
pillow fight /ˈpɪləʊ faɪt/	(die) Kissenschlacht	
fort /fɔːt/	(das) Fort, (die) Festung	
out of /ˈaʊt əv/	aus; außerhalb	
ghost story /ˈgəʊst ˌstɔːri/	(die) Gespenstergeschichte	
alien /ˈeɪliən/	(der/die) Außerirdische	
themed party /ˌθiːmd ˈpɑːti/	(die) Mottoparty	
(to) **dress up** /ˌdres ˈʌp/	(sich) verkleiden	
space /speɪs/	(das) Weltall	
suit /suːt/	(der) Anzug, (das) Kostüm	
helmet /ˈhelmɪt/	(der) Helm	
decoration /ˌdekəˈreɪʃn/	(die) Dekoration, (der) Schmuck	
(to) **put up** /ˌpʊt ˈʌp/	aufhängen, aufstellen	

pillow

experience /ɪkˈspɪəriəns/	(die) Erfahrung	
(to) **take a photo** /ˌteɪk ə ˈfəʊtəʊ/	ein Foto machen	
tree /triː/	(der) Baum	
(to) **hold** /həʊld/	(fest)halten	
treasure hunt /ˈtreʒə hʌnt/	(die) Schatzsuche	
(to) **take to the streets** /ˌteɪk tə ðə ˈstriːts/	auf die Straße gehen	
(to) **get into** /ˌget ˈɪntʊ/	*hier:* bilden	
street light /ˈstriːt laɪt/	(die) Straßenlaterne	
something blue /ˌsʌmθɪŋ ˈbluː/	etwas Blaues	
(to) **hug** /hʌg/	umarmen	
(to) **take a selfie** /ˌteɪk ə ˈselfi/	ein Selfie machen	
the fastest /ðə ˈfɑːstɪst/	der/die/das schnellste	
winner /ˈwɪnə/	(der/die) Gewinner/in	
prize /praɪz/	(der) Preis, (der) Gewinn	

first /fɜːst/ erste(r, s)
second /ˈsekənd/ zweite(r, s)
third /θɜːd/ dritte(r, s)
fourth /fɔːθ/ vierte(r, s)
fifth /fɪfθ/ fünfte(r, s)
sixth /sɪksθ/ sechste(r, s)
seventh /ˈsevnθ/ siebte(r, s)
eighth /eɪtθ/ achte(r, s)
ninth /naɪnθ/ neunte(r, s)
tenth /tenθ/ zehnte(r, s)
eleventh /ɪˈlevnθ/ elfte(r, s)
twelfth /twelfθ/ zwölfte(r, s)

The **winner** gets the first **prize**.

dear /dɪə/	liebe/r *(Anrede)*	
I would like … (= I'd like …) /aɪ ˌwʊd ˈlaɪk, aɪd ˈlaɪk/	Ich würde gern … / Ich hätte gern …	
(to) **invite** /ɪnˈvaɪt/	einladen	
till /tɪl/	bis	
toothbrush /ˈtuːθbrʌʃ/	(die) Zahnbürste	
(to) **expect** /ɪkˈspekt/	erwarten	
adventure /ədˈventʃə/	(das) Abenteuer	

Today's **date** is 5th February.

date /deɪt/	(das) Datum	

(to) **put together** /ˌpʊt təˈgeðə/	zusammenstellen, zusammensetzen	

planning /ˈplænɪŋ/	(das) Planen	
the coolest /ðə ˈkuːlɪst/	der/die/das coolste	

ever /ˈevə/	jemals	
limit /ˈlɪmɪt/	(die) (Höchst)grenze, (das) Limit	
superhero /ˈsuːpə͵hɪərəʊ/	(der/die) Superheld/in	
spooky /ˈspuːki/	schaurig, unheimlich	
spaceship /ˈspeɪsˌʃɪp/	(das) Raumschiff	**spaceship**
character /ˈkærəktə/	*hier:* (die) Figur	

Unit 5 | Part B A day out

p. 100, **1**	**beach** /biːtʃ/	(der) Strand
	last /lɑːst/	letzte(r, s)
	(to) **be scared (of)** /͵biː ˈskeəd ͵əv/	Angst haben (vor)
	(to) **be (good/great) fun** /͵biː ͵gʊd/͵greɪt ˈfʌn/	(viel/großen) Spaß machen
	(to) **be good at doing something** /͵biː gʊd ͵ət ˈduːɪŋ ͵sʌmθɪŋ/	gut darin sein, etwas zu tun
	I'd love to … /aɪd ˈlʌv tə/	Ich würde sehr gern …
	far /fɑː/	weit
	heading /ˈhedɪŋ/	(die) Überschrift, (der) Titel
	crazy /ˈkreɪzi/	verrückt, wahnsinnig
	seagull /ˈsiː͵gʌl/	(die) Möwe
	the next one /ðə ˈnekst wʌn/	der/die/das nächste
	year /jɪə/	(der) Jahrgang
	day trip /ˈdeɪ trɪp/	(der) Tagesausflug
p. 101, **1**	**full** /fʊl/	*hier:* vollständig
p. 101, **2**	**by** /baɪ/	von; mit
	train /treɪn/	(der) Zug
	boat /bəʊt/	(das) Boot
	car /kɑː/	(das) Auto
	lake /leɪk/	(der) See
	mountain /ˈmaʊntɪn/	(der) Berg
	home town /ˈhəʊm ͵taʊn/	(die) Heimatstadt
p. 102, **3**	**sunny** /ˈsʌni/	sonnig
	diary /ˈdaɪəri/	(das) Tagebuch
p. 102, **4**	**summer** /ˈsʌmə/	(der) Sommer
	Italy /ˈɪtəli/	Italien
	France /frɑːns/	Frankreich
	Germany /ˈdʒɜːməni/	Deutschland
	Scotland /ˈskɒtlənd/	Schottland
p. 103, **5**	**sight** /saɪt/	(die) Sehenswürdigkeit
	observation tower /͵ɒbzəˈveɪʃn ͵taʊə/	(der) Aussichtsturm
	announcement /əˈnaʊnsmənt/	(die) Mitteilung, (die) Durchsage
p. 104, **6**	**those** (*pl of* **that**) /ðəʊz/	diese, jene
	that's (= **that is**) /ðæts, ˈðæt͜ɪz/	*hier:* das kostet
	change /tʃeɪndʒ/	(das) Wechselgeld

I **was**   ich war
he **was**   er war
she **was**   sie war
you **were**   du warst,
        ihr wart,
        Sie waren
we **were**   wir waren
they **were**   sie waren

seagull

They are on a **boat**.

by train	mit dem Zug
by boat	mit dem Boot
by bus	mit dem Bus
by car	mit dem Auto

It is often **sunny** in **summer**.

Tower Bridge is a famous **sight** in London.

there was /ðeə ˈwɒz/ dort war; es gab
there were /ðeə ˈwɜː/ dort waren; es gab

	(to) **enjoy** /ɪnˈdʒɔɪ/	genießen	
	postcard /ˈpəʊstˌkɑːd/	(die) Postkarte, (die) Ansichtskarte	**postcard**
	p (= penny, *pl* **pence)** /piː, ˈpeni, pens/	(der) Penny *(britische Währung)*	
	Would you like …? /ˌwʊd juː ˈlaɪk/	Hättest du / Hättet ihr / Hätten Sie gern …?	When you want to buy clothes, you need to know your **size**.
	size /saɪz/	(die) Größe	
	(to) **fit** /fɪt/	passen	
	shopkeeper /ˈʃɒpˌkiːpə/	(der/die) Ladeninhaber/in	
	this one /ˈðɪs wʌn/	dieser / diese / dieses	
	stamp /stæmp/	(die) Briefmarke	
	Just a minute. /ˌdʒʌst ə ˈmɪnɪt/	Einen Moment.	
	(to) **have a look** /ˌhæv ə ˈlʊk/	nachsehen	
	M (= medium) /em, ˈmiːdiəm/	mittel(groß)	
	till /tɪl/	(die) Kasse	
p. 105, **8**	**visit** /ˈvɪzɪt/	(der) Besuch	
	town /taʊn/	(die) Stadt	
	(to) **check out** *(informal)* /ˌtʃekˈaʊt/	sich ansehen	
	British /ˈbrɪtɪʃ/	britisch	
	seaside /ˈsiːˌsaɪd/	(die) (Meeres)küste, (das) Meer	You have a **fantastic** view of the **seaside** from here!
p. 105, **9**	**fantastic** /fænˈtæstɪk/	fantastisch, super	
	not any /ˌnɒtˈeni/	kein(e)	
	the Upside Down House /ðiˌʌpsaɪdˈdaʊn haʊs/	*(das) Haus, das auf dem Kopf steht*	
	view /vjuː/	(die) (Aus)sicht	If you send a **postcard** when you are on **holiday**, you have to write the **address** of the person you are sending it to.
	(to) **be lucky** /ˌbiː ˈlʌki/	Glück haben	
p. 106, **10**	**holiday(s)** /ˈhɒlɪdeɪ(z)/	(die) Ferien, (der) Urlaub	
	past /pɑːst/	(die) Vergangenheit	
p. 107, **13**	**address** /əˈdres/	(die) Adresse	
	what it is like /ˌwɒtˌɪtˌɪz ˈlaɪk/	wie es ist	

Hier findest du alphabetisch sortiert alle Wörter aus dem vorliegenden Buch mit der Angabe der Seitenzahl *(p.)*, auf der das Wort das erste Mal vorkommt oder auf der es zum Lernwort gemacht wird. Die Zahl hinter dem Komma bezeichnet die Aufgabe auf der Seite.

Die **fett** gedruckten Lernwörter solltest du dir merken.

Folgende Abkürzungen werden verwendet: *(pl)* = (unregelmäßige) Mehrzahlform, *(no pl)* = keine Mehrzahlform, *(irr)* = unregelmäßiges Verb

(informal) bedeutet: Dieses Wort oder dieser Ausdruck ist umgangssprachlich.

A

a, an /ə/eɪ, ən/ ein(e) p.7,1
about /əˈbaʊt/ über; an p.8,4
about /əˈbaʊt/ ungefähr p.50
above /əˈbʌv/ über p.75,6
absolutely /ˈæbsəluːtli/ absolut; *hier:* überhaupt p.48
academy /əˈkædəmi/ Akademie; Schule p.30
acrostic /əˈkrɒstɪk/ Akrostichon; Leistenvers p.25,9
(to) **act out** /ˌækt ˈaʊt/ nachspielen; vorspielen p.9,5
action /ˈækʃn/ Handlung p.34,6
(to) activate /ˈæktɪveɪt/ aktivieren p.12,1
activity /ækˈtɪvəti/ Aktivität p.33,3
ad (= advertisement) /æd, ədˈvɜːtɪsmənt/ Anzeige p.83,8
(to) **add** /æd/ hinzufügen p.27,14
address /əˈdres/ Adresse p.107,13
adult /ˈædʌlt/ Erwachsene/r p.28
adventure /ədˈventʃə/ Abenteuer p.97,10
adverb of frequency /ˌædvɜːb ˌəv ˈfriːkwənsi/ Häufigkeitsadverb p.82
after /ˈɑːftə/ nach p.24,8
after /ˈɑːftə/ nachdem p.155
afternoon /ˌɑːftəˈnuːn/ Nachmittag p.33,3
in the afternoon /ˌɪn ði ˌɑːftəˈnuːn/ am Nachmittag p.33,3
in the afternoons /ˌɪn ði ˌɑːftəˈnuːnz/ nachmittags p.155
afterwards /ˈɑːftəwədz/ anschließend; später p.111
again /əˈgen/ wieder; noch einmal p.13,1
against /əˈgenst/ gegen p.50
age /eɪdʒ/ Alter p.28
air /eə/ Luft p.49

alien /ˈeɪliən/ Außerirdische/r p.96,9
all /ɔːl/ alle; alles p.17,10; ganz; völlig p.57,11
all over the place /ˌɔːl ˌəʊvə ðə ˈpleɪs/ überall p.76,7
all over the world /ˌɔːl ˌəʊvə ðə ˈwɜːld/ auf der ganzen Welt p.136
almost /ˈɔːlməʊst/ fast; beinahe p.50
alone /əˈləʊn/ allein p.65,10
alphabetical /ˌælfəˈbetɪkl/ alphabetisch p.16,8
already /ɔːlˈredi/ schon; bereits p.80,2
also /ˈɔːlsəʊ/ auch p.15,6
always /ˈɔːlweɪz/ immer p.12,1
am (= ante meridiem) /ˌeɪˈem, ˌænti məˈrɪdiəm/ morgens, vormittags *(nur hinter Uhrzeit zwischen Mitternacht und 12 Uhr mittags)* p.35,9
and /ænd/ und p.7,2
angry /ˈæŋgri/ verärgert p.49
animal /ˈænɪml/ Tier p.7,1
animal shelter /ˈænɪml ˌʃeltə/ Tierheim p.136
announcement /əˈnaʊnsmənt/ Mitteilung; Durchsage p.103,5
another /əˈnʌðə/ noch ein/e; ein anderer/ein anderes/eine andere p.24,8
for another half hour /fər əˌnʌðə hɑːf ˈaʊə/ noch eine halbe Stunde p.80,1
answer /ˈɑːnsə/ Antwort p.22,3; (be)antworten p.10,6
any /ˈeni/ (irgend)ein(e) p.33,3
anything /ˈeniˌθɪŋ/ irgendetwas p.80,2
anyway /ˈeniweɪ/ jedenfalls p.29
apple /ˈæpl/ Apfel p.38,14
apple pie /ˈæpl ˌpaɪ/ gedeckter Apfelkuchen p.40,1

(to) **apply** /əˈplaɪ/ anwenden p.12,1
April /ˈeɪprəl/ April p.95,7
are /ɑː/ bist, sind, seid p.8,4
Are there …? /ˈɑː ðeə/ Gibt es …? p.139
area /ˈeəriə/ Gebiet; Region p.27,14
around /əˈraʊnd/ *hier:* in, im p.118; um; herum; umher p.136
around the world /əˌraʊnd ðə ˈwɜːld/ weltweit, überall auf der Welt p.136
(to) **arrive** /əˈraɪv/ ankommen p.92,3
art /ɑːt/ Kunst p.35,9
article /ˈɑːtɪkl/ Artikel p.38,14
(to) do arts and crafts /ˌduː ˌɑːts ən ˈkrɑːfts/ basteln p.61,3
as /əz/ als; wie; während p.37,13
(to) **ask** /ɑːsk/ fragen; bitten p.10,6
(to) **ask questions** /ˌɑːsk ˈkwestʃnz/ Fragen stellen p.10,6
assembly /əˈsembli/ Versammlung, Schülerversammlung p.33,3
assembly hall /əˈsembli ˌhɔːl/ Aula p.40,1
at /æt/ an; in; bei; um p.20,1
at home /æt ˈhəʊm/ zu Hause p.71
at least /ət ˈliːst/ mindestens; wenigstens p.65,10
at / in the back /ˌæt/ˌɪn ðə ˈbæk/ hinten p.75,6
at / in the front /ˌæt/ˌɪn ðə ˈfrʌnt/ vorne p.74,5
at the moment /ˌæt ðə ˈməʊmənt/ im Moment p.92,3
at the same time /ˌæt ðə ˌseɪm ˈtaɪm/ gleichzeitig; zur gleichen Zeit p.111
at the weekend /æt ðə ˈwiːkend/ am Wochenende p.51
at the weekends /æt ðə ˈwiːkendz/ an den Wochenenden p.155
(to) **attack** /əˈtæk/ angreifen p.49

August /ˈɔːgəst/ August p. 21, 1
aunt /ɑːnt/ Tante p. 95, 8
away /əˈweɪ/ weg p. 84, 10

B

back /bæk/ zurück p. 31
back /bæk/ Rücken p. 110
at / in the back /ˌæt / ˌɪn ðə ˈbæk/
hinten p. 75, 6
bacon /ˈbeɪkən/ Schinkenspeck
p. 52, 1
bad /bæd/ schlecht; schlimm
p. 24, 8
bag /bæg/ Tasche; Tüte p. 73, 2
(to) **bake** /beɪk/ backen p. 92, 3
baked beans *(pl)* /ˌbeɪkt ˈbiːnz/
Bohnen in Tomatensauce p. 52, 1
balcony /ˈbælkəni/ Balkon p. 90
balloon /bəˈluːn/ Luftballon p. 92, 3
banana /bəˈnɑːnə/ Banane p. 7, 2
(to) **have a barbecue** /ˌhæv ə
ˈbɑːbɪkjuː/ grillen, eine Grillparty
machen p. 92, 2
base /beɪs/ Boden p. 70
bat /bæt/ Fledermaus p. 24, 8
bathroom /ˈbɑːθˌruːm/
Badezimmer p. 55, 7
(to) **be** *(irr)* /biː/ sein p. 7, 2
(to) **be a mess** /ˌbi ə ˈmes/
unordentlich sein p. 76, 7
(to) **be about** /ˌbi əˈbaʊt/ gehen
um; handeln von p. 33, 2
(to) **be fun** /ˌbi: ˈfʌn/ Spaß machen
p. 20, 1
(to) **be going to do something**
/biː ˌgəʊɪŋ tə ˈduː: ˌsʌmθɪŋ/ etwas
tun werden p. 69
(to) **be good at doing something**
/ˌbi gʊd ət ˈduːɪŋ ˌsʌmθɪŋ/
gut darin sein, etwas zu tun
p. 100, 1
(to) **be (good/great) fun**
/ˌbi: ˌgʊd/ˌgreɪt ˈfʌn/ (viel/großen)
Spaß machen p. 100, 1
(to) **be lucky** /ˌbi: ˈlʌki/ Glück
haben p. 105, 9
(to) **be one's turn** /ˌbi: wʌnz ˈtɜːn/
an der Reihe sein p. 80, 2
(to) **be prepared** /ˌbi: prɪˈpeəd/
vorbereitet sein auf p. 111
(to) **be right** /ˌbi: ˈraɪt/ recht haben
p. 57, 11

(to) **be rubbish** /ˌbi: ˈrʌbɪʃ/ Quatsch
sein p. 76, 7
beach /biːtʃ/ Strand p. 100, 1
bear /beə/ Bär p. 150
beautiful /ˈbjuːtəfl/ schön p. 24, 8
because /bɪˈkɒz/ weil; da p. 80, 2
bed /bed/ Bett p. 15, 6
Bed and Breakfast /ˌbed ən
ˈbrekfəst/ Frühstückspension p. 90
bedroom /ˈbedruːm/ Schlafzimmer
p. 76, 7
before /bɪˈfɔː/ bevor p. 19, 15; zuvor,
vorher p. 37, 13; vor p. 41, 2
(to) **begin** *(irr)* /bɪˈgɪn/ anfangen;
beginnen p. 84, 10
beginner /bɪˈgɪnə/ Anfänger/in
p. 23, 7
beginning /bɪˈgɪnɪŋ/ Anfang;
Beginn p. 50
behind /bɪˈhaɪnd/ hinter p. 65, 10
(to) **believe** /bɪˈliːv/ glauben
p. 28
(to) **belong** /bɪˈlɒŋ/ hingehören
p. 83, 8
berry /ˈberi/ Beere p. 70
best /best/ beste(r, s) p. 20, 1
(to) **like best** /ˌlaɪk ˈbest/ am
liebsten mögen p. 43, 7
the best /ðə ˈbest/ der/die/das
beste p. 7, 2
between /bɪˈtwiːn/ zwischen p. 75, 6
big /bɪg/ groß p. 12, 1
bike /baɪk/ Fahrrad p. 157
(to) **ride a bike** /ˌraɪd ə ˈbaɪk/
Fahrrad fahren p. 61, 3
bin /bɪn/ Abfalleimer p. 36, 10
bird /bɜːd/ Vogel p. 150
birthday /ˈbɜːθdeɪ/ Geburtstag p. 91
Happy birthday (to you)!
/ˌhæpi ˈbɜːθdeɪ tʊ juː/ Herzlichen
Glückwunsch zum Geburtstag!
p. 91
biscuit /ˈbɪskɪt/ Keks p. 20, 1
a bit /ə ˈbɪt/ ein bisschen p. 32, 1
a (little) bit /ə ˌlɪtl ˈbɪt/ ein (kleines)
bisschen p. 70
bite /baɪt/ Bissen p. 88
black /blæk/ schwarz p. 153
blackberry /ˈblækbəri/ Brombeere
p. 70
(to) **blend** /blend/ *hier:* mixen p. 70
blender /ˈblendə/ Mixer p. 70

blue /bluː/ blau p. 153
BMX biker /ˌbiːemˈeks ˌbaɪkə/
BMX-Fahrer/in p. 23, 7
board /bɔːd/ Tafel; Brett p. 36, 10
board game /ˈbɔːd geɪm/ Brettspiel
p. 15, 6
boarding house /ˈbɔːdɪŋ haʊs/
Internatstrakt p. 50
boarding school /ˈbɔːdɪŋ skuːl/
Internat p. 50
boat /bəʊt/ Boot p. 101, 2
body /ˈbɒdi/ (der) Körper p. 55, 7
body part /ˈbɒdi pɑːt/ Körperteil
p. 55, 7
book /bʊk/ Buch p. 15, 6
bookshelf /ˈbʊkˌʃelf/ Bücherregal
p. 36, 10
boring /ˈbɔːrɪŋ/ langweilig p. 24, 8
(to) **borrow** /ˈbɒrəʊ/ (aus)leihen
p. 36, 10
both … and … /ˈbəʊθ ænd/
sowohl … als auch … p. 50
bottle /ˈbɒtl/ Flasche p. 36, 10
(to) **bow** /baʊ/ sich verbeugen p. 49
box /bɒks/ Kasten; Kiste p. 17, 9
box /bɒks/ *hier:* Packung p. 75, 6
boy /bɔɪ/ Junge p. 33, 3
brave /breɪv/ mutig p. 29
bread /bred/ Brot p. 138
break /breɪk/ Pause p. 35, 9
breakfast /ˈbrekfəst/ Frühstück
p. 52, 1
for breakfast /fə ˈbrekfəst/ zum
Frühstück p. 52, 1
have breakfast /ˌhæv ˈbrekfəst/
frühstücken p. 138
breath /breθ/ Atem p. 49
(to) breathe /briːð/ atmen; *hier:*
speien p. 48
brilliant /ˈbrɪljənt/ genial, klasse
p. 23, 6
(to) **bring** *(irr)* /brɪŋ/ mitbringen
p. 40, 1
British /ˈbrɪtɪʃ/ britisch p. 105, 8
broccoli /ˈbrɒkəli/ Brokkoli p. 156
brochure /ˈbrəʊʃə/ Broschüre p. 27, 14
brother /ˈbrʌðə/ Bruder p. 8, 4
brothers and sisters /ˈbrʌðəz ænd
ˌsɪstəz/ Geschwister p. 151
brown /braʊn/ braun p. 153
(to) **brush one's teeth** /ˌbrʌʃ wʌnz
ˈtiːθ/ sich die Zähne putzen p. 55, 7

budgie /'bʌdʒi/ Wellensittich p. 150

(to) **build** *(irr)* /bɪld/ bauen p. 96, 9

(to) burn *(irr)* /bɜːn/ (ver)brennen p. 88

burp /bɜːp/ Rülpser p. 108

busy /'bɪzi/ beschäftigt p. 85, 10

but /bʌt/ aber p. 7, 2

(to) **buy** *(irr)* /baɪ/ kaufen p. 20, 1

by /baɪ/ von; mit p. 101, 2

bye /baɪ/ tschüs(s) p. 8, 4

C

cage /keɪdʒ/ Käfig p. 15, 6

cake /keɪk/ Kuchen p. 75, 6

calculator /'kælkjʊˌleɪtə/ Taschenrechner p. 32, 1

calendar /'kælɪndə/ Kalender p. 95, 7

(to) **call** /kɔːl/ anrufen p. 68

phone call /'fəʊn kɔːl/ Telefonanruf p. 68

(to) **be called** /ˌbiː ˈkɔːld/ heißen, genannt werden p. 24, 8

can /kæn/ können p. 7, 1

can't (= cannot) /kɑːnt, ˈkænɒt/ nicht können p. 23, 6

candle /'kændl/ Kerze p. 92, 3

cap /kæp/ Mütze p. 76, 7

car /kɑː/ Auto p. 101, 2

card /kɑːd/ Karte p. 39, 17

care sheet /'keə ʃiːt/ Pflegeanleitung p. 137

carpet /'kɑːpɪt/ Teppich p. 158

carrot /'kærət/ Möhre; Karotte p. 12, 1

castle /'kɑːsl/ Burg; Schloss p. 27, 14

cat /kæt/ Katze p. 18, 14

cat food /'kæt fuːd/ Katzenfutter p. 137

(to) **catch** *(irr)* /kætʃ/ fangen p. 65, 10

shopping centre /'ʃɒpɪŋ ˌsentə/ Einkaufszentrum p. 21, 2

cereal /'sɪəriəl/ Frühstücksflocken p. 52, 1

chair /tʃeə/ Stuhl p. 36, 10

challenge /'tʃæləndʒ/ Herausforderung p. 39, 17

change /tʃeɪndʒ/ Wechselgeld p. 104, 6

chant /tʃɑːnt/ Sprechgesang p. 7, 2

character /'kærəktə/ *hier:* Figur p. 99, 14

cheaper /'tʃiːpə/ billiger p. 90

(to) **check** /tʃek/ überprüfen; kontrollieren p. 13, 1

(to) check out /ˌtʃekˈaʊt/ auschecken p. 10, 7

(to) check out *(informal)* /ˌtʃekˈaʊt/ sich ansehen; ausprobieren p. 72, 1

checklist /'tʃeklɪst/ Checkliste p. 32, 1

cheek /tʃiːk/ Wange p. 108

cheese /tʃiːz/ Käse p. 75, 6

cherry /'tʃeri/ Kirsche p. 156

chicken /'tʃɪkɪn/ Huhn p. 150

child *(pl* **children)** /tʃaɪld, 'tʃɪldrən/ Kind p. 8, 4

chilli con carne /ˌtʃɪli kɒn ˈkɑːni/ *Chili con Carne* p. 40, 1

chilli /'tʃɪli/ Chili; Peperoni; *auch:* Chilligericht p. 89

Chinese /ˌtʃaɪˈniːz/ Chinese / Chinesin; chinesisch p. 138

fish and chips /ˌfɪʃ_ən ˈtʃɪps/ *Fisch mit Pommes* p. 23, 6

chips *(pl)* /tʃɪps/ Pommes frites p. 40, 1

chocolate /'tʃɒklət/ Schokolade p. 7, 2

chocolate cake /'tʃɒklət keɪk/ Schokoladenkuchen p. 17, 10

chocolate spread /'tʃɒklət spred/ Schokoladenaufstrich p. 52, 1

(to) **choose** *(irr)* /tʃuːz/ wählen; sich entscheiden p. 10, 7

chore /tʃɔː/ lästige Aufgabe, Hausarbeit p. 71

chorus /'kɔːrəs/ Refrain p. 37, 13

cinema /'sɪnəmə/ Kino p. 20, 1

cinnamon /'sɪnəmən/ Zimt p. 70

city /'sɪti/ Stadt; Innenstadt p. 11

(to) clap one's hands /ˌklæp wʌnz ˈhændz/ in die Hände klatschen p. 7, 2

class /klɑːs/ Klasse; Unterrichtsstunde p. 16, 8

classmate /'klɑːsˌmeɪt/ Klassenkamerad/in, Mitschüler/in p. 10, 6

classroom /'klɑːsˌruːm/ Klassenzimmer p. 27, 14

claw /klɔː/ Kralle; Klaue p. 29

clean /kliːn/ sauber p. 83, 8

(to) **clean (up)** /kliːn, ˌkliːnˈʌp/ sauber machen p. 52, 1

cleaning /'kliːnɪŋ/ *hier:* beim Reinigen p. 80, 2

clever /'klevə/ klug; schlau p. 136

(to) **climb** /klaɪm/ auf etwas (hinauf)steigen; klettern p. 61, 3

climbing /'klaɪmɪŋ/ Klettern p. 126

climbing wall /'klaɪmɪŋ wɔːl/ Kletterwand p. 63, 7

clock /klɒk/ Uhr p. 34, 7

(to) **close** /kləʊz/ zumachen; schließen p. 7, 2

clothes *(pl)* /kləʊðz/ Kleider; Kleidung p. 20, 1

club /klʌb/ AG; Klub p. 20, 1

coffee /'kɒfi/ Kaffee p. 52, 1

cold /kəʊld/ kalt p. 36, 10

(to) **collect** /kəˈlekt/ sammeln p. 12, 1

colour /'kʌlə/ Farbe p. 7, 1

coloured pencil /ˌkʌləd ˈpensl/ Buntstift p. 154

(to) **comb** /kəʊm/ kämmen p. 55, 7

(to) **come** *(irr)* /kʌm/ kommen p. 21, 1

(to) **come back** /ˌkʌm ˈbæk/ zurückkommen p. 24, 8

Come on! *(informal)* /ˌkʌmˈɒn/ Komm(t) schon! p. 9, 5

command /kəˈmɑːnd/ Befehl p. 34, 6

competition /ˌkɒmpəˈtɪʃn/ Wettbewerb p. 83, 9

(to) **complete** /kəmˈpliːt/ vervollständigen p. 13, 2

comprehensive school /kɒmprɪˈhensɪv skuːl/ Gesamtschule p. 50

concert /'kɒnsət/ Konzert p. 30

conference /'kɒnfrəns/ Konferenz p. 28

console /'kɒnsəʊl/ Konsole p. 65, 10

contest /'kɒntest/ Wettbewerb p. 72, 1

(to) **cook** /kʊk/ kochen p. 43, 7

cooking /'kʊkɪŋ/ Kochen; Koch- p. 40, 1

(to) **do the cooking** /ˌduː ðə ˈkʊkɪŋ/ kochen p. 80, 1

the coolest /ðə ˈkuːlɪst/ der/die/das coolste p. 99, 14

(to) **copy** /'kɒpi/ abschreiben p. 46, 13

corner shop /'kɔːnə ʃɒp/ Laden an der Ecke; Tante-Emma-Laden p. 72, 1

correct /kə'rekt/ richtig, korrekt p. 22, 5; korrigieren p. 13, 1

(to) **cost (irr)** /kɒst/ kosten p. 26, 11

costume /'kɒstjuːm/ Kostüm p. 21, 1

could /kʊd/ könnte(st, n, t) p. 47, 15

country /'kʌntri/ Land p. 136

county /'kaʊnti/ Grafschaft; Bezirk p. 111

mini golf course /'mɪni gɒlf ˌkɔːs/ Minigolfanlage p. 157

court /kɔːt/ Platz p. 65, 10

cousin /'kʌzn/ Cousin/e p. 95, 8

(to) cover /'kʌvə/ bedecken p. 70

cow /kaʊ/ Kuh p. 90

crack /kræk/ Knacken p. 89

crack! /kræk/ *etwa:* knack! p. 109

(to) **crack open** /ˌkræk_'əʊpən/ aufbrechen p. 109

(to) do arts and crafts /ˌduː_ˌɑːts_ən 'krɑːfts/ basteln p. 61, 3

crazy /'kreɪzi/ verrückt; wahnsinnig p. 100, 1

(to) **create** /kri'eɪt/ erschaffen; erzeugen p. 45, 10

creative /kri'eɪtɪv/ kreativ p. 20, 1

creature /'kriːtʃə/ Kreatur; Lebewesen p. 111

credit card /'kredɪt kɑːd/ Kreditkarte p. 68

crisps *(pl)* /krɪsps/ Chips p. 75, 6

crocodile /'krɒkədaɪl/ Krokodil p. 150

cucumber /'kjuːˌkʌmbə/ Salatgurke p. 156

cup /kʌp/ Tasse p. 52, 1

customer /'kʌstəmə/ Kunde/Kundin p. 159

cute /kjuːt/ süß; niedlich p. 76, 7

D

dad /dæd/ Papa; Vati p. 12, 1

daily /'deɪli/ täglich p. 23, 7

(to) **dance** /dɑːns/ tanzen p. 60, 2

dancing /'dɑːnsɪŋ/ Tanzen p. 21, 1

dancing lesson /'dɑːnsɪŋ ˌlesn/ Tanzstunde p. 157

dangerous /'deɪndʒərəs/ gefährlich p. 88

date /deɪt/ Datum p. 97, 11

daughter /'dɔːtə/ Tochter p. 95, 8

day /deɪ/ Tag p. 24, 8

school day /'skuːl ˌdeɪ/ Schultag p. 35, 9

day out /ˌdeɪ_'aʊt/ *Ausflugstag* p. 91

day trip /'deɪ trɪp/ Tagesausflug p. 100, 1

dear /dɪə/ liebe/r *(Anrede)* p. 97, 10

December /dɪ'sembə/ Dezember p. 95, 7

(to) **decide** /dɪ'saɪd/ entscheiden; sich entscheiden p. 47, 15

(to) **decorate** /'dekəreɪt/ schmücken; dekorieren p. 20, 1

decoration /ˌdekə'reɪʃn/ Dekoration; Schmuck p. 96, 9

delicious /dɪ'lɪʃəs/ köstlich, lecker p. 89

(to) **describe** /dɪ'skraɪb/ beschreiben p. 26, 12

(to) **design** /dɪ'zaɪn/ entwerfen p. 45, 10

design /dɪ'zaɪn/ Entwurf; Design p. 76, 7

desk /desk/ Schreibtisch p. 36, 10

dessert /dɪ'zɜːt/ Nachtisch p. 40, 1

detail /'diːteɪl/ Detail; Einzelheit p. 79, 13

detailed /'diːteɪld/ detailliert, genau p. 137

(to) develop /dɪ'veləp/ erarbeiten; entwickeln p. 12, 1

dialogue /'daɪəlɒg/ Gespräch; Dialog p. 10, 7

diary /'daɪəri/ Tagebuch p. 102, 3

different /'dɪfrənt/ andere(r, s); verschiedene(r, s); anders p. 25, 10

difficult /'dɪfɪklt/ schwierig; schwer p. 48

(to) **dig (irr)** /dɪg/ graben p. 84, 10

dinner /'dɪnə/ Abendessen p. 57, 11

for dinner /fə 'dɪnə/ zum Abendessen p. 58, 13

dirty /'dɜːti/ dreckig; schmutzig p. 83, 8

dish /dɪʃ/ Gericht *(Speise)* p. 138

(to) empty /'empti/ ausleeren; ausräumen p. 86, 14

dishwasher /'dɪʃˌwɒʃə/ Spülmaschine p. 80, 2

(to) **display** /dɪ'spleɪ/ aushängen; zeigen p. 27, 14

divorced /dɪ'vɔːst/ geschieden p. 95, 8

(to) **do (irr)** /duː/ tun; machen p. 7, 2

(to) do a survey /ˌduː_ə 'sɜːveɪ/ eine Umfrage machen p. 139

(to) do arts and crafts /ˌduː_ˌɑːts_ən 'krɑːfts/ basteln p. 61, 3

(to) **do athletics** /ˌduː_æθ'letɪks/ Leichtathletik machen p. 61, 3

(to) **do gymnastics** /ˌduː dʒɪm'næstɪks/ **turnen** p. 61, 3

(to) **do research** /ˌduː rɪ'sɜːtʃ/ recherchieren p. 78, 11

(to) do sports /ˌduː 'spɔːts/ Sport treiben p. 30

(to) **do the cooking** /ˌduː ðə 'kʊkɪŋ/ kochen p. 80, 1

(to) **do the shopping** /ˌduː ðə 'ʃɒpɪŋ/ einkaufen p. 80, 1

dog /dɒg/ Hund p. 12, 1

(to) take a dog for a walk /ˌteɪk_ə ˌdɒg fər_ə 'wɔːk/ mit einem Hund Gassi gehen p. 80, 1

game of dominoes /ˌgeɪm_əv 'dɒmɪnəʊz/ Dominospiel p. 37, 12

Don't forget …! /ˌdəʊnt fə'get/ Vergiss nicht … / Vergesst nicht …! p. 32, 1

done /dʌn/ fertig; erledigt p. 76, 7

door /dɔː/ Tür p. 158

double /'dʌbl/ doppelt, Doppel- p. 36, 10

down /daʊn/ hinunter; (nach) unten p. 69

dragon /'drægən/ Drache p. 28

dragon tamer /'drægən ˌteɪmə/ Drachenzähmer/in p. 28

drama /'drɑːmə/ Theater-; Schauspiel- p. 40, 1

(to) **draw (irr)** /drɔː/ zeichnen p. 19, 15

dream /driːm/ Traum p. 33, 2

dress /dres/ Kleid p. 153

(to) **dress up** /ˌdres_'ʌp/ (sich) verkleiden p. 96, 9

drink /drɪŋk/ Trinken; Getränk p. 72, 1; trinken p. 52, 1

E

each /iːtʃ/ jede(r, s) p. 46, 14

each other /ˌiːtʃ_'ʌðə/ einander p. 56, 8

ear /ɪə/ Ohr p. 55, 7

(to) **earn** /ɜːn/ verdienen p. 90

earring /'ɪərɪŋ/ Ohrring p. 69
easy /'iːzi/ leicht; einfach p. 20, 1
(to) **eat** *(irr)* /iːt/ essen p. 46, 13
(to) **edit** /'edɪt/ bearbeiten p. 79, 13
egg /eg/ Ei p. 52, 1
elephant /'elɪfənt/ Elefant p. 150
else /els/ anders; sonst p. 43, 7
(to) **empty** /'empti/ ausleeren; ausräumen p. 80, 2
end /end/ Ende; Schluss p. 79, 13
in the end /ˌɪn ðiˑˌend/ am Ende, schließlich p. 24, 8
English /'ɪŋglɪʃ/ Englisch; englisch p. 27, 14
(to) **enjoy** /ɪn'dʒɔɪ/ genießen p. 104, 6
enough /ɪ'nʌf/ genug p. 41, 2
equipment /ɪ'kwɪpmənt/ Ausrüstung; Ausstattung p. 67, 13
eraser /ɪ'reɪzə/ Radiergummi p. 32, 1
erm *(informal)* /ɜːm/ ähm p. 76, 7
(to) **escape** /ɪ'skeɪp/ fliehen, entkommen p. 72, 1
Europe /'jʊərəp/ Europa p. 48
even /'iːvn/ selbst; sogar p. 12, 1
evening /'iːvnɪŋ/ Abend p. 15, 6
in the evening /ˌɪn ðiˑˌiːvnɪŋ/ am Abend p. 57, 11
in the evenings /ˌɪn ðiˑˌiːvnɪŋz/ abends p. 155
this evening /ðɪsˌiːvnɪŋ/ heute Abend p. 80, 1
event /ɪ'vent/ Ereignis; Veranstaltung p. 23, 7
ever /'evə/ jemals p. 99, 14
every /'evri/ jede(r, s) p. 15, 6
everybody /'evriˌbɒdi/ alle; jeder p. 37, 13
everyone /'evriwʌn/ alle; jeder p. 23, 7
everything /'evriθɪŋ/ alles p. 45, 11
everywhere /'evriweə/ überall p. 76, 7
example /ɪg'zɑːmpl/ Beispiel p. 62, 5
for example /fərˌɪg'zɑːmpl/ zum Beispiel p. 47, 15
excellent /'eksələnt/ ausgezeichnet p. 72, 1
exchange student /ɪks'tʃeɪndʒ ˌstjuːdnt/ Austauschschüler/in p. 45, 11

exciting /ɪk'saɪtɪŋ/ aufregend p. 33, 3
excuse /ɪk'skjuːs/ Entschuldigung p. 84, 10
Excuse me! /ɪk'skjuːz ˌmiː/ Entschuldigung! p. 36, 10
exercise book /'eksəsaɪz ˌbʊk/ Heft p. 32, 1
(to) **expect** /ɪk'spekt/ erwarten p. 97, 10
experience /ɪk'spɪəriəns/ Erfahrung p. 97, 9
experiment /ɪk'sperɪmənt/ Experiment; Versuch p. 40, 1
(to) **explain** /ɪk'spleɪn/ erklären p. 67, 13
extra /'ekstrə/ zusätzlich p. 72, 1
eye /aɪ/ Auge p. 7, 2
I spy with my little eye. /aɪ ˌspaɪ wɪð ˌmaɪ ˌlɪtlˌaɪ/ Ich sehe was, was du nicht siehst. p. 75, 6

F

face /feɪs/ Gesicht p. 96, 9
fact /fækt/ Tatsache; Fakt p. 65, 10
fact file /'fækt faɪl/ Steckbrief p. 27, 14
(to) **fall over** /ˌfɔːlˌəʊvə/ umfallen; *hier:* hinfallen p. 49
false /fɔːls/ falsch p. 13, 1
family /'fæmli/ Familie p. 12, 1
family tree /ˌfæmli 'triː/ Familienstammbaum p. 95, 8
famous /'feɪməs/ berühmt p. 22, 5
fantastic /fæn'tæstɪk/ fantastisch; super p. 105, 9
far /fɑː/ weit p. 100, 1
farm /fɑːm/ Bauernhof p. 90
farmhouse /'fɑːmˌhaʊs/ Bauernhaus p. 90
fast /fɑːst/ schnell p. 20, 1
the fastest /ðə 'fɑːstɪst/ der/die/das schnellste p. 97, 9
father /'fɑːðə/ Vater p. 95, 8
favourite /'feɪvrət/ Liebling; Lieblings- p. 12, 1
February /'februəri/ Februar p. 95, 7
(to) **feed** *(irr)* /fiːd/ füttern p. 150
feedback /'fiːdbæk/ Feedback; Rückmeldung p. 59, 15
feel *(irr)* /fiːl/ (sich) fühlen p. 111

smelly feet *(pl)* /ˌsmeli 'fiːt/ Stinkefüße p. 55, 7
felt-tip /'feltˌtɪp/ Filzstift p. 32, 1
field /fiːld/ Feld p. 65, 10
fiery /'faɪri/ glühend; brennend p. 49
fifth /fɪfθ/ fünfte(r, s) p. 95, 7
(to) **fill in** /ˌfɪlˌɪn/ eintragen, ausfüllen p. 26, 11
final /'faɪnl/ letzte(r, s); endgültig p. 59, 15
finally /'faɪnli/ schließlich; endlich p. 109
(to) **find** *(irr)* /faɪnd/ finden p. 14, 3
(to) **find out** /ˌfaɪndˌaʊt/ herausfinden p. 8, 4
fine /faɪn/ in Ordnung, gut p. 80, 1
(to) **finish** /'fɪnɪʃ/ beenden; enden p. 50
fire /'faɪə/ Feuer p. 29
first /fɜːst/ erste(r, s) p. 32, 1; zuerst p. 41, 2
fish and chip shop /ˌfɪʃ ən 'tʃɪp ʃɒp/ Fischimbiss p. 23, 6
fish and chips /ˌfɪʃ ən 'tʃɪps/ *Fisch mit Pommes* p. 23, 6
fish *(pl fish or fishes)* /fɪʃ, fɪʃ, fɪʃɪz/ Fisch p. 82, 7
(to) **fit** /fɪt/ passen p. 104, 6
flame /fleɪm/ Flamme p. 49
flat /flæt/ Wohnung p. 90
rented flat /ˌrentɪd 'flæt/ Mietwohnung p. 90
flavour /'fleɪvə/ Geschmacksrichtung p. 7, 2
flea market /'fliː ˌmɑːkɪt/ Flohmarkt p. 57, 11
(to) **flip** /flɪp/ wenden p. 70
floor /flɔː/ Fußboden p. 76, 7
flour /'flaʊə/ Mehl p. 70
flower /'flaʊə/ Blume p. 69
(to) **fly** *(irr)* /flaɪ/ fliegen p. 88
(to) fly at /ˌflaɪˌæt/ losgehen auf p. 49
(to) fly up /ˌflaɪˌʌp/ hochfliegen p. 49
(to) **focus on** /'fəʊkəsˌɒn/ sich konzentrieren auf p. 77, 10
folder /'fəʊldə/ Mappe; Ordner p. 32, 1
following /'fɒləʊɪŋ/ folgende(r, s) p. 113

food /fuːd/ Essen p. 7, 1

foot (pl **feet**) /fʊt, fiːt/ Fuß p. 7, 2

on foot /ˌɒn ˈfʊt/ zu Fuß p. 157

(to) stamp one's foot /ˌstæmp wʌnz ˈfʊt/ mit dem Fuß aufstampfen p. 7, 2

football /ˈfʊtˌbɔːl/ Fußball p. 15, 6

football ground /ˈfʊtˌbɔːl graʊnd/ Fußballplatz p. 63, 7

for /fɔː/ für p. 7, 2

for /fɔː/ hier: nach p. 69

for (+ Zeitraum) /fɔː/ ... lang p. 70

for a long time /fər‿ə ˈlɒŋ taɪm/ lange p. 49

for a moment /fər‿ə ˈməʊmənt/ einen Moment lang p. 88

for an hour /fər‿ən‿ˈaʊə/ eine Stunde lang p. 110

for another half hour /fər‿ə‿nʌðə haːf‿ˈaʊə/ noch eine halbe Stunde p. 80, 1

for breakfast /fə ˈbrekfəst/ zum Frühstück p. 52, 1

for dinner /fə ˈdɪnə/ zum Abendessen p. 58, 13

for example /fər‿ɪgˈzaːmpl/ zum Beispiel p. 47, 15

for lunch /fə ˈlʌntʃ/ zum Mittagessen p. 157

forest /ˈfɒrɪst/ Wald p. 29

(to) **forget** (irr) /fəˈget/ vergessen p. 32, 1

fork /fɔːk/ Gabel p. 52, 1

form /fɔːm/ Klasse p. 35, 9

form time /ˈfɔːm taɪm/ Klassenlehrerstunde p. 35, 9

fort /fɔːt/ Fort; Festung p. 96, 9

fourth /fɔːθ/ vierte(r, s) p. 95, 7

France /fraːns/ Frankreich p. 102, 4

free time /friː ˈtaɪm/ Freizeit p. 51

freezer /ˈfriːzə/ Gefrierschrank p. 75, 6

French /frentʃ/ Französisch p. 35, 9

adverb of frequency /ˌædvɜːb‿əv‿ˈfriːkwənsi/ Häufigkeitsadverb p. 82

Fri (= Friday) /ˈfraɪdeɪ/ Freitag p. 80, 1

Friday /ˈfraɪdeɪ/ Freitag p. 35, 9

(on) Fridays /ˈfraɪdeɪz/ freitags p. 45, 9

fridge /frɪdʒ/ Kühlschrank p. 75, 6

friend /frend/ Freund/in p. 8, 4

from /frɒm/ von; aus p. 8, 4

from all over the world /frəm‿ˌɔːl‿ˌəʊvə ðə ˈwɜːld/ aus der ganzen Welt p. 20, 1

at / in the front /æt / ˌɪn ðə ˈfrʌnt/ vorne p. 74, 5

in front of /ˌɪn ˈfrʌnt‿əv/ vor p. 75, 6

fruit /fruːt/ Frucht; Obst p. 52, 1

full /fʊl/ hier: vollständig p. 101, 1; voll; satt p. 136

fun /fʌn/ Spaß p. 80, 2

fun /fʌn/ lustig; witzig p. 79, 13

be fun /ˌbi ˈfʌn/ Spaß machen p. 20, 1

(to) **be (good/great) fun** /ˌbi ˌgʊd/ˌgreɪt ˈfʌn/ (viel/großen) Spaß machen p. 100, 1

funny /ˈfʌni/ lustig; komisch p. 15, 6

furniture /ˈfɜːnɪtʃə/ Möbel(stück) p. 77, 8

G

g (= gram) /græm/ Gramm p. 70

game /geɪm/ Spiel p. 12, 1

game of dominoes /ˌgeɪm‿əv ˈdɒmɪnəʊz/ Dominospiel p. 37, 12

gap /gæp/ Lücke p. 26, 11

garden /ˈgaːdn/ Garten p. 12, 1

genitive /ˈdʒenətɪv/ Genitiv p. 78, 11

geography /dʒiˈɒgrəfi/ Erdkunde p. 35, 9

German /ˈdʒɜːmən/ Deutsch; deutsch p. 17, 11

Germany /ˈdʒɜːməni/ Deutschland p. 102, 4

(to) **get** (irr) /get/ bekommen; holen; kaufen p. 24, 8

(to) **get** (irr) /get/ werden p. 111

(to) get into /ˌget‿ˈɪntʊ/ sich auseinandersetzen mit p. 65, 10; hier: bilden p. 97, 9; einsteigen in p. 110

(to) get ready /ˌget ˈredi/ sich fertig machen p. 7, 2

(to) **get together** /ˌget‿təˈgeðə/ zusammenkommen p. 9, 5

(to) **get up** /ˌget‿ˈʌp/ aufstehen p. 49

ghost story /ˈgəʊst ˌstɔːri/ Gespenstergeschichte p. 96, 9

girl /gɜːl/ Mädchen p. 33, 3

(to) **give** (irr) /gɪv/ geben p. 73, 2

(to) **give a presentation** /ˌgɪv‿ə ˌprezn̩ˈteɪʃn/ eine Präsentation halten p. 67, 13

glass /glaːs/ Glas p. 156

glove /glʌv/ Handschuh p. 153

glue /gluː/ Klebstoff p. 32, 1

(to) **go** (irr) /gəʊ/ gehen; fahren p. 8, 4

(to) go down /ˌgəʊ ˈdaʊn/ hinuntergehen p. 110

(to) go out /ˌgəʊ‿ˈaʊt/ hier: Gassi gehen; hinausgehen p. 55, 7

(to) go red /ˌgəʊ ˈred/ rot werden p. 108

(to) go to sleep /ˌgəʊ tə ˈsliːp/ einschlafen p. 49

(to) go swimming /ˌgəʊ ˈswɪmɪŋ/ schwimmen gehen p. 157

Here we go! /ˌhɪə wiː ˈgəʊ/ Jetzt geht's los! p. 68

goal /gəʊl/ Tor p. 65, 10

goal line /ˈgəʊl ˌlaɪn/ Ziellinie p. 65, 10

gold /gəʊld/ golden p. 69

golden brown /ˌgəʊldn ˈbraʊn/ goldbraun p. 70

goldfish (pl goldfish) /ˈgəʊldˌfɪʃ/ Goldfisch p. 150

good /gʊd/ gut p. 21, 2

I'm good, thanks. /aɪm ˈgʊd ˌθæŋks/ Es geht mir gut, danke. p. 44, 8

Good morning! /ˌgʊd ˈmɔːnɪŋ/ Guten Morgen! p. 33, 3

goodbye /gʊdˈbaɪ/ auf Wiedersehen p. 78, 12

(to) **say goodbye (to somebody)** /ˌseɪ gʊdˈbaɪ tə ˌsʌmbədi/ sich von jemandem verabschieden p. 79, 13

grammar /ˈgræmə/ Grammatik p. 14

granddaughter /ˈgrænˌdɔːtə/ Enkelin p. 95, 8

grandfather /ˈgrænˌfaːðə/ Großvater p. 95, 8

grandma (informal) /ˈgrænˌmaː/ Oma p. 30

grandmother /ˈgrænˌmʌðə/ Großmutter p. 95, 8

grandpa (informal) /ˈgrænˌpaː/ Opa p. 92, 3

grandparents (pl) /ˈgrænˌpeərənts/ Großeltern p. 160

grandson /ˈɡrænˌsʌn/ Enkel p. 95, 8

granny (informal) /ˈɡræni/ Oma, Omi p. 56, 8

(to) grate /ɡreɪt/ raspeln, reiben p. 70

great /ɡreɪt/ groß; großartig p. 8, 4

green /ɡriːn/ grün p. 7, 1

grey /ɡreɪ/ grau p. 153

ground /ɡraʊnd/ Boden p. 69

sports ground /ˈspɔːts ɡraʊnd/ Sportplatz p. 43, 7

group /ɡruːp/ Gruppe p. 9, 5

groups of five /ˌɡruːps əv ˈfaɪv/ Fünfergruppen p. 9, 5

(to) **guess** /ɡes/ (er)raten p. 61, 3

guessing game /ˈɡesɪŋ ˌɡeɪm/ Ratespiel p. 61, 3

guest /ɡest/ Gast p. 92, 3

guide /ɡaɪd/ Führer/in p. 111

guinea pig /ˈɡɪni ˌpɪɡ/ Meerschweinchen p. 150

guitar /ɡɪˈtɑː/ Gitarre p. 15, 6

(you) guys (pl, informal) /ɡaɪz/ Leute (umgangssprachl.) p. 23, 6

gym (= gymnasium) /dʒɪm, dʒɪmˈneɪziəm/ Turnhalle p. 40, 1

H

hair /heə/ Haar; Haare p. 55, 7

(to) style one's hair /ˌstaɪl wʌnz ˈheə/ sich frisieren p. 55, 7

half /hɑːf/ halb p. 33, 3

for another half hour /fər ə ˌnʌðə hɑːf ˈaʊə/ noch eine halbe Stunde p. 80, 1

half brother /ˈhɑːfˌbrʌðə/ Halbbruder p. 160

half sister /ˈhɑːfˌsɪstə/ Halbschwester p. 160

ham /hæm/ Schinken p. 156

(to) clap one's hands /ˌklæp wʌnz ˈhændz/ in die Hände klatschen p. 7, 2

(to) **happen** /ˈhæpən/ geschehen; passieren p. 35, 8

happy /ˈhæpi/ glücklich p. 91

Happy birthday (to you)! /ˌhæpi ˈbɜːθdeɪ tʊ juː/ Herzlichen Glückwunsch zum Geburtstag! p. 91

hard /hɑːd/ hart; anstrengend p. 90

hat /hæt/ Hut p. 153

(to) **hate** /heɪt/ hassen; nicht ausstehen können p. 12, 1

(to) **have (irr)** /hæv/ haben p. 8, 4; essen; trinken p. 56, 8

(to) have (irr) /hæv/ hier: machen p. 96, 9

(to) have a barbecue /ˌhæv ə ˈbɑːbɪkjuː/ grillen, eine Grillparty machen p. 92, 2

(to) have a look /ˌhæv ə ˈlʊk/ nachsehen p. 104, 6

(to) have breakfast /ˌhæv ˈbrekfəst/ frühstücken p. 138

(to) **have got** /ˌhæv ˈɡɒt/ haben p. 8, 4

(to) **have to** /ˈhæv tə/ müssen p. 65, 10

he /hiː/ er p. 8, 4

head /hed/ Kopf p. 109

heading /ˈhedɪŋ/ Überschrift; Titel p. 100, 1

headteacher /ˌhedˈtiːtʃə/ Schulleiter/in; Rektor/in p. 33, 3

(to) **hear (irr)** /hɪə/ hören p. 95, 7

(to) **heat** /hiːt/ erhitzen p. 70

heavy /ˈhevi/ schwer p. 76, 7

helicopter /ˈhelɪˌkɒptə/ Hubschrauber p. 29

hello /həˈləʊ/ hallo p. 10, 6

(to) say hello (to somebody) /ˌseɪ həˈləʊ tʊ ˌsʌmbədi/ jemanden (be)grüßen p. 44, 8

helmet /ˈhelmɪt/ Helm p. 96, 9

help /help/ Hilfe p. 32, 1; helfen p. 52, 1

her /hɜː/ ihr/ihre; sie p. 8, 4

here /hɪə/ hier; hierher p. 12, 1

over here /ˌəʊvə ˈhɪə/ hier (drüben) p. 152

Here we go! /ˌhɪə wiː ˈɡəʊ/ Jetzt geht's los! p. 68

Here you are! /ˌhɪə juː ˈɑː/ Hier, bitte! p. 36, 10

herself /həˈself/ sich (selbst) p. 49

hey there (informal) /ˈheɪ ðeə/ hallo p. 68

(to) say hi to somebody (informal) /ˌseɪ ˈhaɪ tʊ ˌsʌmbədi/ jemanden (be)grüßen p. 110

hi there (informal) /ˈhaɪ ðeə/ hallo p. 88

high /haɪ/ hoch p. 7, 2

ten-mile hike /ˌten maɪl ˈhaɪk/ Wanderung von zehn Meilen p. 17, 10

him /hɪm/ ihm, ihn p. 16, 8

his /hɪz/ sein; seine(r, s) p. 12, 1

history /ˈhɪstri/ Geschichte p. 35, 9

(to) **hit (irr)** /hɪt/ schlagen p. 65, 10

(to) **hold (irr)** /həʊld/ (fest)halten p. 97, 9

hole /həʊl/ Loch p. 84, 10

holiday(s) /ˈhɒlɪdeɪ(z)/ Ferien; Urlaub p. 106, 10

home /həʊm/ nach Hause p. 20, 1; zu Hause; daheim p. 80, 1

home /həʊm/ Zuhause; Haus p. 90

at home /ˌæt ˈhəʊm/ zu Hause p. 71

home town /ˈhəʊm ˌtaʊn/ Heimatstadt p. 101, 2

homework /ˈhəʊmwɜːk/ Hausaufgaben p. 17, 10

honey /ˈhʌni/ Honig p. 70

(to) **hope** /həʊp/ hoffen p. 33, 3

horse /hɔːs/ Pferd p. 90

(to) **ride a horse** /ˌraɪd ə ˈhɔːs/ reiten p. 61, 3

hot /hɒt/ heiß; scharf p. 48

hour /ˈaʊə/ Stunde p. 80, 1

for an hour /fər ən ˈaʊə/ eine Stunde lang p. 110

for another half hour /fər ə ˌnʌðə hɑːf ˈaʊə/ noch eine halbe Stunde p. 80, 1

house /haʊs/ Haus p. 7, 1

houseboat /ˈhaʊsˌbəʊt/ Hausboot p. 90

how /haʊ/ wie p. 8, 4

How about ...? /ˈhaʊ əˌbaʊt/ Was ist / Wie wäre es mit ...? p. 29

How are you? /ˌhaʊ ˈɑː jʊ/ Wie geht es dir / euch / Ihnen? p. 44, 8

How much is it? /ˌhaʊ mʌtʃ ˈɪz ɪt/ Wie viel kostet es? p. 27, 14

(to) **hug** /hʌɡ/ umarmen p. 97, 9

huge /hjuːdʒ/ riesig p. 49

hungry /ˈhʌŋɡri/ hungrig p. 12, 1

(to) **hurry (up)** /ˌhʌri ˈʌp/ sich beeilen p. 55, 7

(to) **hurt (irr)** /hɜːt/ wehtun; schmerzen p. 88

husband /ˈhʌzbənd/ Ehemann p. 95, 8

I

I /aɪ/ ich p. 7, 1

I can't wait! /ˌaɪ ˌkɑːnt ˈweɪt/ Ich kann es nicht erwarten! p. 23, 6

I don't know. /ˌaɪ ˌdəʊnt ˈnəʊ/ Ich weiß es nicht. p. 41, 2

I don't like … /ˌaɪ ˈdəʊnt laɪk/ Ich mag … nicht. p. 24, 8

I'd like … /ˌaɪd ˈlaɪk/ ich hätte gern … p. 159

I'd love to … /ˌaɪd ˈlʌv tə/ Ich würde sehr gern … p. 100, 1

I'll (= I will) /aɪl, ˈaɪ wɪl/ ich werde p. 68

I'm (= I am) /aɪm, ˈaɪ_æm/ ich bin, ich heiße p. 8, 4

I'm good, thanks. /aɪm ˈɡʊd ˌθæŋks/ Es geht mir gut, danke. p. 44, 8

ice cream /ˈaɪs ˌkriːm/ Eis p. 7, 2

ice cream van /ˈaɪs kriːm ˌvæn/ Eiswagen p. 7, 3

ice hockey /ˈaɪs ˌhɒki/ Eishockey p. 157

ice rink /ˈaɪs rɪŋk/ Schlittschuh-bahn p. 63, 7

(to) ice-skate /ˈaɪs ˌskeɪt/ Schlittschuh laufen p. 61, 3

ICT (= Information and Communication Technology) /ˌaɪ siː ˈtiː, ˌɪnfəˈmeɪʃn_ən kəˌmjuːnɪˈkeɪʃn tekˌnɒlədʒi/ Informatik (Schulfach) p. 35, 9

ID (= identification) /ˌaɪˈdiː, aɪˌdentɪfɪˈkeɪʃn/ Ausweis p. 28

idea /aɪˈdɪə/ Idee p. 24, 8; Vorstellung p. 57, 11

identity /aɪˈdentɪti/ Identität p. 28

if /ɪf/ wenn; falls p. 7, 2; ob p. 67, 13

(to) imagine /ɪˈmædʒɪn/ sich etwas vorstellen p. 58, 13

imperative /ɪmˈperətɪv/ Imperativ; Befehlsform p. 34

important /ɪmˈpɔːtnt/ wichtig p. 33, 3

in /ɪn/ in; auf p. 7, 1

in front of /ˌɪn ˈfrʌnt_əv/ vor p. 75, 6

in the afternoon /ˌɪn ðiˌɑːftəˈnuːn/ am Nachmittag p. 33, 3

in the afternoons /ˌɪn ðiˌɑːftəˈnuːnz/ nachmittags p. 155

in the back /ˌɪn ðə ˈbæk/ hinten p. 75, 6

in the end /ˌɪn ðiˈend/ am Ende, schließlich p. 24, 8

in the evening /ˌɪn ðiˈiːvnɪŋ/ am Abend p. 54, 5

in the evenings /ˌɪn ðiˈiːvnɪŋz/ abends p. 155

in the front /ˌɪn ðə ˈfrʌnt/ vorne p. 75, 6

in the morning /ˌɪn ðə ˈmɔːnɪŋ/ am Morgen p. 54

in the mornings /ˌɪn ðə ˈmɔːnɪŋz/ morgens p. 155

in there /ˌɪn ˈðeə/ darin p. 68

in time /ɪn ˈtaɪm/ rechtzeitig; pünktlich p. 108

Indian /ˈɪndiən/ indisch p. 56, 8

indoor /ˈɪnˌdɔː/ Hallen- p. 23, 7

indoor skate park /ˌɪndɔː ˈskeɪt pɑːk/ Hallenskatepark p. 8, 4

indoors /ˌɪnˈdɔːz/ drinnen, im Haus p. 24, 8

information *(no pl)* /ˌɪnfəˈmeɪʃn/ Informationen p. 18, 13

inside /ˈɪnˌsaɪd/ innerhalb p. 65, 10

inspiring /ɪnˈspaɪərɪŋ/ inspirierend, anregend p. 50

instead /ɪnˈsted/ stattdessen p. 111

interesting /ˈɪntrəstɪŋ/ interessant p. 21, 2

searching the Internet /ˌsɜːtʃɪŋ ðiˈɪntənet/ Suchen im Internet p. 64, 9

(to) interview /ˈɪntəˌvjuː/ interviewen, befragen p. 47, 15

into /ˈɪntuː/ in p. 46, 13

(to) introduce /ˌɪntrəˈdjuːs/ einführen; vorstellen p. 79, 13

introduction /ˌɪntrəˈdʌkʃn/ Einleitung p. 79, 13

invitation /ˌɪnvɪˈteɪʃn/ Einladung p. 92, 3

(to) invite /ɪnˈvaɪt/ einladen p. 97, 10

it /ɪt/ es p. 8, 4

it's (= it is) /ɪts, ˈɪt_ɪz/ *hier:* es kostet p. 23, 6

Italy /ˈɪtəli/ Italien p. 102, 4

its /ɪts/ sein(e), ihr(e) *(sächlich)* p. 78, 12

J

jacket /ˈdʒækɪt/ Jacke p. 153

jam /dʒæm/ Marmelade p. 52, 1

January /ˈdʒænjuəri/ Januar p. 95, 7

Japanese /ˌdʒæpəˈniːz/ Japaner/in; japanisch p. 24, 8

jaw /dʒɔː/ Kiefer p. 29

job /dʒɒb/ Aufgabe p. 78, 11

(to) join /dʒɔɪn/ mitmachen (bei) p. 40, 1

juice /dʒuːs/ Saft p. 52, 1

July /dʒʊˈlaɪ/ Juli p. 95, 7

(to) jump /dʒʌmp/ springen p. 7, 2

(to) jump up /ˌdʒʌmp_ˈʌp/ aufspringen p. 49

jumper /ˈdʒʌmpə/ Pullover p. 153

June /dʒuːn/ Juni p. 92, 3

just /dʒʌst/ nur; bloß p. 55, 7

just /dʒʌst/ gerade p. 70; genau p. 110

Just a minute. /ˌdʒʌst_ə ˈmɪnɪt/ Einen Moment. p. 104, 6

K

(to) keep *(irr)* /kiːp/ halten; behalten; aufbewahren p. 65, 10

keyword /ˈkiːˌwɜːd/ Schlüsselwort, Stichwort p. 92, 3

(to) kick /kɪk/ treten p. 65, 10

kid /kɪd/ Kind p. 20, 1

kind /kaɪnd/ Art; Sorte p. 65, 10

kitchen /ˈkɪtʃən/ Küche p. 40, 1

knee /niː/ Knie p. 153

knife /naɪf/ Messer p. 52, 1

(to) know *(irr)* /nəʊ/ wissen; kennen p. 17, 9

I don't know. /ˌaɪ ˌdəʊnt ˈnəʊ/ Ich weiß es nicht. p. 41, 2

L

lab (= laboratory) /læb, ləˈbɒrətri/ Labor p. 24, 8

(to) label /ˈleɪbl/ beschriften p. 37, 11

lake /leɪk/ See p. 101, 2

lamp /læmp/ Lampe p. 76, 7

(to) land /lænd/ landen p. 110

language /ˈlæŋɡwɪdʒ/ Sprache p. 78, 12

large /lɑːdʒ/ groß p. 88

last /lɑːst/ letzte(r, s) p. 100, 1

late /leɪt/ (zu) spät p. 36, 10

(to) stay up (late) /ˌsteɪ_ˌʌp ˈleɪt/ lange aufbleiben p. 57, 11

later /ˈleɪtə/ später p. 55, 7

(to) laugh /lɑːf/ lachen p. 108

(to) **leave** *(irr)* /liːv/ weggehen
p. 55, 7

(to) leave *(irr)* /liːv/ verlassen;
zurücklassen p. 110

on the left /ˌɒn ðə ˈleft/ links, auf
der linken Seite p. 76, 7

leg /leg/ Bein p. 153

lemon /ˈlemən/ Zitrone p. 7, 2

lemonade /ˌleməˈneɪd/ Limonade
p. 73, 2

lesson /ˈlesn/ Stunde; Unterricht
p. 23, 7

(to) **let** *(irr)* /let/ lassen p. 7, 2

(to) let out /ˌletˈ_aʊt/ herauslassen
p. 108

let's (= let us) /lets, ˈletˌ_əs/ lass(t)
uns … p. 7, 2

letter /ˈletə/ Buchstabe p. 25, 9

level /ˈlevl/ Stufe; Level p. 13, 2

library /ˈlaɪbrəri/ Bücherei p. 40, 1

(to) lie down /ˌlaɪ ˈdaʊn/ sich
hinlegen p. 49

life /laɪf/ Leben p. 31

light /laɪt/ Licht p. 96, 9

light /laɪt/ hell p. 48

like /laɪk/ wie p. 65, 10; mögen p. 7, 2

I would like … (= I'd like …)
/aɪ ˌwʊd ˈlaɪk, aɪd ˈlaɪk/ Ich würde
gern … / Ich hätte gern … p. 97, 10

What is … like? /ˌwɒtˌɪz … ˈlaɪk/
Wie ist …? p. 138

what it is like /ˌwɒtˌɪtˌɪz ˈlaɪk/
wie es ist p. 107, 13

… would like /ˌwʊd ˈlaɪk/ … würde
gern … / … hätte gern … p. 115

(to) **like best** /ˌlaɪk ˈbest/ am
liebsten mögen p. 43, 7

(to) **like better** /ˌlaɪk ˈbetə/ lieber
mögen p. 114

(to) like doing something /laɪk
ˈduːɪŋ ˌsʌmθɪŋ/ etwas gern tun p. 30

(to) like something very much
/ˌlaɪk ˌsʌmθɪŋ ˌveri ˈmʌtʃ/ etwas
sehr gern mögen p. 30

like that /ˌlaɪk ˈðæt/ so p. 80, 2

like this /ˌlaɪk ˈðɪs/ so p. 91

limit /ˈlɪmɪt/ (Höchst)grenze; Limit
p. 99, 14

line /laɪn/ Linie; Zeile p. 65, 10

lion /ˈlaɪən/ Löwe p. 150

list /lɪst/ Liste p. 16, 8; auflisten
p. 73, 1

(to) **listen (to)** /ˈlɪsn/ zuhören,
anhören p. 7, 2

listening /ˈlɪsnɪŋ/ Hören p. 16, 7

little /ˈlɪtl/ klein p. 8, 4

a (little) bit /ə ˌlɪtl ˈbɪt/ ein kleines
bisschen p. 70

the little one /ðə ˈlɪtl wʌn/ Kleines
p. 49

(to) **live** /lɪv/ leben; wohnen p. 8, 4

living room /ˈlɪvɪŋ ˌruːm/
Wohnzimmer p. 80, 2

(to) **load** /ləʊd/ laden p. 80, 2

long /lɒŋ/ lang p. 14

for a long time /fərˌə ˈlɒŋ taɪm/
lange p. 49

(to) **look** /lʊk/ aussehen p. 44, 8

(to) look /lʊk/ *hier:* suchen p. 68

(to) **look after** /ˌlʊkˈ_ɑːftə/ sich
kümmern um; aufpassen auf
p. 84, 10

(to) **look around** /ˌlʊkˌəˈraʊnd/
sich umsehen p. 69

(to) **look (at)** /ˈlʊkˌət/ (an)sehen,
(an)schauen p. 9, 5

(to) **look for** /ˈlʊk fə/ suchen nach
p. 84, 10

(to) look up (at) /ˌlʊkˈ_ʌp/ hoch-
schauen, hinaufsehen (zu) p. 49

(to) have a look /ˌhævˌə ˈlʊk/
nachsehen p. 104, 6

a lot /ə ˈlɒt/ viel, sehr; oft p. 44, 8

a lot (of) /ə ˈlɒt/ viel(e), jede
Menge p. 12, 1

thanks a lot /ˌθæŋksˌə ˈlɒt/ vielen
Dank p. 75, 6

lots of /ˈlɒtsˌəv/ viel(e) p. 7, 2

loud /laʊd/ laut p. 15, 6

(to) **love** /lʌv/ lieben, sehr mögen
p. 12, 1

(to) **love doing something** /lʌv
ˈduːɪŋ ˌsʌmθɪŋ/ etwas sehr gern
tun p. 15, 6

I'd love to … /aɪd ˈlʌv tə/ Ich würde
sehr gern … p. 100, 1

love /lʌv/ viele Grüße; alles Liebe
(in Briefen) p. 80, 1

luck /lʌk/ Glück p. 110

lunch /lʌntʃ/ Mittagessen p. 33, 3

for lunch /fə ˈlʌntʃ/ zum
Mittagessen p. 157

lunchbox /ˈlʌntʃbɒks/ Frühstücks-
dose p. 36, 10

lunchtime /ˈlʌntʃtaɪm/ Mittagszeit;
Mittagspause p. 40, 1

M

M (= medium) /em, ˈmiːdiəm/
mittel(groß) p. 104, 6

main /meɪn/ Haupt- p. 79, 13

main (course) /ˈmeɪn kɔːs/
Hauptgericht p. 40, 1

(to) **make** *(irr)* /meɪk/ machen p. 16, 8

(to) make *(irr)* /meɪk/ *hier:*
ausmachen p. 138

(to) **make notes** /ˌmeɪk ˈnəʊts/
sich Notizen machen p. 19, 15

(to) **make sure** /ˌmeɪk ˈʃɔː/ darauf
achten, dass p. 80, 1

(to) **make up** /ˌmeɪkˈ_ʌp/ erfinden,
sich ausdenken p. 55, 7

man (*pl* **men**) /mæn, men/ Mann
p. 95, 8

many /ˈmeni/ viele p. 20, 1

map /mæp/ Karte p. 36, 10

maple syrup /ˌmeɪpl ˈsɪrəp/
Ahornsirup p. 70

March /mɑːtʃ/ März p. 95, 7

market /ˈmɑːkɪt/ Markt p. 20, 1

match /mætʃ/ Spiel p. 40, 1

(to) **match (with/to)** /mætʃ/
zuordnen p. 22, 3

matching /ˈmætʃɪŋ/ zusammen-
passend p. 14, 3

maths *(informal)* /mæθ/ Mathe
(Schulfach) p. 35, 9

mattress /ˈmætrəs/ Matratze p. 96, 9

May /meɪ/ Mai p. 92, 3

maybe /ˈmeɪbi/ vielleicht p. 21, 1

me, to me /miː, tə ˈmiː/ mir; mich;
ich p. 11

meal /miːl/ Mahlzeit; Essen
p. 57, 11

(to) **mean** *(irr)* /miːn/ meinen;
bedeuten p. 29

the media /ðə ˈmiːdiə/ die Medien
p. 136

mediation /ˌmiːdiˈeɪʃn/ Sprach-
mittlung; Mediation p. 17, 11

(to) **meet** *(irr)* /miːt/ treffen; sich
treffen p. 12, 1

Nice to meet you. /ˌnaɪs tə ˈmiːt
jə/ Schön, dich / euch / Sie zu
treffen. p. 9, 5

melon /ˈmelən/ Melone p. 75, 6

(to) melt /melt/ schmelzen p. 70

member /'membə/ Mitglied p. 78, 11

menu /'menju:/ Speisekarte; Menü p. 10, 7

mess /mes/ Unordnung p. 92, 3

(to) be a mess /ˌbi_ə 'mes/ unordentlich sein p. 76, 7

message /'mesɪdʒ/ Nachricht; Botschaft p. 56, 9

messy /'mesi/ unordentlich p. 76, 7

the messy one /ðə 'mesi wʌn/ der / die / das Unordentliche p. 76, 7

miaow /mi'aʊ/ miau p. 108

middle /'mɪdl/ Mitte p. 65, 10

milk /mɪlk/ Milch p. 52, 1

(to) mime /maɪm/ mimen, pantomimisch darstellen p. 34, 6

mini golf course /'mɪni gɒlf ˌkɔ:s/ Minigolfanlage p. 63, 7

Just a minute. /ˌdʒʌst_ə 'mɪnɪt/ Einen Moment. p. 104, 6

(to) **miss** /mɪs/ vermissen; verpassen p. 44, 8

missing /'mɪsɪŋ/ fehlend p. 25, 9

mission /'mɪʃn/ Einsatz p. 29

mistake /mɪ'steɪk/ Fehler p. 137

(to) mix /mɪks/ (ver)mischen p. 70

mixed /mɪkst/ gemischt p. 50

mixture /'mɪkstʃə/ Mischung p. 70

ml (= millilitre) /'mɪlɪˌli:tə/ Milliliter p. 70

modelling /'mɒdlɪŋ/ Modeln p. 72, 1

for a moment /fər_ə 'məʊmənt/ einen Moment lang p. 88

Monday /'mʌndeɪ/ Montag p. 35, 9

(on) Mondays /'mʌndeɪz/ montags p. 40, 1

money /'mʌni/ Geld p. 73, 2

monkey /'mʌŋki/ Affe p. 150

month /mʌnθ/ Monat p. 40, 1

moon /mu:n/ Mond p. 96, 9

more /mɔ:/ mehr; weitere p. 10, 7

morning /'mɔ:nɪŋ/ Morgen p. 33, 3

in the morning /ɪn ðə 'mɔ:nɪŋ/ am Morgen p. 54

in the mornings /ˌɪn ðə 'mɔ:nɪŋz/ morgens p. 155

most /məʊst/ die meisten; am meisten p. 29

mother /'mʌðə/ Mutter p. 86, 13

mountain /'maʊntɪn/ Berg p. 101, 2

the mountains *(pl)* /ðə 'maʊntɪnz/ Gebirge p. 29

mouse (*pl* mice) /maʊs, maɪs/ Maus p. 150

mouth /maʊθ/ Mund p. 153

move /mu:v/ Bewegung p. 7, 2

(to) move /mu:v/ sich bewegen; bewegen p. 90

movement /'mu:vmənt/ Bewegung p. 48

Mr /'mɪstə/ Herr *(Anrede)* p. 33, 3

Mrs /'mɪsɪz/ Frau *(Anrede)* p. 40, 1

much /mʌtʃ/ viel p. 23, 7

(to) like something very much /laɪk ˌsʌmθɪŋ ˌveri 'mʌtʃ/ etwas sehr gern mögen p. 30

muesli /'mju:zli/ Müsli p. 138

mum /mʌm/ Mama; Mutti p. 12, 1

music /'mju:zɪk/ Musik p. 15, 6

musician /mjʊ'zɪʃn/ Musiker/in p. 30

must /mʌst/ müssen p. 48

my /maɪ/ mein(e) p. 8, 4

N

(to) **name** /neɪm/ (be)nennen p. 35, 9

nature /'neɪtʃə/ Natur p. 24, 8

near /nɪə/ nahe, in der Nähe von p. 83, 8

nearly /'nɪəli/ fast; beinahe p. 28

necessary /'nesəsri/ notwendig, erforderlich p. 79, 13

(to) **need** /ni:d/ brauchen p. 40, 1

(to) **need to** /'ni:d_tə/ müssen p. 55, 7

neighbourhood /'neɪbəˌhʊd/ Viertel; Nachbarschaft p. 11

nervous /'nɜ:vəs/ nervös p. 32, 1

net /net/ Netz p. 65, 10

never /'nevə/ nie, niemals p. 15, 6

new /nju:/ neu p. 8, 4

New Zealand /ˌnju: 'zi:lənd/ Neuseeland p. 28

news *(no pl)* /nju:z/ Neuigkeit; Nachrichten p. 88

newspaper /'nju:zˌpeɪpə/ Zeitung p. 28

next /nekst/ nächste(r, s) p. 32, 1

the next one /ðə 'nekst wʌn/ der / die / das nächste p. 100, 1

next time /'nekst_taɪm/ nächstes Mal p. 24, 8

next to /'nekst_tə/ neben p. 75, 6

nice /naɪs/ schön; nett p. 24, 8

nice /naɪs/ *hier:* lecker p. 108

Nice to meet you. /ˌnaɪs tə 'mi:t jə/ Schön, dich / euch / Sie zu treffen. p. 9, 5

no /nəʊ/ kein(e) p. 19, 15; nein p. 21, 2

(to) nod /nɒd/ nicken p. 109

normally /'nɔ:mli/ normalerweise p. 29

north /nɔ:θ/ nördlich, Nord- p. 30

North Wales /ˌnɔ:θ 'weɪlz/ Nordwales p. 111

Northern Ireland /ˌnɔ:ðən_'aɪələnd/ Nordirland p. 111

nose /nəʊz/ Nase p. 7, 2

not /nɒt/ nicht p. 12, 1

not any /ˌnɒt_'eni/ kein(e) p. 105, 9

note /nəʊt/ Nachricht; Notiz p. 19, 15

notepad /'nəʊtˌpæd/ Notizblock p. 32, 1

nothing /'nʌθɪŋ/ nichts p. 49

noticeboard /'nəʊtɪsˌbɔ:d/ Schwarzes Brett p. 33, 3

noun /naʊn/ Hauptwort; Substantiv; Nomen p. 38, 14

November /nəʊ'vembə/ November p. 95, 7

now /naʊ/ jetzt p. 8, 4

number /'nʌmbə/ Zahl; Nummer; Anzahl p. 9, 4

phone number /'fəʊn ˌnʌmbə/ Telefonnummer p. 8, 4

O

o'clock /ə'klɒk/ Uhr *(bei Nennung einer Uhrzeit)* p. 24, 8

oats *(only plural)* /əʊts/ Haferflocken p. 70

observation tower /ˌɒbzə'veɪʃn ˌtaʊə/ Aussichtsturm p. 103, 5

October /ɒk'təʊbə/ Oktober p. 95, 7

odd one out /ˌɒd wʌn_'aʊt/ *Wort, das nicht zu den anderen passt* p. 18, 14

of /əv/ von; aus p. 9, 5

Of course! /əv 'kɔ:s/ Natürlich! p. 75, 6

office /'ɒfɪs/ Büro p. 33, 3

official /ə'fɪʃl/ offiziell p. 68

often /'ɒfn/ oft; häufig p. 73, 3

oh dear /əʊ 'dɪə/ oje p. 108

old /əʊld/ alt p. 8, 4

on /ɒn/ auf; an; in p. 10, 7

on /ɒn/ *hier:* mit p. 20, 1; *hier:* über p. 57, 11; *hier:* zu p. 137

on foot /ˌɒn 'fʊt/ zu Fuß p. 157

What's on? *(informal)* /ˌwɒts‿'ɒn/ Was ist los? p. 40, 1

on one's own /ˌɒn ˌwʌnz‿'əʊn/ allein p. 67, 13

on the left /ˌɒn ðə 'left/ links, auf der linken Seite p. 76, 7

on the right /ˌɒn ðə 'raɪt/ rechts, auf der rechten Seite p. 76, 7

on time /ˌɒn 'taɪm/ pünktlich p. 33, 3

once more /ˌwʌns 'mɔː/ noch einmal p. 37, 13

one /wʌn/ ein(e); eins p. 7, 2

the next one /ðə 'nekst wʌn/ der / die / das nächste p. 100, 1

onion /'ʌnjən/ Zwiebel p. 75, 6

only /'əʊnli/ nur; erst p. 23, 6; einzige(r, s) p. 23, 7

onto /'ɒntə/ auf, in p. 110

oops *(informal)* /uːps/ hoppla p. 93, 3

open /'əʊpən/ offen; geöffnet p. 23, 7

(to) **open** /'əʊpən/ öffnen; aufmachen p. 34, 5

opposite /'ɒpəzɪt/ Gegenteil p. 66, 12

or /ɔː/ oder p. 9, 4

orange /'ɒrɪndʒ/ orange p. 153; Orange; Apfelsine p. 38, 14

order /'ɔːdə/ Reihenfolge p. 155

origin /'ɒrɪdʒɪn/ Ursprung; Herkunft p. 48

other /'ʌðə/ andere(r, s) p. 65, 10

ouch /aʊtʃ/ aua, autsch p. 88

our /aʊə/ unser(e) p. 12, 1

out /aʊt/ heraus, hinaus; aus p. 65, 10

out of /'aʊt‿əv/ aus; außerhalb p. 96, 9

outdoors /ˌaʊt'dɔːz/ draußen; im Freien p. 47, 15

outside /ˌaʊt'saɪd/ außen; (nach) draußen p. 46, 14

over /'əʊvə/ über, hinüber; vorbei p. 21, 1

all over the world /ˌɔːl‿ˌəʊvə ðə 'wɜːld/ auf der ganzen Welt p. 136

over here /ˌəʊvə 'hɪə/ hier (drüben) p. 152

over there /ˌəʊvə 'ðeə/ dort (drüben) p. 23, 6

own /əʊn/ eigene(r, s) p. 33, 4

on one's own /ˌɒn ˌwʌnz‿'əʊn/ allein p. 67, 13

P

p (= penny, *pl* **pence)** /piː, 'peni, pens/ Penny *(brit. Währung)* p. 104, 6

(to) **pack** /pæk/ packen p. 32, 1

packet /'pækɪt/ Packung p. 75, 6

paddle /'pædl/ Paddel; paddeln p. 111

page /peɪdʒ/ Seite p. 10, 7

(to) **paint** /peɪnt/ (an)malen p. 72, 1

painting /'peɪntɪŋ/ Bild; Gemälde p. 27, 14

pair /peər/ Paar p. 153

a pair of shoes /ə ˌpeər‿əv 'ʃuː z/ ein Paar Schuhe p. 153

(a pair of) trousers /ə ˌpeər‿əv 'traʊzəz/ Hose p. 44, 8

pan /pæn/ Pfanne p. 70

pancake /'pæn‿keɪk/ Pfannkuchen p. 57, 11

paper /'peɪpə/ Papier p. 137

paradise /'pærədaɪs/ Paradies p. 23, 7

skater's paradise /ˌskeɪtəz 'pærədaɪs/ *Paradies für Skater* p. 23, 7

parents *(pl)* /'peərənts/ Eltern p. 80, 1

parrot /'pærət/ Papagei p. 150

part /pɑːt/ Teil p. 11

(to) **pass** /pɑːs/ geben, herüberreichen p. 52, 1

past /pɑːst/ nach p. 32, 1; Vergangenheit p. 106, 10

patient /'peɪʃnt/ geduldig p. 28

(to) **pay** *(irr)* /peɪ/ (be)zahlen p. 75, 6

PE (= Physical Education) /ˌpiː 'iː, ˌfɪzɪkl‿edjʊ'keɪʃn/ Sport *(Schulfach)* p. 35, 9

(to) **peel** /piːl/ schälen p. 70

pen /pen/ Stift p. 32, 1

pencil /'pensl/ Bleistift p. 32, 1

pencil case /'pensl ˌkeɪs/ Federmäppchen p. 32, 1

pencil sharpener /'pensl ˌʃaːpnə/ Bleistiftspitzer p. 32, 1

people /'piːpl/ Leute; Menschen p. 7, 1

pepper /'pepə/ Pfeffer p. 70

per /pɜː/ pro p. 23, 7

perfect /'pɜːfɪkt/ perfekt p. 53, 3

perfection /pə'fekʃn/ Perfektion p. 55, 7

(to) **perform** /pə'fɔːm/ spielen p. 30

personal /'pɜːsnəl/ persönlich p. 20, 1

pet /pet/ Haustier p. 16, 8

pet shop /'pet ʃɒp/ Tierhandlung p. 136

phew *(informal)* /fjuː/ puh p. 108

phone /fəʊn/ Telefon p. 14, 4

phone call /'fəʊn kɔːl/ Telefonanruf p. 68

phone number /'fəʊn ˌnʌmbə/ Telefonnummer p. 8, 4

photo /'fəʊtəʊ/ Foto p. 20, 1

(to) **take a photo** /ˌteɪk‿ə 'fəʊtəʊ/ ein Foto machen p. 97, 9

phrase /freɪz/ Satz; Ausdruck p. 38, 15

piano /pi'ænəʊ/ Klavier p. 61, 3

(to) **pick up** /ˌpɪk‿'ʌp/ aufheben; abholen p. 56, 8

picture /'pɪktʃə/ Bild p. 9, 5

(to) **take a picture** /ˌteɪk‿ə 'pɪktʃə/ ein Foto machen p. 19, 15

apple pie /'æpl ˌpaɪ/ gedeckter Apfelkuchen p. 40, 1

pig /pɪg/ Schwein p. 150

pillow /'pɪləʊ/ Kissen p. 96, 9

pillow fight /'pɪləʊ faɪt/ Kissenschlacht p. 96, 9

pink /pɪŋk/ rosa, pink p. 99, 14

place /pleɪs/ Ort; Platz p. 11; *hier:* Haus, Zuhause p. 80, 1

(to) **place** /pleɪs/ platzieren; stellen p. 39, 17

all over the place /ˌɔːl‿ˌəʊvə ðə 'pleɪs/ überall p. 76, 7

(to) **plan** /plæn/ planen p. 56, 8

planner /'plænə/ Kalender p. 56, 8

planning /'plænɪŋ/ Planen p. 99, 14

plate /pleɪt/ Teller p. 52, 1

(to) **play** /pleɪ/ spielen p. 15, 6

player /ˈpleɪə/ Spieler/in p. 39, 17

playground /ˈpleɪˌɡraʊnd/
Spielplatz p. 21, 2

playing /ˈpleɪɪŋ/ Spielen p. 12, 1

please /pliːz/ bitte p. 32, 1

pm (= post meridiem) /ˌpiːˈem,
ˌpəʊst məˈrɪdiəm/ nachmittags;
abends *(nur hinter Uhrzeit
zwischen 12 Uhr mittags und
Mitternacht)* p. 32, 1

poem /ˈpəʊɪm/ Gedicht p. 17, 10

point /pɔɪnt/ Punkt p. 65, 10

(to) **point (at/to)** /pɔɪnt/ deuten
(auf); zeigen (auf) p. 7, 3

Poland /ˈpəʊlənd/ Polen p. 92, 3

policeman *(pl policemen)*
/pəˈliːsmən/ Polizist p. 29

poor /pɔː/ arm p. 108

porridge /ˈpɒrɪdʒ/ Haferbrei p. 70

possessive determiner /pəˌzesɪv
dɪˈtɜːmɪnə/ Possessivbegleiter
p. 78, 11

postcard /ˈpəʊstˌkɑːd/ Postkarte;
Ansichtskarte p. 104, 6

pound (= £) /paʊnd/ Pfund
(britische Währung) p. 23, 6

pour /pɔː/ gießen, schütten p. 70

(to) **practise** /ˈpræktɪs/ üben;
trainieren p. 40, 1

(to) **prepare** /prɪˈpeə/ vorbereiten
p. 47, 15

(to) **prepare** /prɪˈpeə/ zubereiten
p. 138

(to) **be prepared** /ˌbiː prɪˈpeəd/
vorbereitet sein auf p. 111

present /ˈpreznt/ Geschenk p. 92, 3

present progressive /ˌpreznt
prəʊˈɡresɪv/ *Verlaufsform der
Gegenwart* p. 94

(to) **present (to)** /prɪˈzent/
präsentieren, vorstellen p. 46, 14

presentation /ˌpreznˈteɪʃn/
Präsentation; Vortrag p. 47, 15

(to) **give a presentation** /ˌɡɪv ə
ˌpreznˈteɪʃn/ eine Präsentation
halten p. 67, 13

pretty /ˈprɪti/ ziemlich p. 57, 11

prize /praɪz/ Preis; Gewinn p. 97, 9

product /ˈprɒdʌkt/ Produkt p. 139

professional /prəˈfeʃnəl/ Profi
p. 23, 7

project /ˈprɒdʒekt/ Projekt p. 50

(to) **protect** /prəˈtekt/ beschützen
p. 29

puppy /ˈpʌpi/ junger Hund; Welpe
p. 17, 10

purple /ˈpɜːpl/ violett; lila p. 153

(to) **put (irr)** /pʊt/ setzen; stellen;
legen p. 27, 14

(to) **put down** /ˌpʊt ˈdaʊn/ ablegen
p. 69

(to) **put together** /ˌpʊt təˈɡeðə/
zusammenstellen, zusammen-
setzen p. 98, 13

(to) **put up** /ˌpʊt ˈʌp/ aufhängen;
aufstellen p. 96, 9

pyjamas *(pl)* /pəˈdʒɑːməz/
Schlafanzug p. 153

Q

quarter /ˈkwɔːtə/ Viertel p. 32, 1

question /ˈkwestʃn/ Frage p. 22

quickly /ˈkwɪkli/ schnell p. 88

quiet /ˈkwaɪət/ leise; ruhig p. 24, 8

quite /kwaɪt/ ziemlich p. 88

R

rabbit /ˈræbɪt/ Kaninchen p. 15, 6

race /reɪs/ Rennen p. 30

racetrack /ˈreɪsˌtræk/ Rennbahn
p. 63, 7

racket /ˈrækɪt/ Schläger p. 65, 10

white water rafting /ˌwaɪtwɔːtə
ˈrɑːftɪŋ/ Wildwasserrafting p. 111

(to) **rain** /reɪn/ regnen p. 43, 7

rainy /ˈreɪni/ regnerisch p. 73, 3

(to) **rap along** /ˌræp əˈlɒŋ/
mitrappen p. 95, 7

raspberry /ˈrɑːzbəri/ Himbeere p. 70

RE (= Religious Education)
/ˌɑːrˈiː, reˌlɪdʒəsˌedjʊˈkeɪʃn/
Religion *(Schulfach)* p. 35, 9

(to) **read (irr)** /riːd/ lesen p. 20, 1

(to) **read along** /ˌriːd əˈlɒŋ/
mitlesen p. 8, 4

(to) **read out** /ˌriːd ˈaʊt/ (laut)
vorlesen p. 17, 10

reading /ˈriːdɪŋ/ Lesen p. 75, 6

ready /ˈredi/ fertig, bereit p. 23, 6

(to) **get ready** /ˌɡet ˈredi/ sich fertig
machen p. 7, 2

really /ˈrɪəli/ wirklich p. 8, 4

recipe /ˈresəpi/ Rezept p. 70

(to) **record** /rɪˈkɔːd/ aufnehmen
p. 37, 12

recording /rɪˈkɔːdɪŋ/ Aufnahme
p. 87, 15

red /red/ rot p. 153

registration /ˌredʒɪˈstreɪʃn/
Überprüfung der Anwesenheit
p. 33, 3

(to) **relax** /rɪˈlæks/ entspannen
p. 24, 8

(to) **remember** /rɪˈmembə/ sich
erinnern an p. 76, 7

(to) **remember** /rɪˈmembə/ *hier:*
an etwas denken p. 109

(to) **rent** /rent/ mieten p. 111

rented flat /ˌrentɪd ˈflæt/
Mietwohnung p. 90

(to) **repeat** /rɪˈpiːt/ wiederholen
p. 26, 13

(to) **reply** /rɪˈplaɪ/ antworten;
erwidern p. 110

(to) **do research** /ˌduː rɪˈsɜːtʃ/
recherchieren p. 78, 11

result /rɪˈzʌlt/ Ergebnis p. 139

revision /rɪˈvɪʒn/ Wiederholung
p. 74

rhyme /raɪm/ Reim p. 48

rhyming pair /ˈraɪmɪŋ peə/
Reimpaar p. 17, 10

rice /raɪs/ Reis p. 40, 1

riddle /ˈrɪdl/ Rätsel p. 25, 9

(to) **ride** /raɪd/ fahren; reiten p. 62, 5

(to) **ride a bike** /ˌraɪd ə ˈbaɪk/
Fahrrad fahren p. 61, 3

(to) **ride a horse** /ˌraɪd ə ˈhɔːs/
reiten p. 61, 3

riding a bike /ˌraɪdɪŋ ə ˈbaɪk/
Fahrradfahren p. 17, 10

right /raɪt/ richtig p. 57, 11

right /raɪt/ genau; direkt p. 88

right now /ˌraɪt ˈnaʊ/ jetzt; sofort;
gleich p. 43, 7

on the right /ˌɒn ðə ˈraɪt/ rechts,
auf der rechten Seite p. 76, 7

river /ˈrɪvə/ Fluss p. 30

road /rəʊd/ Straße p. 23, 7

robot /ˈrəʊbɒt/ Roboter p. 83, 8

rock /rɒk/ Stein; Fels p. 111

rock pool /ˈrɒk puːl/ Felsenbecken
p. 111

rock pooling /ˈrɒk ˌpuːlɪŋ/ *Schwimmen in Felsenbecken* p. 111

role play /ˈrəʊl pleɪ/ Rollenspiel p. 75, 6

roll /rəʊl/ Brötchen p. 156

room /ruːm/ Platz; Raum; Zimmer p. 12, 1

round /raʊnd/ rund p. 65, 10

rubbish /ˈrʌbɪʃ/ Müll p. 80, 2

(to) be rubbish /ˌbiː ˈrʌbɪʃ/ Quatsch sein p. 76, 7

rule /ruːl/ Regel p. 67, 13

ruler /ˈruːlə/ Lineal p. 32, 1

(to) run (irr) /rʌn/ laufen; rennen p. 30

(to) run away /ˌrʌn_əˈweɪ/ weglaufen p. 49

(to) run up to somebody /ˌrʌn_ˈʌp tə ˌsʌmbədi/ jemandem entgegenlaufen p. 110

S

sad /sæd/ traurig p. 109

safe /seɪf/ sicher; ungefährlich p. 29

salad /ˈsæləd/ Salat p. 108

salt /sɔːlt/ Salz p. 75, 6

the same /ðə ˈseɪm/ der/die/das Gleiche; der-/die-/dasselbe p. 31

at the same time /æt_ðə ˌseɪm ˈtaɪm/ gleichzeitig; zur gleichen Zeit p. 111

Saturday /ˈsætədeɪ/ Samstag p. 52, 1

(on) Saturdays /ˈsætədeɪz/ samstags p. 40, 1

sausage /ˈsɒsɪdʒ/ Wurst; Würstchen p. 52, 1

(to) save /seɪv/ retten p. 28

(to) **say** (irr) /seɪ/ sagen p. 7, 1

(to) say goodbye (to somebody) /ˌseɪ gʊdˈbaɪ tə ˌsʌmbədi/ sich von jemandem verabschieden p. 79, 13

(to) say hello (to somebody) /ˌseɪ həˈləʊ tə ˌsʌmbədi/ jemanden (be)grüßen p. 44, 8

(to) say hi to somebody (informal) /ˌseɪ ˈhaɪ tə ˌsʌmbədi/ jemanden (be)grüßen p. 110

(to) **be scared (of)** /ˌbiː ˈskeəd_əv/ Angst haben (vor) p. 100, 1

scarf (pl scarfs or scarves) /skɑːf, skɑːfs, skɑːvz/ Schal p. 153

scary /ˈskeəri/ Furcht erregend p. 29

scene /siːn/ Szene p. 9, 5

school /skuːl/ Schule p. 21, 2

school day /ˈskuːl ˌdeɪ/ Schultag p. 35, 9

schoolbag /ˈskuːlˌbæg/ Schultasche p. 32, 1

science /ˈsaɪəns/ Natur- wissenschaft p. 35, 9

the Science Museum /ðə ˈsaɪəns mjuːˌziːəm/ Natur- wissenschaftsmuseum p. 24, 8

(a pair of) scissors /ˈsɪzəz/ Schere p. 32, 1

(to) score /skɔː/ einen Punkt machen p. 65, 10

Scotland /ˈskɒtlənd/ Schottland p. 102, 4

(to) scramble /ˈskræmbl/ durcheinander bringen p. 58, 14; rühren p. 70

scrambled /ˈskræmbld/ durcheinander gebracht p. 58, 14

scrambled egg /ˌskræmbld_ˈeg/ Rührei p. 70

(to) script /skrɪpt/ das Drehbuch zu etwas schreiben p. 79, 13

sea /siː/ Meer; See p. 111

seagull /ˈsiːˌgʌl/ Möwe p. 100, 1

search /sɜːtʃ/ Suche p. 25, 9

(to) **search** /sɜːtʃ/ suchen p. 79, 13

(to) **search the Internet** /ˌsɜːtʃ ði_ˈɪntənet/ im Internet suchen p. 79, 13

searching /ˈsɜːtʃɪŋ/ Suchen p. 79, 13

searching the Internet /ˌsɜːtʃɪŋ ði_ˈɪntənet/ Suchen im Internet p. 64, 9

seaside /ˈsiːˌsaɪd/ (Meeres)küste; Meer p. 105, 8

second /ˈsekənd/ Sekunde p. 55, 7; zweite(r, s) p. 95, 7

second-hand /ˌsekənd ˈhænd/ gebraucht p. 20, 1

(to) **see** (irr) /siː/ sehen p. 7, 1

(to) **see** (irr) /siː/ hier: verstehen p. 68

see you tomorrow /ˌsiː jə təˈmɒrəʊ/ bis morgen p. 8, 4

(to) take a selfie /ˌteɪk_ə ˈselfi/ ein Selfie machen p. 97, 9

(to) **sell** (irr) /sel/ verkaufen p. 90

(to) **send** (irr) /send/ schicken p. 92, 3

sentence /ˈsentəns/ Satz p. 13, 2

September /sepˈtembə/ September p. 95, 7

(to) serve /sɜːv/ servieren p. 70

session /ˈseʃn/ Stunde; Session p. 23, 7

(to) **set the table** /ˌset ðə ˈteɪbl/ den Tisch decken p. 52, 1

(to) set up /ˌset_ˈʌp/ aufbauen p. 92, 3

(to) **share** /ʃeə/ teilen p. 72, 1

sharp /ʃɑːp/ scharf, spitz p. 29

she /ʃiː/ sie p. 8, 4

sheep (pl **sheep**) /ʃiːp/ Schaf p. 90

sheet /ʃiːt/ Blatt; Bogen p. 154

shelf /ʃelf/ Regal p. 54, 5

shirt /ʃɜːt/ Hemd p. 44, 8

shocked /ʃɒkt/ schockiert, entsetzt p. 108

shoe /ʃuː/ Schuh p. 88

a pair of shoes /ə ˌpeər_əv ˈʃuːz/ ein Paar Schuhe p. 153

shop /ʃɒp/ Geschäft; Laden p. 11

fish and chip shop /ˌfɪʃ_ən ˈtʃɪp ʃɒp/ Fischimbiss p. 23, 6

shopkeeper /ˈʃɒpˌkiːpə/ Ladeninhaber/in p. 104, 6

shopping /ˈʃɒpɪŋ/ Einkaufen; Einkaufs- p. 75, 6

shopping centre /ˈʃɒpɪŋ ˌsentə/ Einkaufszentrum p. 21, 2

(to) **do the shopping** /ˌduː ðə ˈʃɒpɪŋ/ einkaufen p. 80, 1

short /ʃɔːt/ kurz p. 14

shoulder /ˈʃəʊldə/ Schulter p. 109

(to) **shout** /ʃaʊt/ rufen; schreien p. 68

(to) shout at somebody /ˈʃaʊt_ət ˌsʌmbədi/ jemanden anschreien p. 68

(to) **show** (irr) /ʃəʊ/ zeigen p. 19, 15

shower /ˈʃaʊə/ Dusche p. 158

(to) take a shower /ˌteɪk_ə ˈʃaʊə/ duschen p. 55, 7

shy /ʃaɪ/ scheu, schüchtern p. 28

side /saɪd/ Seite p. 28

side (dish) /ˈsaɪd_dɪʃ/ Beilage p. 40, 1

sight /saɪt/ Sehenswürdigkeit p. 103, 5

simple /ˈsɪmpl/ einfach; simpel p.109

simple past /ˌsɪmpl ˈpɑːst/ einfache Vergangenheit p.102

simple present /ˌsɪmpl ˈpreznt/ einfache Gegenwart p.42

(to) **sing** *(irr)* /sɪŋ/ singen p.7, 2

(to) **sing along** /ˌsɪŋ_əˈlɒŋ/ mitsingen p.37, 13

(to) sing out /ˌsɪŋ_ˈaʊt/ laut singen p.37, 13

single /ˈsɪŋgl/ alleinerziehend p.152

sister /ˈsɪstə/ Schwester p.8, 4

(to) **sit** *(irr)* /sɪt/ sitzen p.109

(to) **sit down** /ˌsɪt_ˈdaʊn/ sich hinsetzen p.36, 10

size /saɪz/ Größe p.104, 6

skateboarding /ˈskeɪtbɔːdɪŋ/ Skateboardfahren p.8, 4

skater's paradise /ˌskeɪtəz ˈpærədaɪs/ *Paradies für Skater* p.23, 7

(to) **ski** /skiː/ Ski fahren, Ski laufen p.157

skill /skɪl/ Fertigkeit; Kompetenz p.16, 7

skirt /skɜːt/ Rock p.44, 8

(to) **sleep** *(irr)* /sliːp/ schlafen p.94, 5

(to) sleep in /ˌsliːp_ˈɪn/ ausschlafen p.56, 8

sleeping bag /ˈsliːpɪŋ bæg/ Schlafsack p.96, 9

sleeping mat /ˈsliːpɪŋ mæt/ Schlafmatte p.96, 9

sleepover /ˈsliːpˌəʊvə/ Übernachtung p.96, 9

(to) **slice** /slaɪs/ in Scheiben schneiden p.70

slowly /ˈsləʊli/ langsam p.49

small /smɔːl/ klein p.12, 1

smell /smel/ Geruch p.17, 10

smelly /ˈsmeli/ stinkend p.55, 7

smelly feet *(pl)* /ˌsmeli ˈfiːt/ Stinkefüße p.55, 7

smooth /smuːð/ *hier:* cremig p.70

snake /sneɪk/ Schlange p.77, 8

(to) **sneeze** /sniːz/ niesen p.69

(to) **sniff** /snɪf/ riechen an p.69

so /səʊ/ also p.8, 4; deshalb; daher p.15, 6

so far /ˈsəʊ fɑː/ bisher p.37, 13

sock /sɒk/ Socke p.15, 6

solution /səˈluːʃn/ Lösung p.83, 8

some /sʌm/ einige, ein paar; etwas p.16, 7

someone /ˈsʌmwʌn/ jemand; irgendwer p.27, 14

something /ˈsʌmθɪŋ/ etwas p.19, 15

something blue /ˌsʌmθɪŋ ˈbluː/ etwas Blaues p.97, 9

sometimes /ˈsʌmtaɪmz/ manchmal p.41, 2

son /sʌn/ Sohn p.95, 8

song /sɒŋ/ Lied p.37, 13

soon /suːn/ bald p.89

sorry /ˈsɒri/ es tut mir leid, Entschuldigung p.36, 10

(to) **sort** /sɔːt/ sortieren p.58, 14

(to) **sound** /saʊnd/ klingen, sich anhören p.41, 2

space /speɪs/ Weltall p.96, 9; Raum; Platz p.109

spaceship /ˈspeɪsˌʃɪp/ Raumschiff p.99, 14

(to) **speak** *(irr)* /spiːk/ sprechen; reden p.27, 14

special /ˈspeʃl/ besondere(r, s); besonders p.10, 7

speciality /ˌspeʃiˈæləti/ Spezialität p.28

(to) **spell** *(irr)* /spel/ buchstabieren p.36, 10

spelling /ˈspelɪŋ/ Buchstabieren; Rechtschreibung p.38, 16

(to) **spend** *(irr)* /spend/ verbringen *(Zeit)*; ausgeben *(Geld)* p.90

spicy /ˈspaɪsi/ würzig; scharf p.48

spinach /ˈspɪnɪdʒ/ Spinat p.17, 10

spooky /ˈspuːki/ schaurig; unheimlich p.99, 14

spoon /spuːn/ Löffel p.52, 1

wooden spoon /ˌwʊdn ˈspuːn/ Holzlöffel, Kochlöffel p.70

sport /spɔːt/ Sport; Sportart p.16, 7

(to) do sports /ˌduː ˈspɔːts/ Sport treiben p.30

sports day /ˈspɔːts deɪ/ *Sportfest* p.50

sports ground /ˈspɔːts graʊnd/ Sportplatz p.43, 7

sports hall /ˈspɔːts hɔːl/ Sporthalle p.46, 14

sportsperson /ˈspɔːtsˌpɜːsn/ Sportler/in p.64, 9

I spy with my little eye. /aɪ ˌspaɪ wɪð ˌmaɪ ˌlɪtl̩ ˈaɪ/ Ich sehe was, was du nicht siehst. p.75, 6

squirrel /ˈskwɪrəl/ Eichhörnchen p.84, 10

stadium (pl stadiums or stadia) /ˈsteɪdiəm(z), ˈsteɪdiə/ Stadion p.30

stall /stɔːl/ Stand p.20, 1

stamp /stæmp/ Briefmarke p.104, 6

(to) stamp one's foot /ˌstæmp wʌnz ˈfʊt/ mit dem Fuß aufstampfen p.7, 2

(to) **stand** *(irr)* /stænd/ stehen p.50

(to) stand up /ˌstænd_ˈʌp/ aufstehen p.95, 7

star /stɑː/ Stern p.96, 9

start /stɑːt/ Anfang; Beginn p.46, 14

(to) **start** /stɑːt/ anfangen; beginnen p.19, 15

starter /ˈstɑːtə/ Vorspeise p.89

statement /ˈsteɪtmənt/ Äußerung, Aussage p.13, 1

station /ˈsteɪʃn/ U-Bahn-Station; Bahnhof p.11

(to) **stay** /steɪ/ bleiben; wohnen p.57, 11

(to) stay up (late) /ˌsteɪ_ˌʌp ˈleɪt/ lange aufbleiben p.57, 11

step /step/ Stufe; Schritt p.19, 15

stepbrother /ˈstepˌbrʌðə/ Stiefbruder p.160

stepfather /ˈstepˌfɑːðə/ Stiefvater p.160

stepmother /ˈstepˌmʌðə/ Stiefmutter p.160

stepsister /ˈstepˌsɪstə/ Stiefschwester p.160

still /stɪl/ (immer) noch p.44, 8

stinky /ˈstɪŋki/ stinkend p.17, 10

stomach /ˈstʌmək/ Magen; Bauch p.153

(to) **stop** /stɒp/ stehen bleiben; anhalten p.21, 2

story /ˈstɔːri/ Geschichte, Erzählung p.40, 1

strawberry /ˈstrɔːbri/ Erdbeere p.70

street /striːt/ Straße p.7, 1

street light /ˈstriːt laɪt/ Straßenlaterne p. 97, 9

(to) take to the streets /ˌteɪk tə ðə ˈstriːts/ auf die Straße gehen p. 97, 9

strong /strɒŋ/ stark p. 29

student /ˈstjuːdnt/ Schüler/in p. 40, 1

exchange student /ɪksˈtʃeɪndʒ ˌstjuːdnt/ Austauschschüler/in p. 45, 11

stuff *(informal)* /stʌf/ Zeug p. 76, 7

(to) stumble /ˈstʌmbl/ stolpern p. 49

(to) style one's hair /ˌstaɪl wʌnz ˈheə/ sich frisieren p. 55, 7

subject /ˈsʌbdʒɪkt/ Schulfach p. 35, 9

sudden /ˈsʌdn/ plötzlich p. 48

suddenly /ˈsʌdnli/ plötzlich p. 49

sugar /ˈʃʊgə/ Zucker p. 70

suit /suːt/ Anzug; Kostüm p. 96, 9

summer /ˈsʌmə/ Sommer p. 102, 4

sun /sʌn/ Sonne p. 96, 9

Sunday /ˈsʌndeɪ/ Sonntag p. 54, 5

(on) Sundays /ˈsʌndeɪz/ sonntags p. 41, 1

sunny /ˈsʌni/ sonnig p. 102, 3

sunshine /ˈsʌnʃaɪn/ Sonnenschein p. 57, 11

superhero /ˈsuːpəˌhɪərəʊ/ Superheld/in p. 99, 14

supermarket /ˈsuːpəˌmɑːkɪt/ Supermarkt p. 152

sure /ʃɔː/ sicher p. 72, 1

sure *(informal)* /ʃɔː/ na klar, natürlich p. 8, 4

(to) make sure /ˌmeɪk ˈʃɔː/ darauf achten, dass p. 80, 1

survey /ˈsɜːveɪ/ Umfrage p. 139

(to) do a survey /ˌduː_ə ˈsɜːveɪ/ eine Umfrage machen p. 139

sweet /swiːt/ süß p. 7, 2

sweet /swiːt/ Süßigkeit p. 77, 9

(to) **swim** *(irr)* /swɪm/ schwimmen p. 62

swimming /ˈswɪmɪŋ/ Schwimmen p. 56, 8

swimming pool /ˈswɪmɪŋ puːl/ Schwimmbad p. 21, 2

(to) **switch on** /ˌswɪtʃ_ˈɒn/ einschalten p. 83, 8

T

table /ˈteɪbl/ Tisch p. 52, 1

table /ˈteɪbl/ Tabelle p. 114

table tennis /ˈteɪbl ˌtenɪs/ Tischtennis p. 61, 3

(to) **set the table** /ˌset ðə ˈteɪbl/ den Tisch decken p. 52, 1

(table)spoon /ˈteɪbl spuːn/ Esslöffel p. 156

(to) tackle /ˈtækl/ angreifen p. 65, 10

tail /teɪl/ Schwanz p. 108

(to) **take** *(irr)* /teɪk/ nehmen; bringen p. 20, 1; benötigen; brauchen p. 55, 7

(to) take a dog for a walk /ˌteɪk_ə ˌdɒg fər_ə ˈwɔːk/ mit einem Hund Gassi gehen p. 80, 1

(to) **take a photo** /ˌteɪk_ə ˈfəʊtəʊ/ ein Foto machen p. 97, 9

(to) **take a picture** /ˌteɪk_ə ˈpɪktʃə/ ein Foto machen p. 19, 15

(to) take a selfie /ˌteɪk_ə ˈselfi/ ein Selfie machen p. 97, 9

(to) take a shower /ˌteɪk_ə ˈʃaʊə/ duschen p. 55, 7

(to) **take notes (on)** /ˌteɪk ˈnəʊts/ sich Notizen machen (zu) p. 57, 11

(to) **take out** /ˌteɪk_ˈaʊt/ hinausbringen p. 80, 2

(to) take somebody on a tour /ˌteɪk ˌsʌmbədi_ɒn_ə ˈtʊə/ mit jemandem einen Rundgang / eine Tour machen p. 21, 1

(to) take to the streets /ˌteɪk tə ðə ˈstriːts/ auf die Straße gehen p. 97, 9

(to) take turns /ˌteɪk ˈtɜːnz/ sich abwechseln p. 15, 6

takeaway /ˈteɪkəˌweɪ/ Essen zum Mitnehmen p. 56, 8

(to) **talk about** /ˈtɔːk_əˌbaʊt/ sprechen über p. 12, 1

(to) **talk (to)** /tɔːk/ sprechen (mit); reden (mit) p. 10, 6

talking /ˈtɔːkɪŋ/ Sprechen p. 53, 2

tame /teɪm/ gezähmt, zahm p. 110

(to) tame /teɪm/ zähmen p. 28

dragon tamer /ˈdrægən ˌteɪmə/ Drachenzähmer/in p. 28

taming /ˈteɪmɪŋ/ Zähmen p. 28

target task /ˈtɑːgɪt ˌtɑːsk/ Zielaufgabe p. 19, 15

task /tɑːsk/ Aufgabe p. 10, 7

tea /tiː/ Tee p. 52, 1

(to) **teach** *(irr)* /tiːtʃ/ unterrichten p. 43, 7

teacher /ˈtiːtʃə/ Lehrer/in p. 33, 4

teaspoon /ˈtiːˌspuːn/ Teelöffel p. 70

(to) **brush one's teeth** /ˌbrʌʃ wʌnz ˈtiːθ/ sich die Zähne putzen p. 55, 7

(to) **tell** *(irr)* /tel/ erzählen p. 17, 11

ten-mile hike /ˌten maɪl ˈhaɪk/ *Wanderung von zehn Meilen* p. 17, 10

tennis court /ˈtenɪs kɔːt/ Tennisplatz p. 63, 7

term /tɜːm/ Trimester p. 43, 7; Begriff p. 79, 13

terrible /ˈterəbl/ schrecklich p. 85, 11

(to) **text** /tekst/ eine Textnachricht schreiben p. 8, 4

text (message) /ˈtekst ˌmesɪdʒ/ Textnachricht p. 80, 1

than /ðæn/ als *(bei Vergleich)* p. 90

(to) thank /θæŋk/ danken, sich bedanken p. 28

thank you /ˈθæŋk ju/ danke p. 76, 7

thanks /θæŋks/ danke p. 32, 1

thanks a lot /ˌθæŋks_ə ˈlɒt/ vielen Dank p. 75, 6

I'm good, thanks. /aɪm ˈgʊd ˌθæŋks/ Es geht mir gut, danke. p. 44, 8

that /ðæt/ das; der / die / das (dort) p. 8, 4; dass p. 80, 1

that /ðæt/ so p. 110

that's (= that is) /ðæts, ˈðæt_ɪz/ *hier:* das kostet p. 104, 6

That's me. /ˌðæts ˈmiː/ Das bin ich. p. 17, 11

the /ðə/ der / die / das p. 7, 1

their /ðeə/ ihr(e) p. 44, 8

them /ðem/ sie; ihnen p. 13, 1

themed party /ˈθiːmd ˌpɑːti/ Mottoparty p. 96, 9

then /ðen/ dann p. 7, 2

there /ðeə/ dort; dahin p. 24, 8

there are /ðeər_ˈɑː/ dort sind; es gibt p. 12, 1

there was /ðeə ˈwɒz/ dort war; es gab p. 102, 3

there were /ðeə ˈwɜː/ dort waren;
es gab p. 102, 3

there's (= there is) /ðeəz, ðeərˈɪz/
dort ist; es gibt p. 8, 4

these (*pl of* **this**) /ðiːz/ diese; das
p. 12, 1

they /ðeɪ/ sie p. 9, 4

thing /θɪŋ/ Ding; Gegenstand p. 11

(to) **think** *(irr)* /θɪŋk/ denken;
glauben p. 10, 7

(to) **think about** /ˈθɪŋk_əˌbaʊt/
denken an, nachdenken über
p. 7, 1

(to) **think of** /ˈθɪŋk_əv/ denken an,
sich ausdenken p. 10, 7

third /θɜːd/ dritte(r, s) p. 95, 7

this /ðɪs/ diese(r, s) p. 9, 5

this evening /ðɪs_ˈiːvnɪŋ/ heute
Abend p. 80, 1

this one /ˈðɪs wʌn/ diese(r, s) p. 104, 6

those (*pl of* **that**) /ðəʊz/ diese,
jene p. 104, 6

(to) **throw** *(irr)* /θrəʊ/ werfen p. 65, 10

Thursday /ˈθɜːzdeɪ/ Donnerstag
p. 35, 9

(on) Thursdays /ˈθɜːzdeɪz/
donnerstags p. 40, 1

the tide is out /ðə ˌtaɪd_ɪz_ˈaʊt/ es
ist Ebbe p. 111

tidy /ˈtaɪdi/ ordentlich;
aufgeräumt p. 76, 7

(to) **tidy (up)** /ˈtaɪdi, ˌtaɪdiˈʌp/
aufräumen p. 80, 2

tie /taɪ/ Krawatte p. 44, 8

till /tɪl/ bis p. 97, 10

till /tɪl/ Kasse p. 104, 6

time /taɪm/ Zeit p. 32, 1; Mal p. 80, 2

at the same time /æt_ðə ˌseɪm
ˈtaɪm/ gleichzeitig; zur gleichen
Zeit p. 111

for a long time /fər_ə ˈlɒŋ taɪm/
lange p. 49

in time /ɪn ˈtaɪm/ rechtzeitig;
pünktlich p. 108

next time /ˈnekst_taɪm/ nächstes
Mal p. 24, 8

on time /ˌɒn ˈtaɪm/ pünktlich p. 33, 3

What time is it? /wɒt_ˈtaɪm_ɪz_ɪt/
Wie spät ist es? p. 34, 7

What's the time, please? /ˌwɒts
ðə ˈtaɪm pliːz/ Wie spät ist es,
bitte? p. 34, 7

timetable /ˈtaɪmteɪbl/ Stundenplan p. 35, 9

tip /tɪp/ Tipp p. 48

to /tʊ/ (um) zu p. 16, 8; in, nach, zu,
an p. 20, 1; bis p. 23, 7; *hier:* vor p. 34, 7

to /tʊ/ *hier:* auf p. 98, 12

to-do list /təˈduː ˌlɪst/ To-do-Liste
p. 161

today /təˈdeɪ/ heute p. 33, 3

toe /təʊ/ Zeh p. 7, 2

together /təˈɡeðə/ zusammen
p. 27, 14

toilet /ˈtɔɪlət/ Toilette p. 36, 10

tomato /təˈmɑːtəʊ/ Tomate p. 52, 1

tomorrow /təˈmɒrəʊ/ morgen p. 8, 4

see you tomorrow /ˌsiː jə təˈmɒrəʊ/
bis morgen p. 8, 4

too /tuː/ auch p. 8, 4; zu p. 24, 8

tooth (*pl* teeth) /tuːθ, tiːθ/ Zahn
p. 29

toothbrush /ˈtuːθbrʌʃ/ Zahnbürste
p. 97, 10

top /tɒp/ beste(r, s) p. 41, 3

topic /ˈtɒpɪk/ Thema p. 47, 15

(to) **touch** /tʌtʃ/ berühren p. 7, 2

(to) take somebody on a tour
/ˌteɪk ˌsʌmbədi_ɒn_ə ˈtʊə/ mit
jemandem einen Rundgang
machen / mit jemandem eine
Tour machen p. 21, 1

towards /təˈwɔːdz/ in Richtung, zu
p. 49

tower /ˈtaʊə/ Turm p. 152

observation tower /ˌɒbzəˈveɪʃn
ˌtaʊə/ Aussichtsturm p. 103, 5

town /taʊn/ Stadt p. 105, 8

toy /tɔɪ/ Spielzeug p. 12, 1

traditional /trəˈdɪʃnəl/ traditionell
p. 138

train /treɪn/ Zug p. 101, 2

(to) **travel** /ˈtrævl/ reisen; fahren
p. 20, 1

travel-around-the-world
/ˌtrævl_ə ˌraʊnd ðə ˈwɜːld/
Reise um die Welt p. 99, 14

treasure hunt /ˈtreʒə hʌnt/
Schatzsuche p. 97, 9

treat /triːt/ Leckerei p. 84, 10

tree /triː/ Baum p. 97, 9

trick /trɪk/ Trick; Kunststück
p. 12, 1

trip /trɪp/ Reise; Fahrt p. 28

(a pair of) trousers /ə ˌpeər_əv
ˈtraʊzəz/ Hose p. 44, 8

true /truː/ wahr p. 13, 1

(to) trust /trʌst/ vertrauen p. 109

(to) **try** /traɪ/ (aus)probieren;
versuchen p. 20, 1

Tuesday /ˈtjuːzdeɪ/ Dienstag
p. 35, 9

(on) Tuesdays /ˈtjuːzdeɪz/
dienstags p. 40, 1

tummy (*informal*) /ˈtʌmi/ Bauch
p. 153

(to) **be one's turn** /ˌbiː wʌnz ˈtɜːn/
an der Reihe sein p. 80, 2

(to) **turn around** /ˌtɜːn_əˈraʊnd/
sich umdrehen p. 109

turn over /ˌtɜːn_ˈəʊvə/ umdrehen
p. 111

(to) **watch TV** /ˌwɒtʃ tiː ˈviː/
Fernsehen gucken p. 54, 4

twenty-first /ˌtwenti ˈfɜːst/
einundzwanzigste(r, s) p. 95, 7

twin /twɪn/ Zwilling; Zwillings-
p. 8, 4

typical /ˈtɪpɪkl/ typisch p. 87, 15

U

ugh (*informal*) /ʌɡ/ i, igitt p. 24, 8

the UK (= United Kingdom)
/ðə ˌjuː ˈkeɪ, juːˌnaɪtɪd ˈkɪŋdəm/
Vereinigtes Königreich p. 50

uncle /ˈʌŋkl/ Onkel p. 43, 7

under /ˈʌndə/ unter p. 76, 7

underground /ˈʌndəˌɡraʊnd/
U-Bahn p. 20, 1

(to) **understand** *(irr)* /ˌʌndəˈstænd/
verstehen p. 45, 11

unit /ˈjuːnɪt/ Kapitel p. 112

(to) **unscramble** /ʌnˈskræmbl/
ordnen, in die richtige
Reihenfolge bringen p. 18, 13

until /ənˈtɪl/ bis p. 70

unusual /ʌnˈjuːʒuəl/ ungewöhnlich
p. 64, 9

up /ʌp/ nach oben; hinauf; oben
p. 7, 2

the Upside Down House
/ðiː_ˌʌpsaɪd_ˈdaʊn haʊs/ *Haus, das
auf dem Kopf steht* p. 105, 9

us /ʌs/ uns p. 7, 2

(to) **use** /juːz/ benutzen p. 17, 9

useful /ˈjuːsfl/ nützlich p. 43, 7

usually /'juːʒuəli/ gewöhnlich; normalerweise p. 80, 2

V

(to) **vacuum** /'vækjuəm/ staubsaugen p. 80, 2

ice cream van /'aɪs kriːm ˌvæn/ Eiswagen p. 7, 3

vanilla /vəˈnɪlə/ Vanille p. 7, 2

vegetable /'vedʒtəbl/ Gemüse p. 138

vegetarian /ˌvedʒəˈteəriən/ vegetarisch p. 52, 1

vegetarian chilli /ˌvedʒəˌteəriən 'tʃɪli/ vegetarisches Chili p. 40, 1

verse /vɜːs/ Strophe; Vers p. 10, 7

version /'vɜːʃn/ Version, Fassung p. 59, 15

very /'veri/ sehr p. 15, 6

(to) like something very much /laɪk ˌsʌmθɪŋ ˌveri 'mʌtʃ/ etwas sehr gern mögen p. 30

view /vjuː/ (Aus)sicht p. 105, 9

vinegar /'vɪnɪgə/ Essig p. 75, 6

visit /'vɪzɪt/ Besuch p. 105, 8

W

(to) **wait** /weɪt/ (er)warten p. 23, 6

walk /wɔːk/ Spaziergang p. 24, 8

(to) **walk** /wɔːk/ gehen p. 21, 2

(to) take a dog for a walk /teɪk ˌə ˌdɒg fər ə 'wɔːk/ mit einem Hund Gassi gehen p. 80, 1

walk up to /ˌwɔːk ˌʌp tʊ/ zugehen auf p. 69

wall /wɔːl/ Wand p. 158

climbing wall /'klaɪmɪŋ wɔːl/ Kletterwand p. 63, 7

wallet /'wɒlɪt/ Brieftasche p. 68

(to) **want (to)** /wɒnt/ wollen p. 9, 4

wardrobe /'wɔːdrəʊb/ Schrank p. 158

was /wɒz/ (ich / er, sie, es) war p. 100, 1

(to) **wash** /wɒʃ/ waschen; sich waschen p. 55, 7

washing machine /'wɒʃɪŋ məˌʃiːn/ Waschmaschine p. 83, 8

(to) **watch** /wɒtʃ/ beobachten; ansehen p. 17, 11

(to) watch TV /ˌwɒtʃ tiː 'viː/ Fernsehen gucken p. 54, 4

water /'wɔːtə/ Wasser p. 75, 6

watermelon /'wɔːtəˌmelən/ Wassermelone p. 57, 11

way /weɪ/ Weg; Art p. 17, 10

we /wiː/ wir p. 8, 4

we've done /ˌwiːv 'dʌn/ wir haben getan p. 37, 13

(to) **wear (irr)** /weə/ tragen (Kleidung) p. 44, 8

weather /'weðə/ Wetter p. 24, 8

web page /'web peɪdʒ/ Webseite, Internetseite p. 20, 1

Wednesday /'wenzdeɪ/ Mittwoch p. 35, 9

(on) Wednesdays /'wenzdeɪz/ mittwochs p. 40, 1

week /wiːk/ Woche p. 41, 1

weekday /'wiːkdeɪ/ Wochentag p. 114

weekend /ˌwiːk'end/ Wochenende p. 51

at the weekend /æt ˌðə 'wiːkend/ am Wochenende p. 51

at the weekends /æt ˌðə 'wiːkendz/ an den Wochenenden p. 155

welcome (to) /'welkəm tʊ/ willkommen (in) p. 6

You're welcome. /jɔː 'welkəm/ Gern geschehen.; Keine Ursache. p. 110

well /wel/ nun p. 32, 1

were /wɜː/ (du) warst / (wir / sie) waren / (ihr) wart p. 100, 1

wet /wet/ nass p. 111

what /wɒt/ was; welche(r, s) p. 7, 1

What about ...? /ˌwɒt ˌəˌbaʊt '.../ Was ist mit ...? / Wie wäre es mit ...? p. 13, 2

What is ... like? /ˌwɒt ˌɪz ... 'laɪk/ Wie ist ...? p. 138

what it is like /ˌwɒt ˌɪt ˌɪz 'laɪk/ wie es ist p. 107, 13

What time is it? /ˌwɒt ˌtaɪm ˌɪz ˌɪt/ Wie spät ist es? p. 35, 9

What ... would you like? /ˌwɒt ... wəd jə 'laɪk/ Was für ein/e ... hättest du / hättet ihr / hätten Sie gern? p. 75, 6

What's on? (informal) /ˌwɒts ˌ'ɒn/ Was ist los? p. 40, 1

What's the time, please? /ˌwɒts ðə 'taɪm pliːz/ Wie spät ist es, bitte? p. 34, 7

when /wen/ wann p. 23, 7; wenn; als p. 43, 7

where /weə/ wo; wohin p. 8, 4

which /wɪtʃ/ welche(r, s); was p. 7, 2

while /waɪl/ während p. 111

white /waɪt/ weiß p. 153

white water rafting /ˌwaɪtwɔːtə 'rɑːftɪŋ/ Wildwasserrafting p. 111

who /huː/ wer p. 9, 4; der/die/das p. 27, 14

whole /həʊl/ ganz, gesamt p. 69

whose /huːz/ wessen p. 76, 7

why /waɪ/ warum p. 72, 1

wife /waɪf/ Ehefrau p. 95, 8

will /wɪl/ werden p. 109

(to) **win (irr)** /wɪn/ gewinnen p. 68

window /'wɪndəʊ/ Fenster p. 36, 10

wing /wɪŋ/ Flügel p. 29

winner /'wɪnə/ Gewinner/in p. 97, 9

(to) wish /wɪʃ/ wünschen p. 110

with /wɪð/ mit; bei p. 12, 1

without /wɪð'aʊt/ ohne p. 44, 8

woman (pl women) /'wʊmən, 'wɪmɪn/ Frau p. 95, 8

wooden spoon /ˌwʊdn 'spuːn/ Holzlöffel, Kochlöffel p. 70

word /wɜːd/ Wort p. 12, 1

word order /'wɜːd ˌɔːdə/ Satzstellung p. 54

word web /'wɜːd web/ Wortnetz p. 16, 8

wordbank /'wɜːdbæŋk/ Wortsammlung p. 33, 4

work /wɜːk/ Arbeit; Werk p. 47, 15

(to) **work** /wɜːk/ arbeiten p. 13, 1

(to) work /wɜːk/ hier: funktionieren p. 68

(to) work late /ˌwɜːk 'leɪt/ länger arbeiten p. 80, 1

workbook /'wɜːkbʊk/ Arbeitsheft p. 7, 1

working /'wɜːkɪŋ/ Arbeiten p. 33, 4

It's not working. /ˌɪts nɒt 'wɜːkɪŋ/ Es funktioniert nicht. p. 68

workout /'wɜːkaʊt/ Training p. 111

world /wɜːld/ Welt p. 96, 9

from all over the world /frəmˌɔːl ˌəʊvə ðə 'wɜːld/ aus der ganzen Welt p. 20, 1

all over the world /ˌɔːl ˌəʊvə ðə 'wɜːld/ auf der ganzen Welt p. 136

around the world /ə,raʊnd ðə
'wɜːld/ weltweit, überall auf der
Welt p. 136

(to) **worry** /'wʌri/ sich Sorgen
machen p. 32, 1

would /wʊd/ würde(st, n, t) p. 19, 15

I would like ... (= I'd like ...)
/aɪ ,wʊd 'laɪk, aɪd 'laɪk/ Ich würde
gern ... / Ich hätte gern ... p. 97, 10

Would you like ...? /,wʊd ju: 'laɪk/
Hättest du / Hättet ihr / Hätten
Sie gern ...? p. 104, 6

(to) **write** *(irr)* /raɪt/ schreiben
p. 10, 7

(to) **write down** /,raɪt‿'daʊn/
aufschreiben p. 13, 1

writing /'raɪtɪŋ/ Schreiben p. 17, 9

Y

year /jɪə/ Jahr p. 12, 1

year /jɪə/ Jahrgang p. 100, 1

(to) yell /jel/ laut schreien; brüllen
p. 17, 10

yellow /'jeləʊ/ gelb p. 153

yes /jes/ ja p. 9, 5

you /ju:/ du; dich; dir; man; ihr;
euch; Sie; Ihnen p. 7, 1

You're welcome. /,jɔː 'welkəm/
Gern geschehen.;
Keine Ursache. p. 110

young /jʌŋ/ jung p. 48

the young one /ðə 'jʌŋ wʌn/
Junges p. 48

younger /'jʌŋgə/ jüngere(r, s) p. 90

your /jɔː/ dein(e); euer/eure;
Ihr(e) p. 7, 2

yourself /jɔː'self/ dir, dich; sich
p. 19, 15

yuck *(informal)* /jʌk/ i, igitt p. 68

yum *(informal)* /jʌm/ lecker p. 108

yummy *(informal)* /'jʌmi/ lecker
p. 7, 2

Names

Girls / Women

Aisha /aɪˈiːʃə/
Ameera /əˈmiːrə/
Amy /ˈeɪmi/
Anna /ˈænə/
Anousa /əˈnuːzə/
Ava /ˈeɪvə/
Cho /tʃəʊ/
Edyta /əˈdiːtə/
Eila /ˈeɪlə/
Ellen /ˈelən/
Fiona /fiˈəʊnə/
Gracie /ˈgreɪsi/
Hannah /ˈhænə/
Helen /ˈhelən/
Julia /ˈdʒuːliə/
Kate /keɪt/
Kora /ˈkɔːrə/
Libby /ˈlɪbi/
Lily /ˈlɪli/
Maya /ˈmeɪə/
Melissa /məˈlɪsə/
Mia /ˈmiːə/
Olivia /əˈlɪviə/
Sarah /ˈseərə/
Sophia /səʊˈfiːə/
Sophie /ˈsəʊfi/
Stevie /ˈstiːvi/
Tazzy /ˈtæzi/
Volta /ˈvɒltə/

Boys / Men

Aaron /ˈeərən/
Alex /ˈælɪks/
Andrew /ˈændruː/
Ben /ben/
Blaze /bleɪz/
Callum /ˈkæləm/
Daniel /ˈdænjəl/
David /ˈdeɪvɪd/
Eric /ˈerɪk/
Fergus /ˈfɜːgəs/
Finn /fɪn/
George /dʒɔːdʒ/
Harry /ˈhæri/
Ignus /ˈɪgnəs/
Israh /ˈɪzrə/
Jonah /ˈdʒəʊnə/
Joshua /ˈdʒɒʃjuə/

Kai /kaɪ/
Lee /liː/
Leo /ˈliːəʊ/
Mark /maːk/
Noah /ˈnəʊə/
Ollie /ˈɒli/
Philipp /ˈfɪlɪp/
Robert /ˈrɒbət/
Rohan /ˈrəʊən/
Sami /ˈsæmi/
Sebastian /səˈbæstiən/
Tarek /ˈtærɪk/
Thomas /ˈtɒməs/
Tim /tɪm/
Tom /tɒm/

Families

Adil /əˈdiːl/
Baker /ˈbeɪkə/
Elliott /ˈeliət/
Fisher /ˈfɪʃə/
Hu /huː/
Kogan /ˈkəʊgən/
Miller /ˈmɪlə/
Norris /ˈnɒrɪs/
Patel /pəˈtel/
Price /praɪs/
Walker /ˈwɔːkə/

Other Names

Acklam /ˈækləm/
Arsenal /ˈaːsnl/
BaySixty6 /ˌbeɪ sɪksti ˈsɪks/
Biscuit /ˈbɪskɪt/
Biscuiteers /ˌbɪskəˈtɪəz/
Brighton Pier
  /ˌbraɪtn ˈpɪə/
Brighton Rock
  /ˌbraɪtn ˈrɒk/
the Brixton Academy
  /ðə ˌbrɪkstən əˈkædəmi/
Chelsea /ˈtʃelsi/
Don McClean
  /ˌdɒn məˈkliːn/
Double /ˈdʌbl/
Ecology Centre
  /ɪˈkɒlədʒi ˌsentə/
Electric Cinema
  /ɪˌlektrɪk ˈsɪnəmə/

escape game
  /ɪˈskeɪp geɪm/
Euro /ˈjʊərəʊ/
Feli-Rhymus
  /ˌfeli ˈraɪməs/
Gate Picturehouse
  /ˌgeɪt ˈpɪktʃəhaʊs/
Holland Park
  /ˌhɒlənd ˈpaːk/
i360 /ˌaɪ θriː ˈsɪksti/
Kids' Club /ˈkɪdz klʌb/
the National Library
  of Scotland
  /ðə ˌnæʃnl ˌlaɪbrəri əv
  ˈskɒtlənd/
the National Museum of
  Scotland
  /ðə ˌnæʃnl mjuːˌziːəm əv
  ˈskɒtlənd/
Notting Hill /ˌnɒtɪŋ ˈhɪl/
Notting Hill Carnival
  /ˌnɒtɪŋ hɪl ˈkaːnɪvl/
Notting Hill Gate
  /ˌnɒtɪŋ hɪl ˈgeɪt/
Portobello Road
  /ˌpɔːtəˌbeləʊ ˈrəʊd/
Premier League
  /ˌpremiə ˈliːg/
Queen's College
  /ˌkwiːnz ˈkɒlɪdʒ/
Queens /kwiːnz/
the Science Museum
  /ðə ˈsaɪəns mjuːˌziːəm/
Skkaddraa /ˌskæˈdraː/
Summerhill /ˈsʌməhɪl/
Trouble /ˈtrʌbl/
the Upside Down House
  /ði ˌʌpsaɪd ˈdaʊn haʊs/
Wembley /ˈwembli/
West Derby /ˌwest ˈdaːbi/
Wonderlab /ˈwʌndəlæb/

Geographical Names

Blackwater
  /ˈblækˌwɔːtə/
Brighton /ˈbraɪtn/
Bristol /ˈbrɪstl/
Brixton /ˈbrɪkstən/
Cardiff /ˈkaːdɪf/

Cornwall /ˈkɔːnwɔːl/
Edinburgh /ˈedɪnbərə/
England /ˈɪŋglənd/
Europe /ˈjʊərəp/
Fistral Bay /ˌfɪstrəl ˈbeɪ/
France /fraːns/
Fulham /ˈfʊləm/
Germany /ˈdʒɜːməni/
Italy /ˈɪtəli/
Japan /dʒəˈpæn/
Liverpool /ˈlɪvəpuːl/
London /ˈlʌndən/
New York /njuː ˈjɔːk/
New Zealand
  /ˌnjuː ˈziːlənd/
North Wales /ˌnɔːθ ˈweɪlz/
Northern Ireland
  /ˌnɔːðən ˈaɪələnd/
Paris /ˈpærɪs/
Poland /ˈpəʊlənd/
Putney /ˈpʌtni/
Scotland /ˈskɒtlənd/
Tyrone /tɪˈrəʊn/
the UK (= the United
  Kingdom) /ðə ˌjuː ˈkeɪ,
  ðə ˌjuːˌnaɪtɪd ˈkɪŋdəm/
Wales /weɪlz/

Numbers

0	oh, zero, nil /əʊ, ˈzɪərəʊ, nɪl/		
1	one /wʌn/	1st	**first** /fɜːst/
2	two /tuː/	2nd	**second** /ˈsekənd/
3	three /θriː/	3rd	**third** /θɜːd/
4	four /fɔː/	4th	fourth /fɔːθ/
5	five /faɪv/	5th	**fif**th /fɪfθ/
6	six /sɪks/	6th	sixth /sɪksθ/
7	seven /sevn/	7th	seventh /sevnθ/
8	eight /eɪt/	8th	**eigh**th /eɪtθ/
9	nine /naɪn/	9th	**nin**th /naɪnθ/
10	ten /ten/	10th	tenth /tenθ/
11	eleven /ɪˈlevn/	11th	eleventh /ɪˈlevnθ/
12	twelve /twelv/	12th	**twelf**th /twelfθ/
13	**thir**teen /ˌθɜːˈtiːn/	13th	thirteenth /ˌθɜːˈtiːnθ/
14	fourteen /ˌfɔːˈtiːn/	14th	fourteenth /ˌfɔːˈtiːnθ/
15	**fif**teen /ˌfɪfˈtiːn/	15th	fifteenth /ˌfɪfˈtiːnθ/
16	sixteen /ˌsɪksˈtiːn/	16th	sixteenth /ˌsɪksˈtiːnθ/
17	seventeen /ˌsevnˈtiːn/	17th	seventeenth /ˌsevnˈtiːnθ/
18	**eigh**teen /ˌeɪˈtiːn/	18th	eighteenth /ˌeɪˈtiːnθ/
19	nineteen /ˌnaɪnˈtiːn/	19th	nineteenth /ˌnaɪnˈtiːnθ/
20	**twen**ty /ˈtwenti/	20th	twent**ie**th /ˈtwentiəθ/
21	twenty-one /ˌtwentiˈwʌn/	21st	twenty-first /ˌtwentiˈfɜːst/
22	twenty-two /ˌtwentiˈtuː/	22nd	twenty-second /ˌtwentiˈsekənd/
30	**thir**ty /ˈθɜːti/	23rd	twenty-third /ˌtwentiˈθɜːd/
33	thirty-three /ˌθɜːtiˈθriː/		
34	thirty-four /ˌθɜːtiˈfɔː/	30th	thirt**ie**th /ˈθɜːtiəθ/
40	**for**ty /ˈfɔːti/	40th	fort**ie**th /ˈfɔːtiəθ/
45	forty-five /ˌfɔːtiˈfaɪv/	50th	fift**ie**th /ˈfɪftiəθ/
50	**fif**ty /ˈfɪfti/	60th	sixt**ie**th /ˈsɪkstiəθ/
56	fifty-six /ˌfɪftiˈsɪks/	70th	sevent**ie**th /ˈsevntiəθ/
60	sixty /ˈsɪksti/	80th	eight**ie**th /ˈeɪtiəθ/
67	sixty-seven /ˌsɪkstiˈsevn/	90th	ninet**ie**th /ˈnaɪntiəθ/
70	seventy /ˈsevnti/	100th	hundredth /ˈhʌndrədθ/
78	seventy-eight /ˌsevntiˈeɪt/		
80	**eigh**ty /ˈeɪti/		
89	eighty-nine /ˌeɪtiˈnaɪn/		
90	ninety /ˈnaɪnti/		

100 a/one hundred
/ə/wʌn ˈhʌndrəd/

101 one hundred and one
/wʌn ˌhʌndrəd‿ən ˈwʌn/

102 one hundred and two
/wʌn ˌhʌndrəd‿ən ˈtuː/

110 one hundred and ten
/wʌn ˌhʌndrəd‿ən ˈten/

200 two hundred
/tuː ˈhʌndrəd/

North Sea

Shetland Islands

Orkney Islands

Aberdeen

Balmoral

Scotland

▲ **Ben Nevis**
1344 m

Edinburgh

Tweed

Glasgow

Lewis

Skye

Outer Hebrides

Atlantic Ocean